Glencoe
Middle School Spanish

¿Cómo te va?

A

Conrad J. Schmitt

Mc Graw Hill **Glencoe**

New York, New York   Columbus, Ohio   Chicago, Illinois   Peoria, Illinois   Woodland Hills, California

About the Front Cover

(left) **Guanajuato, México** Guanajuato was once an important silver mining city. It is a stunning city with beautiful colonial architecture and lovely, narrow cobblestoned streets. The unique downtown area is navigable mainly on foot, as there are relatively few traffic lights and the streets are narrow and twist through the mountainous terrain. The cathedral seen in this photo is the **Basílica de Nuestra Señora de Guanajuato,** located on the **Plaza de la Paz,** in downtown Guanajuato.

(right) **Machu Picchu, Perú** The imposing ruins of the beautiful Inca city of Machu Picchu, discovered by United States Senator Hiram Bingham in 1911, are perched high upon a rock foundation between two sharp mountain peaks of the Peruvian Andes at an elevation of 2,300 meters. The city spreads over five square miles and some 3,000 steps link its many different levels.

 **Glencoe**

*The **McGraw-Hill** Companies*

Send all inquiries to:
Glencoe/McGraw-Hill
8787 Orion Place
Columbus, OH 43240-4027

ISBN-13: 978-0-07-876973-3
ISBN-10: 0-07-876973-6

Printed in the United States of America.

13 DOW 15 14

About the Author

Conrad J. Schmitt

Conrad J. Schmitt received his B.A. degree from Montclair State University in Montclair, New Jersey. He received his M.A. from Middlebury College, Middlebury, Vermont. He did additional graduate work at New York University.

Mr. Schmitt has taught Spanish and French at all levels from elementary school to university graduate courses. He taught at the Middle School in Hackensack, New Jersey, prior to becoming Coordinator of Foreign Languages for all the schools in the city. He also taught methodology at the Graduate School of Education, Rutgers University, New Brunswick, New Jersey.

Mr. Schmitt has authored or coauthored more than one hundred books, all published by the McGraw-Hill Companies. He has addressed teacher groups and given workshops throughout the United States. In addition, he has lectured and presented seminars in Japan, People's Republic of China, Taiwan, Philippines, Singapore, Thailand, Iran, Egypt, Spain, Portugal, Germany, Haiti, Jamaica, Mexico, Panama, Colombia, and Brazil.

Mr. Schmitt has traveled extensively throughout Spain and all of Latin America.

CONTENIDO

Lecciones preliminares Bienvenidos

Objetivos

In these preliminary lessons you will learn to:

- greet people
- say good-bye to people
- find out and tell the days of the week
- find out and tell the months of the year
- find out and tell the date
- count from 1 to 60
- tell time
- express simple courtesies
- tell about the seasons and weather

Unidad ❶ Amigos y alumnos

Objetivos

In this unit you will learn to:

- ask or tell who someone is
- ask or tell what something is
- ask or tell where someone is from
- ask or tell what someone is like
- count from 1 to 30
- describe people and things
- tell what subjects you take in school and express some opinions about them
- discuss differences between schools in the United States and in Spanish-speaking countries

Unidad 2 Mi familia y mi casa

Objetivos

In this unit you will learn to:

- talk about your family
- count from 31 to 100
- describe your home
- tell what you and others have
- tell your age and find out someone else's age
- speak to people informally and formally
- tell what belongs to you and to others
- talk about families in Spanish-speaking countries

CONTENIDO

Unidad ③ En casa y en clase

Objetivos

In this unit you will learn to:

- talk about what you and others do at home
- talk about going to school
- talk about some school activities
- talk about parties
- count from 100 to 1000
- describe where you and others go
- describe where you and others are
- discuss differences between schools in the United States and in Spanish-speaking countries

CONTENIDO

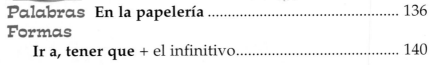

Unidad 4 De compras

Objetivos

In this unit you will learn to:

- identify and describe school supplies
- count from 1000 to 2,000,000
- identify and describe articles of clothing
- state color and size preferences
- tell what you are going to do and what you have to do
- express amazement
- tell what belongs to you and to others
- talk about clothing preferences in Spanish-speaking countries

CONTENIDO

Unidad 5 En el café y en el mercado

Objetivos

In this unit you will learn to:

- order food or a beverage at a café
- identify some foods
- shop for food
- talk about what you and others do
- talk about foods of the Spanish-speaking world
- talk about differences between eating habits in the United States and in the Spanish-speaking countries

CONTENIDO

Unidad 6 Los deportes

Literary Companion

Handbook

Guide to Symbols

Throughout **¿Cómo te va?** you will see these symbols, or icons. They will tell you how to best use the particular part of the unit or activity they accompany. Following is a key to help you understand these symbols.

Audio link This icon indicates material in the unit that is recorded on compact disc format.

Recycling This icon indicates sections that review previously introduced material.

Paired Activity This icon indicates sections that you can practice orally with a partner.

Group Activity This icon indicates sections that you can practice together in groups.

Un poco más This icon indicates additional practice activities that review knowledge from current units.

¡Adelante! This icon indicates the end of new material in each section and the beginning of the recombination section at the end of the unit.

El mundo hispanohablante

Spanish is the language of more than 350 million people around the world. Spanish had its origin in Spain. It is sometimes fondly called the "language of Cervantes," the author of the world's most famous novel and character, *Don Quijote*. The Spanish **conquistadores** and **exploradores** brought their language to the Americas in the fifteenth and sixteenth centuries. Spanish is the official language of almost all the countries of Central and South America. It is the official language of Mexico and several of the larger islands in the Caribbean. Spanish is also the heritage language of some forty million people in the United States.

▼ Trujillo, Perú

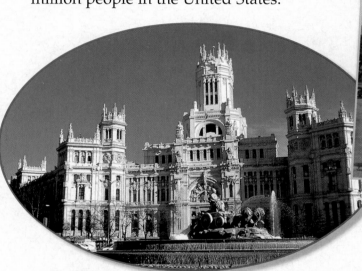

▲ Cibeles, Madrid

▲ El Zócalo, México

▲ Santiago de Chile

El mundo

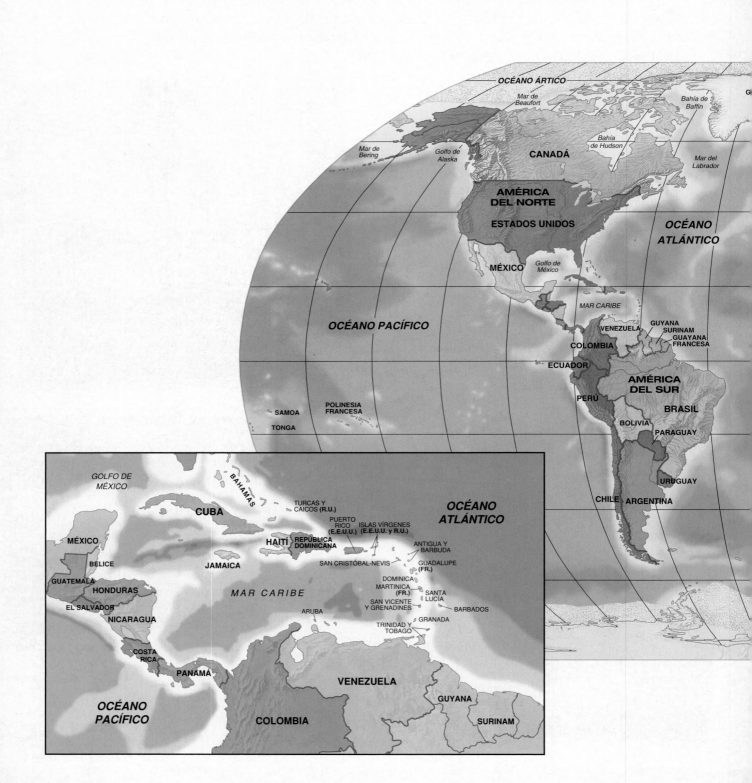

OCÉANO ÁRTICO

Mar de Beaufort

Bahía de Baffin

Mar de Bering

Golfo de Alaska

CANADÁ

Bahía de Hudson

Mar del Labrador

AMÉRICA DEL NORTE

ESTADOS UNIDOS

OCÉANO ATLÁNTICO

MÉXICO

Golfo de México

MAR CARIBE

VENEZUELA

GUYANA
SURINAM
GUAYANA FRANCESA

COLOMBIA

ECUADOR

OCÉANO PACÍFICO

AMÉRICA DEL SUR

PERÚ

BRASIL

BOLIVIA

PARAGUAY

SAMOA

POLINESIA FRANCESA

TONGA

URUGUAY

CHILE   ARGENTINA

GOLFO DE MÉXICO

BAHAMAS

TURCAS Y CAICOS (R.U.)

OCÉANO ATLÁNTICO

CUBA

PUERTO RICO (E.E.U.U.)

ISLAS VÍRGENES (E.E.U.U. y R.U.)

MÉXICO

HAITÍ   REPÚBLICA DOMINICANA

ANTIGUA Y BARBUDA

BELICE

JAMAICA

SAN CRISTÓBAL-NEVIS

GUADALUPE (FR.)

GUATEMALA

HONDURAS

MAR CARIBE

DOMINICA
MARTINICA (FR.)

SANTA LUCÍA

EL SALVADOR

SAN VICENTE Y GRENADINES

BARBADOS

NICARAGUA

ARUBA

GRANADA

TRINIDAD Y TOBAGO

COSTA RICA

PANAMÁ

OCÉANO PACÍFICO

VENEZUELA

GUYANA

COLOMBIA

SURINAM

OCÉANO ÁRTICO

GROENLANDIA
Mar de Groenlandia
ISLANDIA
Mar de Barents
Mar de Kara
Mar de Láptiev

RUSIA

ASIA
Mar de Ojotsk

Mar del Norte

EUROPA

KAZAJSTÁN
MONGOLIA

Mar Negro
GEORGIA
ARMENIA
UZBEKISTÁN
KIRGUIZITÁN

CHINA

COREA DEL NORTE
Mar del Japón
JAPÓN

TURQUÍA
TURKMENISTÁN
TAYIKISTÁN

COREA DEL SUR

CEUTA
MELILLA
LÍBANO
SIRIA
AZERBAIJÁN
AFGANISTÁN

OCÉANO PACÍFICO

MARRUECOS
TÚNEZ
MAR MEDITERRÁNEO
ISRAEL
IRAK
JORDANIA
IRÁN
NEPAL
BHUTÁN

Mar de la China oriental

SÁHARA OCCIDENTAL
KUWAIT
BAHREIN
PÁKISTÁN
TAIWÁN

ARGELIA
LIBIA
EGIPTO
QATAR
ARABIA SAUDITA
EMIRATOS ÁRABES UNIDOS
INDIA

CABO VERDE
MAURITANIA
MALÍ
NÍGER
CHAD
SUDÁN
ERITREA
OMÁN
BANGLADESH
MYANMAR
LAOS
Mar de la China meridional

SENEGAL
GAMBIA
GUINEA-BISSAU
BURKINA FASO
NIGERIA
ÁFRICA
YEMEN
DJIBOUTI
Golfo de Bengala
TAILANDIA
FILIPINAS
MARSHALL

GUINEA
GHANA
BENIN
ETIOPÍA
VIETNAM
MICRONESIA

SIERRA LEONA
REPÚBLICA CENTROAFRICANA
SRI LANKA
CAMBOYA
BRUNEI
PALAU

COSTA DE MARFIL
LIBERIA
TOGO
CAMERÚN
SOMALIA
MALASIA
KIRIBATI

SAN TOMÉ E PRÍNCIPE
UGANDA
KENYA
MALDIVAS

GUINEA ECUATORIAL
GABÓN
REP. DEL CONGO
RUANDA
REP. DEM. DEL CONGO
BURUNDI
SINGAPUR
INDONESIA
PAPÚA-NUEVA GUINEA
NAURÚ

TANZANIA
SEYCHELLES
OCÉANO ÍNDICO
SALOMÓN
TUVALU

ANGOLA
MALAWI
ZAMBIA
MOZAMBIQUE
ISLAS COMORES
WALLIS Y FUTUNA
VANUATU

NAMIBIA
ZIMBABWE
MADAGASCAR
MAURICIO
Mar del Coral
ISLAS FIJI

OCÉANO ATLÁNTICO
BOTSWANA
REUNIÓN
NUEVA CALEDONIA

SUDÁFRICA
SWAZILANDIA
LESOTHO
AUSTRALIA
Mar de Tasmania

ANTÁRTIDA
NUEVA ZELANDIA

NORUEGA
FINLANDIA
SUECIA
ESTONIA

IRLANDA
REINO UNIDO
DINAMARCA
LETONIA
RUSIA

LITUANIA
RUSIA

PAÍSES BAJOS
BELARÚS

BÉLGICA
ALEMANIA
POLONIA

LUXEMBURGO
REPÚBLICA CHECA
UCRANIA

OCÉANO ATLÁNTICO
FRANCIA
SUIZA
ESLOVAQUIA
MOLDOVA

AUSTRIA
HUNGRÍA

ANDORRA
ESLOVENIA
CROACIA
RUMANIA

PORTUGAL
MÓNACO
BOSNIA-HERZOGOVINA
YUGOSLAVIA (Fed. Rep.)
GEORGIA

ESPAÑA
ITALIA
BULGARIA
Mar Negro

ALBANIA
MACEDONIA

MELILLA
Mar Mediterráneo
GRECIA
TURQUÍA

CEUTA

ÁFRICA
MALTA
CHIPRE
SIRIA
LÍBANO

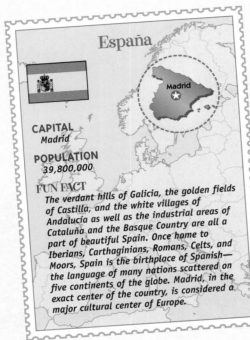

España

CAPITAL
Madrid

POPULATION
39,800,000

FUN FACT
The verdant hills of Galicia, the golden fields of Castilla, and the white villages of Andalucía as well as the industrial areas of Cataluña and the Basque Country are all a part of beautiful Spain. Once home to Iberians, Carthaginians, Romans, Celts, and Moors, Spain is the birthplace of Spanish—the language of many nations scattered on five continents of the globe. Madrid, in the exact center of the country, is considered a major cultural center of Europe.

México

CAPITAL
Ciudad de México

POPULATION
99,600,000

FUN FACT
Beautiful Mexico shares a border with the United States. This magnificent nation of Aztec, Mayan, and Spanish heritage is a country of contrasts: cosmopolitan cities such as Mexico City; industrial centers such as Monterrey; quaint towns such as Taxco and San Miguel de Allende; world-famous beaches like Acapulco and Cancún; as well as magnificent vestiges of pre-Columbian civilization in Chichén Itzá and Tulum.

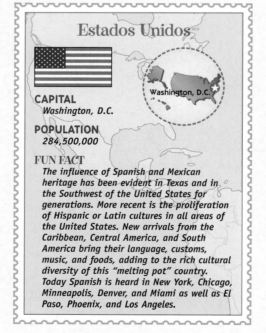

Estados Unidos

CAPITAL
Washington, D.C.

POPULATION
284,500,000

FUN FACT
The influence of Spanish and Mexican heritage has been evident in Texas and in the Southwest of the United States for generations. More recent is the proliferation of Hispanic or Latin cultures in all areas of the United States. New arrivals from the Caribbean, Central America, and South America bring their language, customs, music, and foods, adding to the rich cultural diversity of this "melting pot" country. Today Spanish is heard in New York, Chicago, Minneapolis, Denver, and Miami as well as El Paso, Phoenix, and Los Angeles.

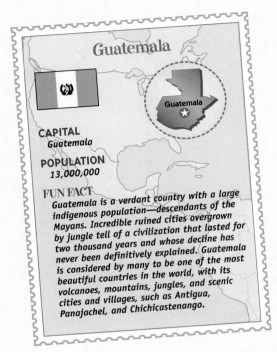

Guatemala

CAPITAL
Guatemala

POPULATION
13,000,000

FUN FACT
Guatemala is a verdant country with a large indigenous population—descendants of the Mayans. Incredible ruined cities overgrown by jungle tell of a civilization that lasted for two thousand years and whose decline has never been definitively explained. Guatemala is considered by many to be one of the most beautiful countries in the world, with its volcanoes, mountains, jungles, and scenic cities and villages, such as Antigua, Panajachel, and Chichicastenango.

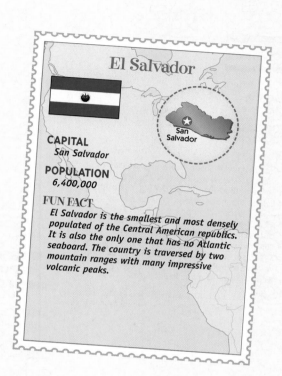

El Salvador

CAPITAL
San Salvador

POPULATION
6,400,000

FUN FACT
El Salvador is the smallest and most densely populated of the Central American republics. It is also the only one that has no Atlantic seaboard. The country is traversed by two mountain ranges with many impressive volcanic peaks.

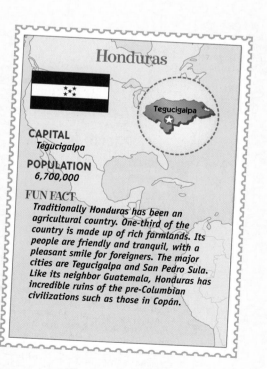

Honduras

CAPITAL
Tegucigalpa

POPULATION
6,700,000

FUN FACT
Traditionally Honduras has been an agricultural country. One-third of the country is made up of rich farmlands. Its people are friendly and tranquil, with a pleasant smile for foreigners. The major cities are Tegucigalpa and San Pedro Sula. Like its neighbor Guatemala, Honduras has incredible ruins of the pre-Columbian civilizations such as those in Copán.

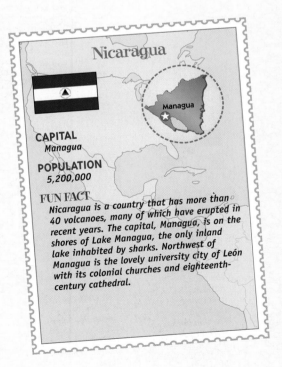

Nicaragua

CAPITAL
Managua

POPULATION
5,200,000

FUN FACT
Nicaragua is a country that has more than 40 volcanoes, many of which have erupted in recent years. The capital, Managua, is on the shores of Lake Managua, the only inland lake inhabited by sharks. Northwest of Managua is the lovely university city of León with its colonial churches and eighteenth-century cathedral.

Costa Rica

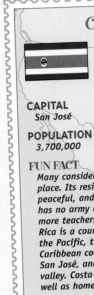

CAPITAL
San José

POPULATION
3,700,000

FUN FACT
Many consider Costa Rica a very special place. Its residents, Ticos, are polite, peaceful, and extremely friendly. Costa Rica has no army and prides itself on having more teachers than police officers. Costa Rica is a country of sun-drenched beaches on the Pacific, tropical jungles along the Caribbean coast, cosmopolitan cities such as San José, and high mountains in the central valley. Costa Rica is a tourist's paradise as well as home to many expatriates.

Panamá

CAPITAL
Panamá

POPULATION
2,900,000

FUN FACT
Panama is a country of variety—a variety of races, customs, natural wonders, and attractions. It is a country of tropical forests, mountains, beautiful beaches, excellent fishing, picturesque lakes, rivers, two oceans, and—the most incredible engineering feat—the Panama Canal. Panama is also the largest financial center of Latin America. All this in a mere 77,432 square kilometers!

Cuba

CAPITAL
La Habana

POPULATION
11,300,000

FUN FACT
Havana, the capital of Cuba, is known for its gorgeous colonial architecture. This lush island, not far from Florida, is one of the world's greatest producers of sugar cane. Cuba has been ruled by Fidel Castro since 1959 when he overthrew the dictator Fulgencio Batista.

La República Dominicana

CAPITAL
Santo Domingo

POPULATION
8,600,000

FUN FACT
The Dominican Republic shares with Haiti the island of Hispaniola in the greater Antilles. The oldest university in our hemisphere, la Universidad de Santo Domingo, was founded in Santo Domingo. The Dominicans are ardent fans or aficionados of baseball, and this rather small island nation has produced some of the finest major league players.

Puerto Rico

CAPITAL
San Juan

POPULATION
3,900,000

FUN FACT
Puerto Ricans have an endearing term for their beloved island—la isla del encanto—island of enchantment. A commonwealth of the United States, Puerto Rico is a lush, tropical island with beaches along its Atlantic and Caribbean shores and gorgeous mountains with Alpine-like views in its interior. Puerto Rico is the home of the beloved coquí—a little frog that lives only in Puerto Rico and who lets no one see him.

Venezuela

CAPITAL
Caracas

POPULATION
24,600,000

FUN FACT
Venezuela was the name given to this country by Spanish explorers in 1499, when they came across indigenous villages where people lived on the water and where all commerce was conducted by dugout canoes. The waterways reminded them of Venice, Italy. Caracas is a teeming cosmopolitan city of high-rises surrounded by mountains and tucked in a narrow nine-mile valley. Angel Falls in southern Venezuela is the highest waterfall in the world, reaching a height of 3,212 feet with an unbroken fall of 2,648 feet.

Colombia

CAPITAL
Bogotá

POPULATION
43,100,000

FUN FACT
Colombia covers over 440,000 square miles of tropical and mountainous terrain. Bogotá is situated in the center of the country in an Andean valley 8,640 feet above sea level. The Caribbean coast in the North boasts many beautiful beaches; the South is covered by jungle, and the southern port of Leticia is on the Amazon River.

Ecuador

CAPITAL
Quito

POPULATION
12,900,000

FUN FACT
Ecuador takes its name from the equator, which cuts right across the country. Ecuador is the meeting place of the high Andean sierra in the center, the tropical coastal plain to the west, and the Amazon Basin jungle to the east. Snowcapped volcanoes stretch some 400 miles from north to south. The beautiful colonial section of the capital, Quito, is sometimes called "the Florence of the Americas."

Perú

CAPITAL
Lima

POPULATION
26,100,000

FUN FACT
Peru, like Ecuador, is divided into three geographical areas—a narrow coastal strip of desert along the Pacific, the Andean highlands where nearly half the population lives, and the Amazon jungle to the east. Lima is on the coast, and for almost nine months out of the year it is enshrouded in a fog called la garúa. Peru is famous for its Incan heritage. Nothing can prepare visitors for the awe-inspiring view of the Incan city of Machu Picchu, an imposing architectural complex high in the Andes.

Bolivia

CAPITAL
La Paz

POPULATION
8,500,000

FUN FACT
Bolivia is one of two landlocked countries in South America. Mountains dominate the Bolivian landscape. La Paz is the highest city in the world at an altitude of 12,500 feet. Bolivia also has the world's highest navigable lake, Lake Titicaca, which is surrounded by the picturesque villages of the Aymara Indians.

Chile

CAPITAL
Santiago

POPULATION
15,400,000

FUN FACT
Chile, a "string bean" country never more than 111 miles wide, stretches 2,666 miles from north to south along the Pacific Coast. The imposing Andes isolate it from Bolivia and Argentina. The northern part of the country is characterized by the super-arid Atacama desert, the South by the spectacular wind-swept glaciers and fjords of Patagonia. Over one-third of the country's population lives in the Santiago area.

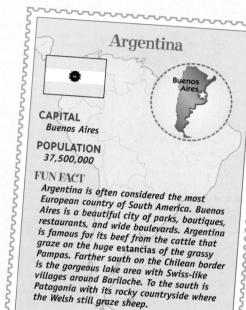

Argentina

CAPITAL
Buenos Aires

POPULATION
37,500,000

FUN FACT
Argentina is often considered the most European country of South America. Buenos Aires is a beautiful city of parks, boutiques, restaurants, and wide boulevards. Argentina is famous for its beef from the cattle that graze on the huge estancias of the grassy Pampas. Farther south on the Chilean border is the gorgeous lake area with Swiss-like villages around Bariloche. To the south is Patagonia with its rocky countryside where the Welsh still graze sheep.

Paraguay

CAPITAL
Asunción

POPULATION
5,700,000

FUN FACT
Paraguay, like Bolivia, is landlocked. Asunción, situated on seven small hills on the east bank of the río Paraguay, is home to one-fifth of the country's total population. Located in the center of South America, this somewhat quaint city is nearly equidistant from the Atlantic and the Andes. The area to the west of the río Paraguay is called the Chaco—a very dry, hot, windy area of grasslands and scrubby forests.

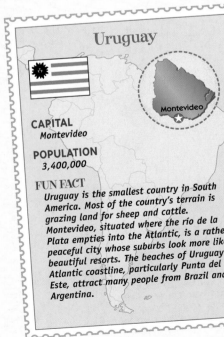

Uruguay

CAPITAL
Montevideo

POPULATION
3,400,000

FUN FACT
Uruguay is the smallest country in South America. Most of the country's terrain is grazing land for sheep and cattle. Montevideo, situated where the río de la Plata empties into the Atlantic, is a rather peaceful city whose suburbs look more like beautiful resorts. The beaches of Uruguay's Atlantic coastline, particularly Punta del Este, attract many people from Brazil and Argentina.

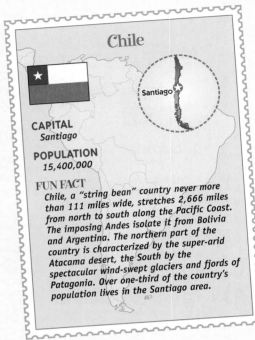

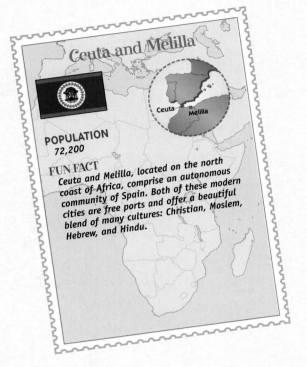

Ceuta and Melilla

Ceuta Melilla

POPULATION
72,200

FUN FACT
Ceuta and Melilla, located on the north coast of Africa, comprise an autonomous community of Spain. Both of these modern cities are free ports and offer a beautiful blend of many cultures: Christian, Moslem, Hebrew, and Hindu.

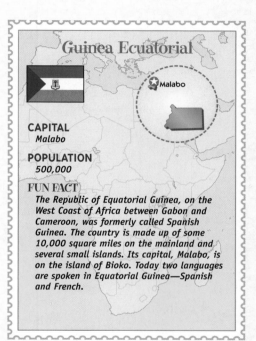

Guinea Ecuatorial

Malabo

CAPITAL
Malabo

POPULATION
500,000

FUN FACT
The Republic of Equatorial Guinea, on the West Coast of Africa between Gabon and Cameroon, was formerly called Spanish Guinea. The country is made up of some 10,000 square miles on the mainland and several small islands. Its capital, Malabo, is on the island of Bioko. Today two languages are spoken in Equatorial Guinea—Spanish and French.

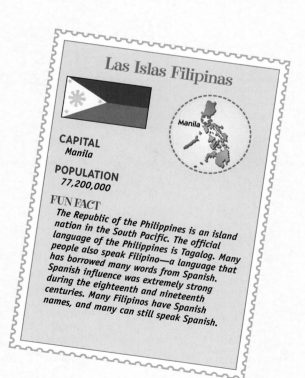

Las Islas Filipinas

Manila

CAPITAL
Manila

POPULATION
77,200,000

FUN FACT
The Republic of the Philippines is an island nation in the South Pacific. The official language of the Philippines is Tagalog. Many people also speak Filipino—a language that has borrowed many words from Spanish. Spanish influence was extremely strong during the eighteenth and nineteenth centuries. Many Filipinos have Spanish names, and many can still speak Spanish.

España

OCÉANO ATLÁNTICO

FRANCIA

MAR CANTÁBRICO

Golfo de Vizcaya

ANDORRA

La Coruña

Santander

San Sebastián

Oviedo
Asturias
Cantabria

Bilbao

Roncesvalles

Santiago de Compostela

CORDILLERA CANTÁBRICA

País Vasco

LOS PIRINEOS

Galicia

León

Burgos

Pamplona

Navarra

Río Ebro

Rioja

Cataluña

Castilla y León

Valladolid

Río Duero

Zaragoza

Barcelona

Aragón

Salamanca

Segovia

Río Tajo

SIERRA DE GUADARRAMA

Ávila

Madrid

Madrid

Menorca

Palma

PORTUGAL

ESPAÑA

Comunidad Valenciana

Islas baleares

Mallorca

Castilla-la Mancha

Valencia

Lisboa

Río Guadiana

Ibiza

Extremadura

Formentera

Alicante

MAR MEDITERRÁNEO

Río Guadalquivir

Murcia

Córdoba

Murcia

Sevilla

Granada

Cartagena

Andalucía

SIERRA NEVADA

Jerez de la Frontera

Málaga

COSTA DEL SOL

Cádiz

Marbella

Estepona

Gibraltar (R.U.)

Estrecho de Gibraltar

Ceuta (Esp.)

Tánger

Melilla (Esp.)

OCÉANO ATLÁNTICO

ARGELIA

Islas Canarias

La Palma

Santa Cruz de Tenerife

Lanzarote

Gomera

Las Palmas

Fuerteventura

MARRUECOS

Hierro

Tenerife

Gran Canaria

ÁFRICA

OCÉANO ATLÁNTICO

SAHARA OCCIDENTAL

MARRUECOS

MAR CARIBE

OCÉANO
ATLÁNTICO

Barranquilla
Maracaibo
Caracas
Cartagena
Lago de
Maracaibo
Río Orinoco
Medellín
VENEZUELA
GUYANA
Río Magdalena
Santafé de
Bogotá
SURINAM
GUAYANA
FRANCESA
Cali
COLOMBIA

Ecuador
Otavalo
Quito
Río Amazonas
Islas Galápagos
(Ecuador)
ECUADOR
Guayaquil
Cuenca

PERÚ
BRASIL

El Callao
Lima
Cuzco
CORDILLERA
Lago
Titicaca
BOLIVIA
La Paz
Cochabamba
Brasília
Santa Cruz
Sucre

Trópico de Capricornio
DE
PARAGUAY
LOS
CHILE
Asunción
ANDES

Vicuña
Córdoba
Río Paraná

OCÉANO
PACÍFICO
Valparaíso
Rosario
URUGUAY
Santiago
Buenos Aires
Montevideo
La Plata
Río de la Plata
ARGENTINA
Mar del Plata

OCÉANO
ATLÁNTICO
Puerto Montt

PATAGONIA

Estrecho de
Magallanes
Islas Malvinas
(R.U.)
Tierra del
Fuego
Punta Arenas

Cabo de Hornos

México, la América Central y el Caribe

OCÉANO PACÍFICO

OCÉANO ATLÁNTICO

ESTADOS UNIDOS

MÉXICO

Golfo de México

Golfo de California

MAR CARIBE

GUATEMALA
BELICE
HONDURAS
EL SALVADOR
NICARAGUA
COSTA RICA
PANAMÁ
CUBA
JAMAICA
HAITÍ
REPÚBLICA DOMINICANA
PUERTO RICO (EE.UU.)
BAHAMAS
COLOMBIA
VENEZUELA

Los Ángeles
San Diego
Tijuana
Mexicali
Nogales
Tucson
Phoenix
Santa Fe
Chihuahua
Ciudad Juárez
El Paso
Nuevo Laredo
San Antonio
Dallas
La Paz
Puerto Vallarta
Guadalajara
Guanajuato
San Luis Potosí
México
San Miguel de Allende
Puebla
Oaxaca
Acapulco
Veracruz
San Cristóbal de las Casas
Mérida
Campeche
Nueva Orleans
Tampa
Miami
La Habana
Matanzas
Cienfuegos
Camagüey
Santiago de Cuba
Guantánamo
Santo Domingo
Arecibo
San Juan
Ponce
Guatemala
Antigua
San Salvador
Tegucigalpa
Managua
Puntarenas
San José
Puerto Limón
Colón
Panamá
Cartagena
Barranquilla
Medellín
Caracas
Washington, D.C.

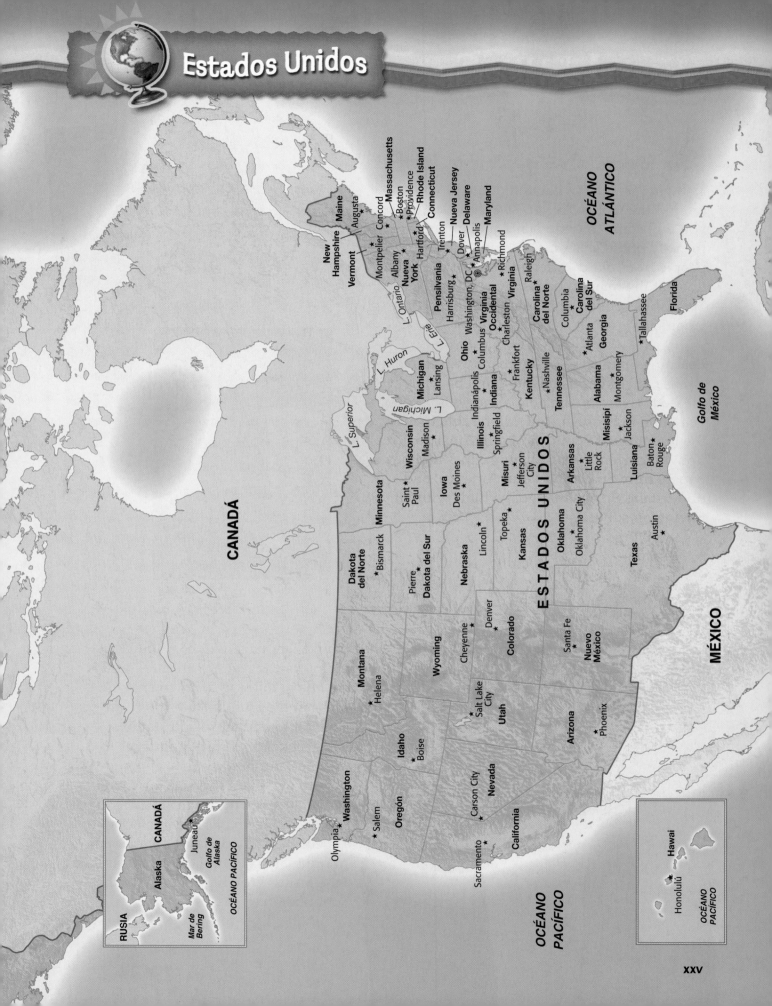

Estados Unidos

OCÉANO ATLÁNTICO

Maine
Augusta ★
New Hampshire
Vermont
Concord ★
Montpelier ★
Massachusetts
Boston ★
Providence ★
Rhode Island
Connecticut
Hartford ★
Nueva Jersey
Trenton ★
Dover ★
Delaware
Maryland
Annapolis ★
Washington, DC ★
Richmond ★
Virginia
Raleigh ★
L. Ontario
Albany ★
Nueva York
Pensilvania
Harrisburg ★
Virginia Occidental
Charleston ★
Frankfort ★
Carolina del Norte
Columbia ★
Carolina del Sur
L. Erie
Ohio
Columbus ★
Atlanta ★
Georgia
L. Huron
Michigan
Lansing ★
Kentucky
Nashville ★
Tennessee
Alabama
Montgomery ★
Florida
Tallahassee ★
L. Michigan
Indianápolis ★
Indiana
Illinois
Springfield ★
Misisipí
Jackson ★
Golfo de México
L. Superior
Wisconsin
Madison ★
Iowa
Des Moines ★
Misuri
Jefferson City ★
Arkansas
Little Rock ★
Luisiana
Baton Rouge ★
Saint Paul ★
Minnesota
Lincoln ★
Topeka ★
Kansas
Oklahoma
Oklahoma City ★
Austin ★
ESTADOS UNIDOS
Dakota del Norte
Bismarck ★
Dakota del Sur
Pierre ★
Nebraska
Denver ★
Colorado
Santa Fe ★
Nuevo México
Texas
CANADÁ
Montana
Helena ★
Wyoming
Cheyenne ★
Salt Lake City ★
Utah
Arizona
Phoenix ★
Washington
Olympia ★
Idaho
Boise ★
Carson City ★
Nevada
Sacramento ★
California
Salem ★
Oregón
OCÉANO PACÍFICO
MÉXICO

RUSIA
CANADÁ
Juneau ★
Alaska
Golfo de Alaska
Mar de Bering
OCÉANO PACÍFICO

Hawai
Honolulú ★
OCÉANO PACÍFICO

The Spanish-Speaking World

Knowing Spanish will open doors to you around the world. As you study the language, you will come to understand and appreciate the way of life, customs, values, and cultures of people from many different areas of the world. Look at the map on pages xiv–xv to see where Spanish is spoken, either as a first or second language.

Learning Spanish can be fun and will bring you a sense of accomplishment. You'll be really pleased when you are able to carry on a conversation in Spanish. You will be able to read the literature of Spain and Latin America, keep up with current events in magazines and newspapers from Spain and Latin America, and understand Spanish-language films without relying on subtitles.

The Spanish language will be a source of enrichment for the rest of your life—and you don't have to leave home to enjoy it. In all areas of the United States there are Hispanic radio and television stations, Latin musicians, Spanish-language magazines and newspapers, and a great diversity of restaurants serving foods from all areas of the Spanish-speaking world. The Latin or Hispanic population of the United States today totals more than forty million people and is the fastest growing segment of the population.

Career Opportunities

Your knowledge of Spanish will also be an asset to you in a wide variety of careers. Many companies from Spain and Latin America are multinational and have branches around the world, including the United States. Many U.S. corporations have great exposure in the Spanish-speaking countries. With the growth of the Hispanic population in the United States, bilingualism is becoming an important asset in many fields including retail, fashion, cosmetics, pharmaceutical, agriculture, automotive, tourism, airlines, technology, finance, and accounting.

You can use your Spanish in all these fields, not only abroad but also in the United States. On the national scene there are innumerable possibilities in medical and hospital services, banking and finance, law, social work, and law enforcement. The opportunities are limitless.

Language Link

Another benefit to learning Spanish is that it will improve your English. Once you know another language, you can make comparisons between the two and gain a greater understanding of how languages function. You'll also come across a number of Spanish words that are used in English. Just a few examples are: **adobe, corral, meseta, rodeo, poncho, canyon, llama, alpaca**. Spanish will also be helpful if you decide to learn yet another language. Once you learn a second language, the learning process for acquiring other languages becomes much easier.

Spanish is a beautiful, rich language spoken on many continents. Whatever your motivation is for choosing to study it, Spanish will expand your horizons and increase your job opportunities. **¡Viva el español!**

a avión

b bebé

c cesta

d dedo

e elefante

f foto

g gemelos

h hamaca

i iglesia

j jabón

k kilo

l lago

m mono

n nariz

ñ 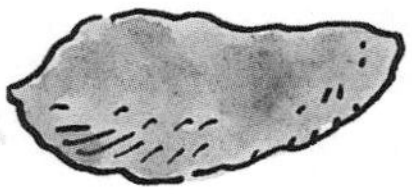
*ñ*ame

o 
*o*so

p 
*p*elo

q 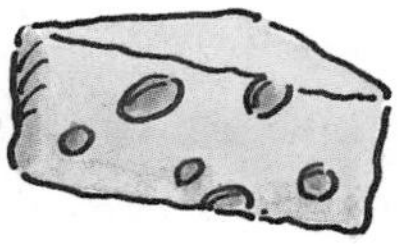
*q*ueso

r 
*r*ana

s 
*s*ala

t 
*t*é

u 
*u*va

v 
*v*aca

w 
*W*ashington, D.C.

x 
e*x*amen

y 
*y*eso

z 
*z*apato

ch 
*ch*icle

ll 
*ll*uvia

rr 
guita*rr*a

Ch, ll, and **rr** are not letters of the Spanish alphabet. However, it is important for you to learn the sounds they represent.

Lecciones preliminares

Bienvenidos

Objetivos

In these preliminary lessons you will learn to:

- greet people
- say good-bye to people
- find out and tell the days of the week
- find out and tell the months of the year
- find out and tell the date
- count from 1 to 60
- tell time
- express simple courtesies
- tell about the seasons and weather

Casa de la fam.
Ordaz desde 1932
Hospicio 33
Bienvenidos

Saludos

Greeting people 🎧

¡Hola!
¿Qué tal?

¡Hola!

Muy bien.

Bien, gracias.
¿Y tú?

1 **¡Hola!** Get up from your desk and walk around the classroom. Say **¡Hola!** to each classmate you meet.

2 **¿Qué tal?** Work in groups of two. Greet one another in Spanish and find out how things are going.

Some Spanish greetings are more formal than ¡**Hola!** When you greet someone, particularly an older person, you can say:

Buenos días, señora.

Buenas tardes, señorita.

Buenas noches, señor.

Cultura

1. When speaking Spanish, the titles **señor, señora,** and **señorita** are frequently used without the last name of the person.

2. In Spanish-speaking countries, young people almost always shake hands when they greet one another.

Manos a la obra

3 **Buenos días** Draw five stick figures. Give each one a name. They will represent your friends, family, and teachers. Greet each of your stick figures properly in Spanish.

4 **Saludos** Look at these photographs of people in Spain and Mexico. As they greet one another, they do some things that are different from what we do when we greet each other. What do you notice in the photographs?

Adiós
Saying good-bye

1. The usual expression to use when saying good-bye to someone is ¡**Adiós!**

2. If you plan to see the person again soon, you can say ¡**Hasta pronto!** or ¡**Hasta luego!** If you plan to see the person the next day, you can say ¡**Hasta mañana!**

3. You will frequently hear the informal expression ¡**Chao!,** especially in Spain as well as in some countries of Latin America.

1 **¡Chao!** Go over to a classmate and say good-bye to him or her.

2 **¡Hasta luego!** Work with a classmate. Say **Chao** to one another and let each other know that you will be getting together again soon.

3 **¡Adiós!** Say good-bye to your Spanish teacher. Then say good-bye to a friend. Use a different expression with each person.

Conversación

¡Hola, Pedro!
¡Hola, Elena! ¿Qué tal?

Bien. ¿Y tú?
Muy bien, gracias.

Chao, Pedro.
Chao, Elena. ¡Hasta luego!

 4 **¡Hola, amigo(a)!** Work with a friend. Speak Spanish together. Have fun saying as much as you can to one another.

 Cultura

The following are some common names for boys and girls in Spanish.

Muchachos
Álvaro, Ángel, Antonio, Alejandro, Daniel, David, Eduardo, Emilio, Enrique, Felipe, Fernando, Francisco, Gabriel, Gerardo, Ignacio, Jaime, Javier, José, Juan, Lucas, Luis, Manuel, Mario, Miguel, Moisés, Pablo, Pedro, Raúl, Ricardo, Roberto, Tomás, Vicente

Muchachas
Adela, Alejandra, Alicia, Ana, Andrea, Beatriz, Catalina, Clara, Claudia, Cristina, Débora, Elena, Elisa, Esther, Esperanza, Guadalupe, Isabel, Josefina, Juana, Julia, Leonor, Luisa, Maïte, Mar, María, Marisa, Marta, Patricia, Paz, Pilar, Rosa, Sandra, Teresa

Los días de la semana
Telling the days of the week 🎧

Los días de la semana son:

lunes	martes	miércoles	jueves	viernes	sábado	domingo
1	2	3	4	5	6	7
8	9	10	11	12	13	14

To find out and give the day, you say:

¿Qué día es hoy? Hoy es lunes.

1 **¿Qué día es?** Answer in Spanish.
1. ¿Qué día es hoy?
2. ¿Qué día es mañana?
3. ¿Cuáles son los días de la semana?

Cultura

The first day of the week in Spanish is **lunes,** not **domingo.**

Procesión religiosa durante la
Semana Santa en Sevilla, España

La fecha

Telling the months 🎧

Los meses del año son:

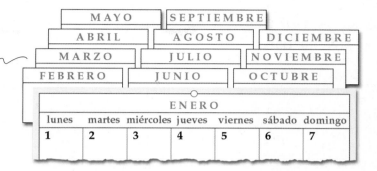

MAYO	SEPTIEMBRE	
ABRIL	AGOSTO	DICIEMBRE
MARZO	JULIO	NOVIEMBRE
FEBRERO	JUNIO	OCTUBRE

ENERO						
lunes	martes	miércoles	jueves	viernes	sábado	domingo
1	2	3	4	5	6	7

Los números

To give the date you have to know how to count from 1 to 31.

1	uno	11	once	21	veintiuno
2	dos	12	doce	22	veintidós
3	tres	13	trece	23	veintitrés
4	cuatro	14	catorce	24	veinticuatro
5	cinco	15	quince	25	veinticinco
6	seis	16	dieciséis	26	veintiséis
7	siete	17	diecisiete	27	veintisiete
8	ocho	18	dieciocho	28	veintiocho
9	nueve	19	diecinueve	29	veintinueve
10	diez	20	veinte	30	treinta
				31	treinta y uno

Finding out and giving the date

¿Cuál es la fecha de hoy?

Hoy es el diez de septiembre.

You use **primero** for the first of the month.

Es el primero de octubre.

 Mi cumpleaños Each of you will stand up and give the date of your birthday in Spanish. Listen and keep a record of how many of you were born in the same month.

2 La fecha, por favor. Look at these calendars and give the dates.

enero

lunes	martes	miércoles	jueves	viernes	sábado	domingo
		1	2	3	4	5
6	7	8	9	(10)	11	12
13	14	15	16	17	18	19
20	21	22	23	24		
27	28	29	30	31		

1.

marzo

lunes	martes	miércoles	jueves	viernes	sábado	domingo
				1	2	3
4	5	6	7	8	9	10
11	12	13	14	15	16	17
18	19	20	(21)	22	23	24
25	26	27	28	29	30	31

2.

julio

lunes	martes	miércoles	jueves	viernes	sábado	domingo
1	2	3	4	5	(6)	7
8	9	10	11	12	13	14
15	16	17	18	19	20	21
22	23	24	25	26		
	30	31				

3.

septiembre

lunes	martes	miércoles	jueves	viernes	sábado	domingo
	1	2	3	4	5	6
7	8	9	10	11	12	13
(14)	15	16	17	18	19	20
21	22	23	24	25	26	27
28	29	30				

4.

Cultura

Fiestas

Some **fiestas** of Hispanic origin are celebrated in the United States.

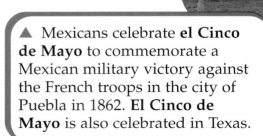

▲ Mexicans celebrate **el Cinco de Mayo** to commemorate a Mexican military victory against the French troops in the city of Puebla in 1862. **El Cinco de Mayo** is also celebrated in Texas.

▲ **El Día de los Muertos** is either **el primero** or **el dos de noviembre.** Mexican Americans decorate their homes with **esqueletos** that symbolize the spirits of the dead. It is a day to visit the cemetery.

Spanish Online

For more information about holidays in the Spanish-speaking world, go to the Glencoe Spanish Web site: Spanish.glencoe.com.

La hora

Telling time

Más números

Let's learn the numbers from 31 to 60 so we can tell time in Spanish.

31	treinta y uno	41	cuarenta y uno	51	cincuenta y uno
32	treinta y dos	42	cuarenta y dos	52	cincuenta y dos
33	treinta y tres	43	cuarenta y tres	53	cincuenta y tres
34	treinta y cuatro	44	cuarenta y cuatro	54	cincuenta y cuatro
35	treinta y cinco	45	cuarenta y cinco	55	cincuenta y cinco
36	treinta y seis	46	cuarenta y seis	56	cincuenta y seis
37	treinta y siete	47	cuarenta y siete	57	cincuenta y siete
38	treinta y ocho	48	cuarenta y ocho	58	cincuenta y ocho
39	treinta y nueve	49	cuarenta y nueve	59	cincuenta y nueve
40	cuarenta	50	cincuenta	60	sesenta

1 **El número, por favor.** Count from one to ten.

2 **De diez en diez** Count from 10 to 60 by tens.

3 **¿Qué número es?**
Give the following numbers.

1. 12
2. 21
3. 28
4. 32
5. 36
6. 41
7. 44
8. 53
9. 57
10. 60

To find out the time, you ask:

Perdón, ¿qué hora es?

Es la una.

Son las dos.

Son las tres.

To tell time you say:

Son las cuatro.

Son las cinco.

Son las seis.

Son las siete.

Son las ocho.

Son las nueve.

Son las diez.

Son las once.

Son las doce.

Es la una y cinco.

Son las dos y diez.

Son las cinco cuarenta.

Son las siete y cuarto.

Son las ocho y media.

4 **La hora, por favor.** Give the following times.

5 **Perdón** Walk up to a classmate and ask for the time. Your classmate will answer you.

To find out at what time something takes place you ask:

¿A qué hora es la clase de español?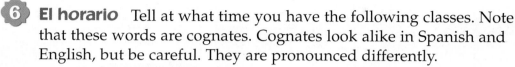
Es a la una *o* **Es a las diez y media.**

6 **El horario** Tell at what time you have the following classes. Note that these words are cognates. Cognates look alike in Spanish and English, but be careful. They are pronounced differently.

La clase de matemáticas es...

1. matemáticas
2. historia
3. educación física
4. ciencias
5. español
6. inglés

Manos a la obra

La rutina Draw pictures of some of your daily activities such as getting up in the morning, eating breakfast, walking or riding the bus to school, going to after-school sports, eating dinner, going to bed, etc. Then compare your pictures with those of a classmate. Both of you will tell when you do these activities.

The Twenty-Four-Hour Clock

1. In Spain and in many areas of Latin America, it is common to use the twenty-four-hour clock for formal activities, such as cultural events, reservations and train and airplane departures. Read the times and guess what time it is in the United States.

    A las dieciocho horas
    A las veinte cuarenta

2. In most Spanish-speaking countries it is not considered rude to arrive a little late for an appointment. If you have a 10:00 A.M. appointment, you would be expected sometime around 10:30.

La cortesía

Speaking politely

1. There are several ways to express *You're welcome*.

> **No hay de qué.**
> **De nada.**
> **Por nada.**

2. When you want to find out how much something is you can ask:

> **¿Cuánto es, por favor?**

Be sure to be polite and add **por favor.**

1 **La cortesía** With a classmate, go over the conversation aloud. Use as much expression as possible.

Café Haití,
Miraflores, Perú

2 **Una cola, por favor.**   You are at the Café Haití in Miraflores, Perú. Order the following things. A classmate will be the server. Don't forget to find out how much it is and to be polite.

1. un sándwich

2. un té

3. una soda

4. una limonada

5. una ensalada

6. una pizza

3 **Por favor.**   You are at a Mexican restaurant in the United States. Order the following foods. Be polite when you order.

1. tacos

2. enchiladas

3. una tostada

4. una chimichanga

5. un burrito

Cultura

Monetary Systems

When you travel, you will use different currencies.

Spain uses the **euro,** the currency of all countries of the European Common Market.

In many Latin American countries, such as Mexico, the currency is the **peso.**

Venezuela uses the **bolívar,** named in honor of the Latin American hero Simón Bolívar.

In Guatemala, the currency is named after the beautiful national bird—**el quetzal.**

However, in some countries such as Panama the monetary unit is the U.S. dollar.

El tiempo y las estaciones
Telling the seasons

Hay cuatro estaciones en el año. Son:

el invierno

el verano

la primavera

el otoño

1 **La estación, por favor.** Give the season in Spanish.

1. when school starts
2. when school ends
3. when Valentine's Day takes place
4. your birthday
5. U.S. Independence Day

Describing the weather

¿Qué tiempo hace?   Hay (Hace) sol.   Hace mal tiempo.
Hace buen tiempo.   Hace calor.   Llueve.

Hace frío.   Hace fresco.
Nieva.   Hace viento.

 2 ¿Qué tiempo hace hoy?   Tell in Spanish what the weather is like today.

 3 El tiempo   Answer.
1. ¿Qué tiempo hace en el verano?
2. ¿Qué tiempo hace en el invierno?
3. ¿Qué tiempo hace en la primavera?
4. ¿Qué tiempo hace en el otoño?

 ## Manos a la obra

 4 ¿Calor o frío?   Draw a picture of your favorite type of weather. Then describe your picture to the class in Spanish.

Vocabulario

Greeting people

¡Hola!

Buenos días.

Buenas tardes.

Buenas noches.

¿Qué tal?

Muy bien.

Identifying titles

señor

señora

señorita

Saying good-bye

¡Adiós!

¡Chao!

¡Hasta luego!

¡Hasta pronto!

¡Hasta mañana!

Identifying the days of the week

la semana	jueves	hoy
lunes	viernes	mañana
martes	sábado	
miércoles	domingo	

Identifying the months of the year

enero	abril	julio	octubre
febrero	mayo	agosto	noviembre
marzo	junio	septiembre	diciembre

Identifying the seasons

la primavera

el verano

el otoño

el invierno

Telling time

¿Qué hora es?

Es la una.

Son las dos (tres, cuatro…).

¿A qué hora es… ?

A la una.

A las dos.

Being courteous

Por favor.

Gracias.

De (Por) nada.

No hay de qué.

Unidad 1

Amigos y alumnos

Objetivos

In this unit you will learn to:

- ask or tell who someone is
- ask or tell what something is
- ask or tell where someone is from
- ask or tell what someone is like
- count from 1 to 30
- describe people and things
- tell what subjects you take in school and express some opinions about them
- discuss differences between schools in the United States and in Spanish-speaking countries

Café con Libros

Palabras ¿Quién es?

cómico, gracioso cómica, graciosa serio seria

guapo guapa, bonita feo fea

moreno morena rubio rubia

pelirrojo pelirroja

alto alta

bajo baja

Pablo es muy alto. No es bajo.

La muchacha es de Argentina.
Ella es argentina.

Juanito es un amigo de Paula.
Juanito es un amigo muy bueno.
Él es simpático.

Paula es una amiga de Juanito.
Paula es una amiga muy buena.
Ella es simpática.

Los números de 1 a 30

1	uno	16	dieciséis
2	dos	17	diecisiete
3	tres	18	dieciocho
4	cuatro	19	diecinueve
5	cinco	20	veinte
6	seis	21	veintiuno
7	siete	22	veintidós
8	ocho	23	veintitrés
9	nueve	24	veinticuatro
10	diez	25	veinticinco
11	once	26	veintiséis
12	doce	27	veintisiete
13	trece	28	veintiocho
14	catorce	29	veintinueve
15	quince	30	treinta

El muchacho es de Puerto Rico.
Él es puertorriqueño.

¿Qué palabra necesito?

1 Historieta Roberto Gómez

Contesten. *(Answer.)*

1. ¿Es guapo Roberto?
2. ¿Es alto o bajo?
3. ¿Es cómico o tímido?
4. ¿Es moreno o rubio?
5. ¿Es peruano o colombiano?

2 Historieta La amiga de Paco

Contesten. *(Answer.)*

1. ¿Es Susana una amiga de Paco?
2. ¿Es bonita Susana?
3. ¿Es ella tímida o graciosa?
4. ¿Es morena o rubia?
5. Susana, ¿es una amiga simpática?
6. Y Paco, ¿es él simpático también?

3 Historieta Manolo es cubano. Contesten. *(Answer.)*

El muchacho alto es de Cuba.

1. ¿Quién es el muchacho?
   ¿Es Manolo o Roberto?
2. ¿Cómo es Manolo?
3. ¿De dónde es Manolo?
4. ¿Quién es de Cuba?
5. ¿De qué nacionalidad
   es Manolo?

Mercado en la Plaza de la Catedral,
La Habana, Cuba

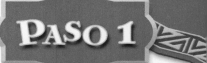
4 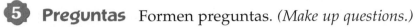 **Historieta** **¿Cómo es la muchacha?**

Contesten. *(Answer.)*

1. ¿Cómo es la muchacha? ¿Es alta o baja?
2. ¿Cómo es la muchacha? ¿Es graciosa o tímida?
3. ¿Cómo es la muchacha? ¿Es pelirroja o morena?
4. ¿Cómo es la muchacha? ¿Es simpática?

5 **Preguntas** Formen preguntas. *(Make up questions.)*

Rafael es *muy gracioso*. →
¿Cómo es Rafael?

1. *María* es de Chile.
2. Paco es *muy serio*.
3. Felipe es *de Cuba*.
4. La amiga de Felipe es *Sofía*.
5. Bárbara es *americana*.

6 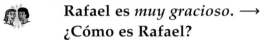 **¿Quién es?** Work in small groups. One person describes someone in class. The others have to guess who is being described. Take turns.

7 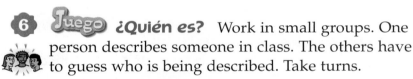 **R o m p e c a b e z a s**

¿Y qué... ? The two words in each line suggest a pattern. Can you think of another word to continue each pattern? With a partner, make up some of your own.

1. dos, tres, ...
2. diez, veinte, ...
3. uno, tres, ...
4. cinco, diez, ...
5. cuatro, ocho, ...
6. treinta, venticinco, ...

 Manos a la obra

8 **Caras** Draw several faces and label the trait of each person you draw.

PASO 1

 Formas Artículos—**el**, **la**, **un**, **una**

Referring to one person or thing

1. The name of a person, place, or thing is a noun. In Spanish, every noun has a gender, either masculine or feminine. Almost all nouns that end in **o** are masculine. Almost all nouns that end in **a** are feminine. In Spanish *the* is either **el** or **la**. You use **el** with masculine nouns and **la** with feminine nouns.

   el muchacho   **la muchacha**
   el amigo   **la amiga**

2. In Spanish *a* or *an* is either **un** or **una**. You use **un** with masculine nouns and **una** with feminine nouns.

   un muchacho   **una muchacha**
   un amigo   **una amiga**

¿Cómo lo digo?

9 **Historieta** El muchacho y la muchacha

Contesten con **sí**. *(Answer with sí.)*

1. ¿Es americano el muchacho?
2. ¿Y la muchacha? ¿Es ella americana?
3. ¿Es guapo el muchacho?
4. ¿Es bonita la muchacha?
5. El muchacho, ¿es Felipe?
6. La muchacha, ¿es Anita?
7. ¿Es Felipe un amigo de Anita?
8. ¿Es Felipe un amigo bueno?
9. ¿Es Anita una amiga de Felipe?
10. ¿Es ella una amiga simpática?

 Adjetivos en el singular
Describing a person or thing

An adjective is a word that describes or modifies a noun. In Spanish, the adjective must agree with the noun it modifies or describes. Study the following examples.

El muchacho americano es alto.   **La muchacha americana es alta.**
Él es un amigo bueno y simpático.   **Ella es una amiga buena y simpática.**

¿Cómo lo digo?

10 ![Historieta] **Un muchacho mexicano**

Contesten. *(Answer.)*

1. ¿Es Antonio mexicano?
2. ¿Es él un muchacho guapo?
3. ¿Cómo es? ¿Es serio o gracioso?
4. ¿Es rubio o moreno?
5. ¿Es Antonio un amigo sincero?

El Zócalo, Ciudad de México

11 ![Historieta] **María**   Cambien **José** a **María**. *(Change José to María.)*

José es colombiano. Él es de la isla de San Andrés. José es moreno. No es rubio. Él es bastante gracioso. No es muy serio. José es un amigo muy bueno.

12 **Un muchacho**   Look at this photograph of a boy from Mexico. Give him a name and say as much as you can about him.

13 **Una muchacha**   Look at this photograph of a girl from Puerto Rico. Give her a name and say as much as you can about her.

PASO 1

 **El verbo ser—formas singulares**

Identifying a person or thing

1. Every sentence has a subject. Let's learn some subjects.

> You use **yo** when you talk *about* yourself.

> You use **tú** when you talk *to* a friend.

> You use **él** or **ella** when you talk *about* someone.

2. Read the following sentences.

> **Yo soy americano(a).**
> **Tú eres americano(a) también.**
> **Él es americano y ella es colombiana.**

The highlighted word in each sentence is the verb. Notice that when the subject of the sentence changes, the verb also changes. Study the following forms of the verb **ser** *(to be)*.

ser	
yo	soy
tú	eres
él	es
ella	

3. To make a sentence negative, you put **no** before the verb.

> **Él no es rubio. Es moreno.**
> **Ella no es baja. Es alta.**

El mar Caribe, Isla de
San Andrés, Colombia

¿Cómo lo digo?

14 ¿Eres americano también?

 Practiquen la conversación. *(Practice the conversation.)*

¡Hola!

¡Hola! ¿Quién eres?

¿Quién? ¿Yo?

Sí, tú.

Pues, yo soy Madela. Madela Ortiz. Y tú, ¿quién eres?

Yo soy Rafael. Rafael Salas.

¿Eres americano, Rafael?

No. Soy de México.

¿De México? ¡Increíble! Yo soy de México también.

15 **Madela y Rafael** Contesten.
(Answer based on the conversation.)

1. ¿Quién es la muchacha?
2. ¿Y quién es el muchacho?
3. ¿De dónde es Rafael?
4. Y Madela, ¿de dónde es ella?
5. ¿De qué nacionalidad es Rafael?
6. ¿De qué nacionalidad es Madela?

PASO 1

 16 **Historieta** Yo soy...

Contesten. *(Answer about yourself.)*

1. ¿Quién eres?
2. ¿Eres americano(a)?
3. ¿De qué nacionalidad eres?
4. ¿De dónde eres?
5. ¿Eres gracioso(a) o serio(a)?
6. ¿Eres moreno(a) o rubio(a)?

 17 **Historieta** José Ayerbe

Ask José questions about himself.
Remember to use **eres.**

1. puertorriqueño
2. de San Juan
3. amigo de Teresa Torres
4. gracioso o serio

Playa de Guajataca, Puerto Rico

18 **Juego** ¿Eres... ?

Toss a ball to another student as you ask any question with **eres.** The person you throw the ball to must be able to answer **no** to your question. He or she will then toss the ball to another student and say something about that student, as in the model.

 19 **Hagan una frase** Use each word in an original sentence.

1. cómica
2. serio
3. pelirroja
4. rubio
5. alto
6. bajo

20 Rompecabezas

¿Quién es el | la culpable?   Look at the following people.
Read the clues to find out who is to blame for eating all the cookies.

Es pelirroja. Es baja. Es seria. ¿Quién es?

Ana   **Paco**   **Carlos**   **Elena**

21 Juego ¿Es una frase?   Put the words in
the right order to form a sentence.

1. yo   amigo(a)   **Paula**   de   soy   un(a)
2. **una**   Teresa   muchacha   venezolana   es
3. **tú**   dónde   **de**   eres
4. no   ella   **fea**   es   es   **bonita**
5. yo   **de**   no   Puerto Rico   soy

*For more practice using words and
forms from **Paso 1**, do Activity 1 on
page H2 at the end of this book.*

El Viejo San Juan,
Puerto Rico

Palabras ¿Quiénes son? 🎧

los alumnos

las alumnas

¡Oye, tú! ¿Quién eres?

¿Yo? Soy Mario. Mario Unimundo. Soy un alumno nuevo aquí.

la escuela

Los alumnos son puertorriqueños.
Son alumnos en una escuela intermedia.

Son alumnos en la misma escuela.
Ellos son amigos también.

Es una clase grande.
Es la clase de español.
Los alumnos son muy inteligentes.
Son muy buenos. No son malos.

¿Quiénes son inteligentes?

Los alumnos.

la clase   el profesor

¿Cómo son los alumnos?

Inteligentes.

la profesora

Es una clase pequeña.
Es una clase interesante.
El curso es bastante difícil (duro).
No es fácil.

Nota

A cognate is a word that looks and means the same in two or more languages. But be careful. Although they look alike, they are pronounced differently. Can you guess what the following school subjects are?

el español   las matemáticas
el inglés   la música
la ciencia   el arte, el dibujo
los estudios sociales   la educación física
la historia

PASO 2

¿Qué palabra necesito?

1 **Historieta** **Dos amigos peruanos**

Contesten. (*Answer.*)

1. ¿Son amigos Roberto y Fernando?
2. ¿Son ellos peruanos?
3. ¿Son ellos alumnos en una escuela en Trujillo?
4. ¿Son muy inteligentes?
5. ¿Son alumnos buenos o malos?

Plaza de Armas, Trujillo, Perú

2 **Historieta** **La clase de español** Contesten.
(Answer about your Spanish class.)

1. ¿Es grande o pequeña la clase de español?
2. ¿Quién es el profesor de español?
3. ¿Es interesante el curso de español?
4. ¿Es fácil o difícil?
5. ¿Son inteligentes los alumnos?

3 **Lo contrario** Completen. *(Complete.)*

1. No son alumnos buenos. Son _____.
2. La clase no es grande. Es _____.
3. El curso no es fácil. Es _____.
4. Ellos no son bajos. Son _____.
5. Ellos no son rubios. Son _____.

4 **Juego** **¿Es fácil o difícil?** Work with a classmate.
Tell one another which courses are easy and which
are difficult. See if you agree.

 Manos a la obra

5 **El horario** Write out your school
schedule in Spanish.

PASO 2

 Formas Sustantivos, artículos y adjetivos en el plural
Describing more than one

1. Plural means *more than one*. In Spanish you add an **s** to most nouns to form the plural.

singular	plural
el muchacho	los muchachos
el curso	los cursos
la amiga	las amigas
la escuela	las escuelas
la clase	las clases

2. Note the plural forms of **el**, **la**, **un**, and **una**.

el curso	**los** cursos
la escuela	**las** escuelas
un alumno	**unos** alumnos
una amiga	**unas** amigas

3. To form the plural of adjectives ending in **o**, **a**, or **e**, add an **s** to the singular form.

El alumno es serio.	**Los alumnos son serios.**
La muchacha es peruana.	**Las muchachas son peruanas.**
La clase es grande.	**Las clases son grandes.**

4. To form the plural of an adjective that ends in a consonant, add **es**.

El curso es fácil.	**Los cursos son fáciles.**

¿Cómo lo digo?

6 **Historieta** Unos amigos

 Contesten con **sí**. (*Answer with* sí.)

1. ¿Son amigos Mara y Roberto?
2. ¿Son mexicanos los dos muchachos?
3. ¿Son alumnos en una escuela secundaria?
4. ¿Son alumnos serios?
5. ¿Son ellos alumnos muy buenos?

7 **En el plural** Cambien al plural.
(*Change each sentence to the plural.*)

1. El muchacho es de México.
2. El muchacho es mexicano.
3. El muchacho es alumno.
4. La muchacha es alumna también.
5. La muchacha es una amiga de Roberto.

San Miguel de Allende. México

8 **¿Quiénes son y cómo son?**

 Give the people in the illustrations names and describe them.

1.   2.   3.   4.

 El verbo ser—formas plurales

Talking about more than one

1. Let's learn some more subjects.

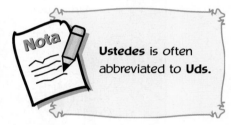

Nota

Ustedes is often abbreviated to **Uds.**

You use **nosotros, nosotras** when you speak *about* yourself and someone else.

You use **ustedes** when you speak *to* more than one person.

You use **ellos** when you speak *about* two or more people.

You use **ellas** when you speak *about* two or more females.

2. Note the plural forms of the verb **ser.**

nosotros(as)	**somos**
ellos	
ellas	**son**
ustedes	

¿Cómo lo digo?

9 **Somos alumnos.** Practiquen la conversación. *(Practice the conversation.)*

10 **Nuevos amigos** Completen según la conversación.
(Complete based on the conversation.)

    Los muchachos ___1___ americanos. Ellos no ___2___ amigos.
Ellos ___3___ alumnos. ¡Qué coincidencia! Ellos ___4___ alumnos
en la misma escuela—Martin Luther King. Ahora ellos ___5___
amigos. La escuela Martin Luther King ___6___ una escuela
muy grande.

11 **Historieta** **Mi amigo(a) y yo**

Contesten. *(Answer about yourself and a friend.)*

1. ¿De qué nacionalidad son ustedes?
2. ¿Son ustedes alumnos(as)?
3. ¿En qué escuela son alumnos(as)?
4. ¿Son ustedes amigos(as) muy buenos(as)?
5. ¿Son ustedes alumnos(as) en la misma clase de español?

12 **¿Y ustedes?** Sigan el modelo.
(Follow the model.)

americanos / mexicanos →
—¿Son ustedes americanos o mexicanos?
—Somos _____.

1. americanos / colombianos
2. alumnos buenos / alumnos malos
3. amigos nuevos / amigos buenos

Santo Domingo, La República Dominicana

13 **Historieta** El amigo de Paco
Completen con **ser.** *(Complete with ser.)*

¡Hola! Yo ___1___ un amigo de Paco. Paco y
yo ___2___ muy buenos amigos. Paco ___3___ de
Puerto Rico y yo ___4___ de la República
Dominicana. Puerto Rico y la República
Dominicana ___5___ dos islas en el mar Caribe.
___6___ dos islas tropicales.

Ahora nosotros ___7___ alumnos en una
escuela intermedia en Nueva York. Nosotros
___8___ alumnos muy buenos. Paco ___9___ un
alumno muy bueno en matemáticas y yo
___10___ un alumno bueno en historia. Y
nosotros dos ___11___ alumnos muy buenos
en español.

Y ustedes, ¿de dónde ___12___? ¿Y quiénes
___13___? ¿___14___ ustedes alumnos muy buenos
en español también?

14 **Mi amigo(a) y yo** Talk to a classmate. Tell
him or her as much as you can about you
and a good friend.

UN POCO MÁS
*For more practice using words and
forms from **Paso 2**, do Activity 2 on
page H3 at the end of this book.*

Andas bien. ¡Adelante!

Conversación
Un alumno nuevo

José	Hola, Ricardo. ¿Qué tal, amigo?
Ricardo	Muy bien, José. ¿Y tú?
José	Bien. Oye, Ricardo, ¿quién es el muchacho allí?
Ricardo	¿Quién? ¿El rubio?
José	Sí, él.
Ricardo	Pues, es Carlos García. Él es un alumno nuevo aquí, pero él y yo somos amigos. ¡C-a-r-l-o-s!
Carlos	¡Hola, Ricardo!
Ricardo	Carlos, José.
Carlos	Mucho gusto, José.
José	Mucho gusto, Carlos. ¿De dónde eres?
Carlos	¿Yo? Soy de Puerto Rico.
José	¿De Puerto Rico? ¡Increíble! Yo también soy puertorriqueño.

¿Comprendes?

A. Contesten. *(Answer.)*

1. ¿Son amigos José y Ricardo?
2. ¿Quién es el muchacho rubio?
3. ¿Es Ricardo un amigo de Carlos?
4. ¿Es Carlos un alumno nuevo en la escuela?
5. ¿De dónde es Carlos?
6. ¿Y de dónde es José?
7. ¿De qué nacionalidad son los dos muchachos?

B. Opinión Do you think Carlos and José will be friends? Why?

Las vocales **a, e, i, o, u**

When you speak Spanish, it is important to pronounce the vowels carefully. The vowel sounds in Spanish are very short, clear, and concise. The vowels in English have several different pronunciations, but in Spanish they have only one sound. Note that the pronunciation of **a** is similar to the *a* in *father*. The pronunciation of **e** is similar to *a* in *mate*. The pronunciation of **i** is similar to the *ee* in *bee* or *see*. The **o** is similar to the *o* in *most,* and **u** is similar to the *u* in *flu.* Imitate carefully the pronunciation of the vowels **a, e, i, o,** and **u.**

a	e	i	o	u
Ana	Elena	Isabel	o	uno
baja	peso	Inés	no	mucha
amiga	Felipe	italiano	Paco	mucho
alumna	feo	tímido	amigo	muchacho

Trabalenguas

Repeat the following.

Ana es alumna.
Adán es alumno.
Ana es una amiga de Adán.
Elena es una amiga de Felipe.
Inés es tímida.
Sí, Isabel es italiana.

Refrán

Can you guess what the following proverb means?

Un amigo sincero es un tesoro divino.

Cultura y lectura
Escuelas

Reading Strategy

Making comparisons As we study Spanish, we will learn many things that are either similar or the same in the Spanish-speaking countries and in the United States. We will also learn things that are different. A good reading strategy is to look for similarities and differences and make comparisons as we read.

Carlos Irizarry es un muchacho alto y guapo. Carlos es de San Juan, la capital de Puerto Rico. Él es alumno en una escuela intermedia en San Juan. Las escuelas públicas en Puerto Rico son como[1] las escuelas en Estados Unidos (EE.UU.). Hay[2] escuelas primarias, escuelas intermedias y escuelas superiores.

[1]como *like*   [2]Hay *There are*

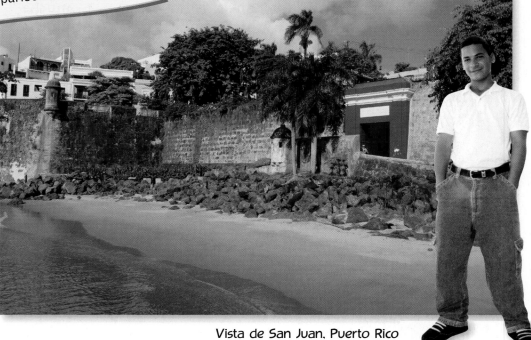

Vista de San Juan, Puerto Rico

Mara Crespo es una alumna muy buena. Ella es una muchacha seria. Es alumna en un colegio en Santiago, la capital de Chile. Pero, ¿qué es un colegio? En muchos países hispanos un colegio es una escuela secundaria. No es una universidad como en Estados Unidos. A veces el colegio es una escuela primaria. Otras palabras para un colegio son «una academia» o «un instituto».

Mara es simpática.

Unidad 1: Amigos y alumnos

Vista de Santiago de Chile

¿Comprendes?

A. ¿Sí o no? *(True or false?)*

1. San Juan es la capital de la República Dominicana.
2. Carlos Irizarry es puertorriqueño.
3. Las escuelas en Puerto Rico son como las escuelas en Chile.
4. Hay escuelas intermedias en Puerto Rico.
5. Un colegio es una universidad en Estados Unidos.
6. Un colegio es una universidad en Chile también.

B. Comparen. *(Compare.)*

1. In what area of the Spanish-speaking world are schools referred to by the same terms as those in the United States?
2. What is **un colegio** in the United States? What is **un colegio** in many Spanish-speaking countries?
3. What are other words that can be used instead of **colegio?**
4. Is **un colegio, una academia,** or **un instituto** always a secondary school?

Repaso

1. In this unit, I learned the important verb **ser.**

singular	plural
soy	**somos**
eres	
es	**son**

2. I also learned that nouns in Spanish are either masculine or feminine.
   Any word or adjective that modifies or describes a noun must agree with it.

el amigo   **los amigos**
un amigo   **unos amigos**

la escuela   **las escuelas**
una alumna   **unas alumnas**

El amigo es sincero.   **Los amigos son sinceros.**
La muchacha es seria.   **Las muchachas son serias.**
La escuela es grande.   **Las escuelas son grandes.**
El curso es difícil.   **Los cursos son difíciles.**

Vista parcial. Plaza de Armas. Lima, Perú

¡Pongo todo junto!

1 **Alumnos** Completen con **ser.** *(Complete with* ser.*)*

1. Yo _____ alumno(a).
2. Carlos _____ un muchacho chileno.
3. Ellos _____ alumnos en un colegio en Santiago.
4. Nosotros _____ alumnos muy buenos en español.
5. ¿Tú _____ un(a) alumno(a) muy bueno(a) en español también?
6. ¿De dónde _____ ustedes?

Alumnos en San Juan, Puerto Rico

2 **¿Singular o plural?** Cambien las frases.
(Change each sentence to the singular or plural.)

1. Las clases son interesantes y grandes.
2. La escuela no es pequeña.
3. El curso es bastante fácil.
4. Los amigos son simpáticos.

¡Te toca a ti!

Hablar

1 Un amigo nuevo

✓ *Describe your new friend*

Work with a classmate. Here is a photograph of your new friend, Sergio Álvarez. Sergio is from Chile. Say as much as you can about him. In addition, answer any questions your partner may have about Sergio.

La alumna panameña es muy bonita, ¿no?

Hablar

2 La escuela y los cursos

✓ *Talk about school and subjects you take*

You recently met Isabel Cortés, a student from Panamá. She does not know much about schools in the United States. Tell her something about your school. Tell her what courses are interesting, hard, or easy. Also, tell her which courses are required (**obligatorios**) or optional (**opcionales**).

Hablar

3 ¿Eres un alumno nuevo?

✓ *Talk about yourself and get information about someone else*

Miguel Orjales (a classmate) is new to your school. He just arrived from Costa Rica. Make him feel at home. Find out as much as you can about Miguel. Tell him similar information about yourself, too.

4 Una postal

✓ *Write a postcard*

You're vacationing with your family in Ecuador. Write a postcard to a friend at home telling him or her about some new friends in Ecuador. Their names are Nando, Antonio, Lupe, and Sandra.

Writing Strategy

Describing Much of the writing we do deals with description. For example, we often write a description of a person. To put some order to your description you may want to start by giving a physical description of the person. You may then want to state some of his or her traits and background. When you describe a person in Spanish, remember to stick to the words you know. Remember also that any word you use must agree with the person you are describing. When you finish writing your description, be sure to check the endings of the words you use to describe the person.

5 Un amigo y una amiga

Write a description of a boy and a girl. Write as much as you can about each one.

PASO 3

Assessment

¿Estoy listo(a)?

Palabras

1 Completen. *(Complete.)*

1. El muchacho es _____. No es alto.
2. Ella no es muy seria. Es bastante _____.
3. Carlos es un _____ muy bueno en matemáticas.
4. Rosita es una _____ muy buena y sincera.
5. El _____ de español es interesante y fácil.
6. La clase es pequeña. No es _____.

To review words from **Paso 1** and **Paso 2**, turn to pages 20–21 and 30–31.

2 Escojan. *(Choose.)*

7. ¿Quién es?
   a. Carlos   **b.** la clase   **c.** grande
8. ¿Cómo es él?
   a. mexicano   **b.** José   **c.** alto
9. ¿De dónde es?
   a. la escuela   **b.** Puerto Rico   **c.** sincero
10. ¿Quiénes son?
   a. los cursos   **b.** José y Tomás   **c.** el profesor

Formas

3 Completen con **ser.** *(Complete with* ser.*)*

11. ¡Hola! Yo _____ Madela.
12. ¿De dónde _____ tú?
13. Nosotros _____ amigos.
14. ¿_____ ustedes alumnos?
15. Él _____ un alumno muy bueno en español.
16. Los cursos _____ interesantes.

To review the use of **ser,** turn to pages 26 and 35.

Unidad 1: Amigos y alumnos

4 Escojan. *(Choose.)*

17. _____ muchacho es de Guatemala.

   a. El   **b.** La   **c.** Los

18. Carlos es _____ amigo sincero.

   a. una   **b.** unos   **c.** un

19. _____ escuelas son grandes.

   a. Las   **b.** Los   **c.** La

To review the use of articles, turn to pages 24 and 34.

5 Completen. *(Complete.)*

20–21. Los alumnos son _____ y _____.
   (inteligente, bueno)

22. La amiga de Pablo es _____. (rubio)

23. Los cursos son _____. (difícil)

To review the agreement of adjectives, turn to pages 24 and 34.

Cultura

6 ¿Sí o no? *(True or false?)*

24. Una academia es una escuela intermedia en Puerto Rico.

25. Un colegio es una escuela primaria o secundaria en muchos países latinoamericanos.

To review this cultural information, turn to pages 40–41.

Una pirámide maya.
Tikal, Guatemala

PASO 4

Diversiones

Canta con Justo
Eres tú

Co - mou - na pro - me - sa   e - res tú,   e - res   tú,

co - mou - na ma - ña - na   de ve - ra_____ no,_____

co - mou - na son - ri - sa   e - res tú,   e - res tú,_____ a - sí___ , a-

sí   e - res   tú,

Como una esperanza eres tú, eres tú
como lluvia fresca en mis manos
como fuerte brisa eres tú, eres tú
así, así eres tú.

Eres tú como el agua de mi fuente;
eres tú el fuego de mi hogar.

Como mi poema eres tú, eres tú
como una guitarra en la noche
como mi horizonte eres tú, eres tú
Así, así eres tú.

Algo así eres tú,
Algo así como el fuego de mi hoguera
Algo así eres tú
En mi vida va a decir eres tú.

Pamplona

U - no de e - ne - ro, dos de fe - bre - ro, tres de mar - zo, cua - tro de a - bril, cin - co de ma - yo, seis de ju - nio, sie - te de ju - lio, San Fer - mín

Uno de enero, dos de febrero
tres de marzo, cuatro de abril,
cinco de mayo, seis de junio
siete de julio, San Fermín
a Pamplona hemos de ir
con una bota, con una bota,
con una bota y un tamborín.

Investigaciones

Puerto Rico In this unit, you learned that the schools in Puerto Rico follow the same system as those in the United States. In Puerto Rico there are elementary, intermediate or middle, and high schools. Puerto Rico has a very special relationship with the United States. It is called **un estado libre asociado** or *commonwealth* in English. Do some research to learn about the history of Puerto Rico.

Spanish Online

For more information about Puerto Rico, go to the Glencoe Spanish Web site: spanish.glencoe.com.

Una *escuela* en Dorado, Puerto Rico

Teatro

Have some fun. You are going to be a mime and mimic the meaning of the following words. See who can be the most original.

feo(a)   serio(a)   guapo(a)   difícil

tímido(a)   alto(a)   gracioso(a)

 Manos a la obra

1. Un mapa Draw an outline map of any Spanish-speaking country. Locate its capital and write the name of the capital on your map. On your map you must also include a picture (drawing or photograph) of a person. In your own words, say everything you can about this fictitious person.

2. Descripciones Draw a series of faces that illustrate some personal traits or physical characteristics you learned in this lesson. Label each face with the appropriate Spanish word.

Rompecabezas

¿Cuántas frases? How many sentences can you make from these words? Use each word only once in a sentence.

alumnos   los   son

puertorriqueños   amigos   inteligentes

Entrevista

¿Quién eres?
¿De dónde eres?
¿De qué nacionalidad eres?
¿Cómo eres?
¿En qué escuela eres alumno(a)?
¿Qué tipo de alumno(a) eres?

PLEGABLES™
Study Organizer

La geografía Use this *pocket book* organizer in your ongoing study of all the countries in the Spanish-speaking world.

Step 1 **Fold** a sheet of paper (8 1/2″ x 11″) in half like a *hamburger.*

Step 2 **Open** the folded paper and fold one of the long sides up two inches to form a pocket. Refold the *hamburger* fold so that the newly formed pockets are on the inside.

Step 3 **Glue** the outer edges of the two-inch fold with a small amount of glue.

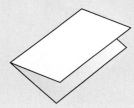

Step 4 **Make a multipaged booklet** by gluing six pockets side-by-side. Glue a cover around the multipaged *pocket book.*

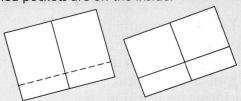

Step 5 **Label** five pockets with the following geographical areas: **Europa, la América del Norte, la América del Sur, la América Central,** and **Islas del Caribe.** Use index cards inside the pockets to record information each time you learn something new about a specific country. Be sure to include the name of the country (in Spanish, of course) and its capital.

Más cultura y lectura

Personajes latinos famosos

Muchos cantantes famosos en Estados Unidos son de ascendencia hispana.

▲ Es una fotografía de Enrique Iglesias. Enrique es un cantante muy popular. Él es de España. Es un muchacho guapo, ¿no? Los conciertos de Enrique son fantásticos.

▲ ¡Hola! Yo soy Gloria Estefan. Yo soy cantante también. Soy de Miami. Soy cubanoamericana. En Florida y en muchas otras partes de Estados Unidos hay mucha gente[1] de ascendencia cubana.

[1]gente *people*

¿Comprendes?

Identifiquen. *(Identify.)*

1. de donde es Enrique Iglesias
2. la profesión de Enrique Iglesias
3. la nacionalidad de Gloria Estefan

Conexiones
Las matemáticas

La aritmética

We seldom do a great deal of arithmetic in a foreign language. We normally do arithmetic in the language in which we learned it. However, it is fun to do some simple arithmetic in Spanish. You can because all you need to know is the verb **ser,** which you have already learned.

La aritmética en español

$2 + 2 = 4$ Dos y dos <mark>son</mark> cuatro.
$10 + 5 = 15$ Diez y cinco <mark>son</mark> quince.

$4 - 3 = 1$ Cuatro menos tres <mark>es</mark> uno.
$10 - 4 = 6$ Diez menos cuatro <mark>son</mark> seis.

$2 \times 5 = 10$ Dos por cinco <mark>son</mark> diez.
$5 \times 4 = 20$ Cinco por cuatro <mark>son</mark> veinte.

$15 \div 3 = 5$ Quince entre tres <mark>son</mark> cinco.
$24 \div 6 = 4$ Veinticuatro entre seis <mark>son</mark> cuatro.

¿Comprendes?

La aritmética en español
(Do the following problems aloud in Spanish.)

1. $2 + 2 = 4$ **5.** $4 \times 4 = 16$
2. $14 + 6 = 20$ **6.** $8 \times 3 = 24$
3. $30 - 8 = 22$ **7.** $27 \div 9 = 3$
4. $14 - 13 = 1$ **8.** $24 \div 3 = 8$

¡Hablo como un pro!

Tell all you can about the following illustration.

Colegio Simón Bolívar

Vocabulario

Identifying a person or thing

el muchacho	el alumno	el colegio
la muchacha	la alumna	la escuela
el amigo	el profesor	la clase
la amiga	la profesora	el curso

Identifying school subjects

el español	los estudios sociales	la música
el inglés	la historia	el arte, el dibujo
la ciencia	las matemáticas	la educación física

Describing a person

alto(a)	rubio(a)	serio(a)
bajo(a)	moreno(a)	tímido(a)
guapo(a)	pelirrojo(a)	simpático(a)
bonito(a)	gracioso(a)	sincero(a)
feo(a)	cómico(a)	ser

Describing teachers and courses

pequeño(a)	intermedio(a)	inteligente
bueno(a)	mismo(a)	interesante
malo(a)	difícil, duro(a)	grande
nuevo(a)	fácil	

Stating nationalities

americano(a)	colombiano(a)	peruano(a)
argentino(a)	cubano(a)	puertorriqueño(a)
chileno(a)	mexicano(a)	venezolano(a)

Finding out information

¿quién? ¿quiénes?	¿de dónde?
¿qué?	¿de qué nacionalidad?
¿cómo?	

Other useful expressions

también	bastante
muy	

Unidad

2

Mi familia y mi casa

Objetivos

In this unit you will learn to:

- talk about your family
- count from 31 to 100
- describe your home
- tell what you and others have
- tell your age and find out someone else's age
- speak to people informally and formally
- tell what belongs to you and to others
- talk about families in Spanish-speaking countries

Las Terrazas
San Miguel

Santo Domingo 3

Palabras Mi familia 🎧

> Soy Melinda Lagos.
> Es mi padre.
> Yo soy la hija de mi padre.
> Julio es mi hermano.

> Soy Julio Lagos.
> Es mi madre.
> Yo soy el hijo de mi madre.
> Melinda es mi hermana.

> Mi padre tiene una hermana.
> Su hermana es Laura.
> Su hermana es mi tía Laura.
> Yo soy el sobrino de mi tía.

> Mi madre tiene un hermano.
> Su hermano es Alejandro.
> Su hermano es mi tío Alejandro.
> Yo soy la sobrina de mi tío.

Mi tía tiene un hijo.
Su hijo es mi primo.
Mi primo tiene trece años.

Mi tío tiene una hija.
Su hija es mi prima.
Mi prima tiene once años.

Son los padres de mis padres.
Sus padres son mis abuelos.
Y yo soy su querido nieto.

Mi perrito y mi gato son otros miembros de mi familia.

un perrito

un gato

Más números 🎧

31	treinta y uno	39	treinta y nueve
32	treinta y dos	40	cuarenta
33	treinta y tres	50	cincuenta
34	treinta y cuatro	60	sesenta
35	treinta y cinco	70	setenta
36	treinta y seis	80	ochenta
37	treinta y siete	90	noventa
38	treinta y ocho	100	ciento, cien

Nota

You may have a step-parent or stepbrother or stepsister. In Spanish, you can say:

mi padrastro

mi madrastra

mi hermanastro

mi hermanastra

¿Qué palabra necesito?

1 Historieta Mis parientes Contesten. *(Answer.)*

1. ¿Eres la hija o el hijo de tu madre?
2. ¿Eres la sobrina o el sobrino de tu tía?
3. ¿Eres el nieto o la nieta de tus abuelos?
4. ¿Eres el primo o la prima de la hija de tu tío?

2 Un diccionario

Completen. *(Complete.)*

1. mi _____: el hijo de mi padre o de mi madre
2. mi _____: la hija de mi padre o de mi madre
3. mi _____: el hermano de mi madre
4. mi _____: la hija de mi tío o de mi tía
5. mi _____: el padre de mi madre
6. mi _____: la madre de mi padre

3 Historieta Juan y Adela Torres

Contesten según se indica. *(Answer as indicated.)*

1. ¿Tiene Juan una hermana? (sí)
2. ¿Tiene Adela un hermano? (sí)
3. ¿Cuántos años tiene Juan? (once)
4. Y, ¿cuántos años tiene Adela? (trece)
5. ¿Quién es menor? (Juan)
6. ¿Quién es mayor? (Adela)

4 Los dos o todos Completen. *(Complete.)*

Mi madre y mi padre son mis padres.

1. Mi hermano y mi hermana son mis _____.
2. Mi tío y mi tía son mis _____.
3. Mi primo y mi prima son mis _____.
4. Mi abuelo y mi abuela son mis _____.
5. Mis parientes son mis _____, mis _____ y mis _____.

Abuelita con su nieto en el parque.
Ronda, España

PASO 1

5 R o m p e c a b e z a s

¡Adivina! ¿Quién es la nieta de Isabel?

    Teresa es la hija de Isabel.
    Juana es la hermana de Teresa.
    Sofía es la hermana de Paco.
    Teresa es la madre de Paco.

Es María, María Unimundo. Ella es mi hermana.

6 Juego ¿Qué pariente es?

Give a definition of a relative in Spanish. Your partner will tell you who it is.

7 R o m p e c a b e z a s

El intruso Choose the word in each group that does not belong. The first letter in each **intruso** will reveal the secret word.

1. bonita   baja   guapa   feo
2. abuelo   prima   hija   tía
3. padre   abuelo   primo   madre
4. tío   padre   hermana   inteligente
5. los abuelos   las hijas   las nietas   las tías
6. hija   italiana   nieta   sobrina
7. amigo   hermano   tío   primo

Es mi _____.

PASO 1

 Formas El verbo **tener**—formas singulares

Telling what you and others have

Study the singular forms of the verb **tener**.

yo	tengo
tú	tienes
él ella	tiene

Nota You use **tener** to tell age.
Yo tengo trece años.
Mi hermano menor
tiene once años.

¡Alguien Cumple Años!

¡Y lo vamos a festejar!

De Alba González
Fecha 5 de diciembre Hora 4 de la tarde
Lugar Residencia González
c/ Poeta Guillermo Colón, 6
Ofrecida por Julio y María González
Teléfono 20-47-12

¿Cómo lo digo?

 8 **Historieta** **Juan Salas** Contesten. (*Answer.*)

1. ¿Tiene Juan una familia grande o pequeña?
2. ¿Tiene Juan dos hermanos o siete hermanos?
3. ¿Cuántos años tiene Juan?
4. ¿Tiene Juan un gato o un perrito?
5. ¿Tiene Juan muchos amigos en la escuela?
6. ¿Tiene un excelente profesor de español?

Una familia dominicana,
Santo Domingo

9 **¿Tienes un hermano?** Practiquen la conversación.
(Practice the conversation.)

10 **Historieta** **Mi familia**

Contesten. *(Answer.)*

1. ¿Tienes una familia grande o pequeña?
2. ¿Tienes hermanos?
3. ¿Cuántos hermanos tienes?
4. ¿Y tú? ¿Cuántos años tienes?
5. ¿Tienes un perro?
6. ¿Tienes un gato?

11 **Miniconversación**

Sigan el modelo. *(Follow the model.)*

una familia grande →
—¿Tienes una familia grande?
—Sí, (No, no) tengo una
familia grande.

1. un hermano
2. una hermana
3. muchos primos
4. muchos amigos
5. un perro adorable
6. un gato cómico

Estatuas de perros en una plaza,
Las Palmas de Gran Canaria, España

Ana López
Antonio López
Carlos López
Marisa López
Juan López
Maja
Elisa López
Chispa

12 **Juego** **La familia** Work in small
groups. Take turns asking questions
about the relatives to the left. Follow
the model.

—¿Quién es la hermana de Juan?
—Elisa es la hermana de Juan.

13 **Juego** **¿Tienes... ?** Take turns
throwing a ball to another student as
you ask if he or she has something.
He or she will answer *no,* throw the
ball to someone else, and tell you
that that person has it.

14 **Juego** **Tengo hermanos.**
Work with a classmate. Take turns
asking one another questions about
your family or someone else's family.

 Tú o usted

Talking informally and formally

1. In Spanish you use **tú** when you talk to a friend, a family member, anyone your own age, or someone you know well.

> **Carlos, ¿eres amigo de Luisa Torres?**
> **¿Tienes un hermano, Enrique?**

2. You use **usted,** often abbreviated **Ud.,** when you speak to an adult whom you do not know well. **Usted** is more respectful than **tú.**

> **Señora, ¿de dónde es usted?**
> **¿Tiene usted familia aquí?**

¿Cómo lo digo?

15 **¿Tú o usted?** Look at the photos. Ask each person where he or she is from and if he or she has a large family.

1. 2. 3.

4. 5.

*For more practice using words and forms from **Paso 1**, do Activity 3 on page H4 at the end of this book.*

Palabras   Mi casa 🎧

una casa

un jardín

el carro

La familia Solís tiene una casa privada.
Ellos tienen una casa grande.
La casa de los Solís tiene seis cuartos.

Su casa tiene un jardín bonito.
Pero no tiene un garaje.

Los Solís tienen un carro.
Su carro es nuevo.
No es viejo.

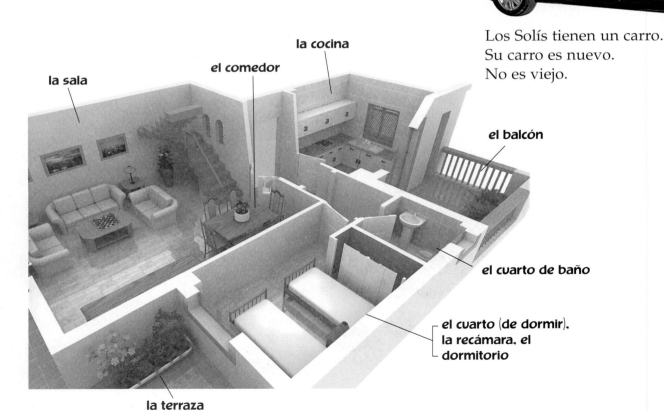

la sala

el comedor

la cocina

el balcón

el cuarto de baño

el cuarto (de dormir),
la recámara, el
dormitorio

la terraza

un edificio alto

un apartamento

un piso

la planta baja

Los Gómez tienen un apartamento.
Tienen un apartamento en un edificio alto.
El edificio tiene seis pisos.
Cada piso tiene varios apartamentos.

Hoy es el cumpleaños de Susana Gómez.
Ella tiene quince años.
Hay una fiesta.
Todos sus parientes tienen regalos para
la quinceañera.
Hay también una torta.
En la torta hay quince velas.

el cumpleaños

el regalo

la vela

la torta, el pastel

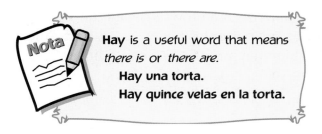

Nota

Hay is a useful word that means
there is or *there are*.
Hay una torta.
Hay quince velas en la torta.

PASO 2

¿Qué palabra necesito?

1 **Historieta** **La casa de los Pidal**

Contesten. (*Answer.*)

1. ¿Tienen los Pidal una casa privada?
2. ¿Tienen una casa bastante grande?
3. ¿Cuántos cuartos tiene su casa?
4. ¿Cuántos dormitorios hay en su casa?
5. ¿Es bonita la casa?
6. ¿Tiene un jardín?
7. ¿Tienen los Pidal un carro?
8. ¿Es nuevo su carro?

Una casa privada.
San Isidro. Lima. Perú

2 **Historieta** **Un apartamento**

Contesten. (*Answer.*)

1. ¿Tienen los Ugarte un apartamento?
2. ¿Tienen un apartamento en un edificio alto?
3. ¿Es bastante grande el apartamento?
4. ¿Cuántos cuartos tiene?
5. ¿Tiene muchos pisos el edificio?
6. ¿Cuántos pisos tiene?
7. ¿Es muy alto el edificio?
8. ¿Hay varios apartamentos en cada piso?

3 **Historieta** **Una celebración en honor de la quinceañera**

Completen. (*Complete.*)

1. Alicia _____ quince años.
2. Hoy es el _____ de Alicia.
3. Alicia es una _____.
4. Hay una _____ en honor de la quinceañera.
5. Todos sus parientes tienen _____ para Alicia.
6. También hay un(a) _____ con quince _____ para Alicia.

Casas de departamentos.
Miraflores. Lima. Perú

4 Rompecabezas

¿Qué cuarto es? Use the floor plan to identify each room of the house. Then unscramble the circled letters to reveal the hidden message.

1. _ _ _Ⓞ Ⓞ Ⓞ
2. _ _Ⓞ _ _Ⓞ _ _
3. _Ⓞ _ _ _ _ _
4. _ _ _ _Ⓞ _ _ _ Ⓞ _ _ _
5. Ⓞ _Ⓞ Ⓞ
6. _ _ _ _Ⓞ _ _

_ _ _ _ _ _ _ _ _ _ _ _

Casas bonitas en Estepona, España

Manos a la obra

5 Mi casa o mi apartamento Draw a plan of a house or an apartment. Think about all you can say in Spanish about "your" house or apartment. Then get together with a classmate. Ask one another questions about your "architectural plan."

Paso 2: Palabras

sesenta y nueve ✿ 69

Formas El verbo **tener**—formas plurales
Telling what you and others have

Now study the plural forms of **tener.**

mi hermano y yo nosotros(as)	tenemos

| ellos
ellas
Uds. | tienen |

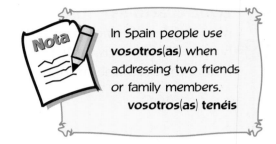

¿Cómo lo digo?

6 **¿Casa o apartamento?** Practiquen la conversacíon.
(Practice the conversation.)

7 Historieta **Nuestra familia** Contesten. *(Answer.)*

1. ¿Tienen ustedes una familia grande o pequeña?
2. ¿Tienen ustedes una casa privada o un apartamento?
3. ¿Tienen ustedes un carro?
4. ¿Tienen un carro nuevo?
5. ¿Tienen ustedes un gato?
6. ¿Tienen un perrito?

8 ¿Qué tienen ustedes?

Sigan el modelo. *(Follow the model.)*

> **muchos o pocos primos** →
> —_____ y _____, ¿tienen ustedes
> **muchos o pocos primos?**
> —Tenemos _____ primos.

1. una familia grande o pequeña
2. una casa o un apartamento
3. un perro o un gato
4. un carro o una bicicleta

Jóvenes en Órgiva, España

San Miguel de Allende, México

9 Historieta **La familia Obregón**

Completen con **tener.** *(Complete with* tener.*)*

Aquí __1__ (nosotros) una fotografía de la familia Obregón. La familia Obregón __2__ una casa muy bonita en México. Su casa __3__ ocho cuartos. Los Obregón __4__ dos hijos, Lupita y Marcos.

Lupita: Hola, mi hermano Marcos __5__ once años y yo __6__ quince. Marcos y yo __7__ un perro. Nuestro perro es Merlín. Es adorable y cómico.

Marcos: Y tú, ¿cuántos años __8__? ¿__9__ (tú) hermanos? ¿Cuántos hermanos __10__ (tú)? ¿__11__ ustedes una casa o un apartamento? ¿__12__ (ustedes) un gato o un perro?

10 Juego ¿Qué tienen ustedes?

Get a ball. Throw the ball to a classmate and ask what he or she and his or her brother or friend have. The person who catches the ball will answer. Then he or she will throw the ball and ask another question. Keep going.

Los adjetivos posesivos
Telling what belongs to whom

1. A possessive adjective tells who owns or possesses something—*my book* and *your pencil*. Study the possessive adjectives in Spanish.

yo	**mi** padre	**mi** prima	**mis** padres	**mis** primas
tú	**tu** padre	**tu** prima	**tus** padres	**tus** primas

él ella él y ella Ud., Uds.	**su** padre	**su** prima	**sus** padres	**sus** primas

2. The possessive adjectives **mi, tu,** and **su** have only two forms—singular and plural. The adjective **su** can refer to many different people

el libro de Juan	**el libro de él**	**su libro**
los libros de María	**los libros de ella**	**sus libros**
la casa de mis padres	**la casa de ellos**	**su casa**
la casa de usted	**la casa de ustedes**	**su casa**

3. The possessive adjective **nuestro**, like any other adjective that ends in **o**, has four forms.

nosotros(as)	**nuestro** padre	**nuestra** prima
	nuestros padres	**nuestras** primas

Nota: In Spain people also use **vuestro** with the **vosotros(as)** form of the verb.

¿Cómo lo digo?

 11 **Historieta** **Mi familia** Contesten. *(Answer.)*

1. ¿Es grande o pequeña tu familia?
2. ¿Cuántos años tiene tu hermano o tu hermana?
3. ¿Tiene tu familia un gato o un perro?
4. ¿Cómo es tu gato o tu perro?
5. ¿Tiene tu familia una casa o un apartamento?
6. ¿Es grande o pequeña(o) tu casa o tu apartamento?

Jaime y su hermana son de
Puerto Limón, Costa Rica.

12 **Historieta** **Unas preguntas**

 Sigan los modelos. *(Follow the models.)*

> **Yo tengo una prima.** →
> —**¿Ah, sí? ¿Quién es tu prima?**
> —**Mi prima es _____.**
>
> **Yo tengo dos primas.** →
> —**¿Ah, sí? ¿Quiénes son tus primas?**
> —**Mis primas son _____ y _____.**

1. Yo tengo un primo.
2. Yo tengo dos primos.
3. Yo tengo una amiga.
4. Yo tengo dos amigos.
5. Yo tengo un(a) excelente profesor(a) de español.

PASO 2

13 **Historieta** **Los parientes**

Contesten según el modelo. *(Answer according to the model.)*

> **¿El hijo de tu tío es tu primo?** →
> **Sí, sí. Su hijo es mi primo.**

1. ¿Los hijos de tu tío son tus primos?
2. ¿El padre de tu madre es tu abuelo?
3. ¿Los padres de tus padres son tus abuelos?
4. ¿La hermana de tu madre es tu tía?
5. ¿El primo de tu hermana es tu primo también?

14 **Historieta** **La casa de nuestra familia**

Contesten. *(Answer.)*

1. ¿Tienen ustedes una casa?
2. ¿Es grande o pequeña su casa?
3. ¿Cuántos cuartos tiene su casa?
4. ¿Y cuántas personas hay en su familia?
5. ¿Tiene su casa un jardín?
6. Y sus primos, ¿tienen ellos una casa o un apartamento?
7. ¿Tienen sus primos un perro o un gato?
8. Y ustedes, ¿tienen un perro o un gato?
9. ¿Cómo es su perro o gato?

RIVIERA

232

Excelente villa
en construcción, 3 dorms., 3 baños, gran salón. Con garaje y piscina propia. Parcela de 500 m2

Tel. 952.493.474

Precio: 420.708 €

RIVIERA

266

Piso
de 2 dormitorios en estupenda zona, ascensor y aire acondicionado, piscina y parking comunitario

Tel. 952.493.474

Desde: 102.172 €

15 **Historieta** **Nuestra escuela** Contesten. *(Answer.)*

1. ¿Es grande o pequeña la escuela de ustedes?
2. Su clase de español, ¿es grande o pequeña?
3. En general, ¿son grandes o pequeñas sus clases?
4. ¿Sus cursos son muy interesantes?

Alumnas en Arecibo, Puerto Rico

16 **¿De quién?** Get together with a classmate. Talk to him or her about some things that you have, he or she has, or a friend or some friends have. Here are some words you may want to use.

casa   apartamento   carro

perro   gato   clase   escuela

amigo   CD   profesor   profesora

amiga   DVD

For more practice using words and forms from **Paso 2,** *do Activity 4 on page H5 at the end of this book.*

Andas bien. ¡Adelante!

Conversación
¿Tienes un hermano?

Felipe Lucas, ¿tienes un hermano?

Lucas Yo, no. No tengo hermano. Pero tengo una hermana.

Felipe ¿Ah, sí? ¿Quién es tu hermana?

Lucas ¿Mi hermana? Es Leonora.

Felipe ¿Leonora? ¿La amiga de Maripaz?

Lucas Sí, Leonora es una amiga de Maripaz.

Felipe ¿Cuántos años tiene tu hermana?

Lucas ¡Oye, Felipe! Tienes muchas preguntas, ¿no?

¿Comprendes?

A. Contesten. *(Answer.)*

1. ¿Tiene Lucas un hermano?
2. ¿Qué tiene?
3. ¿Quién es su hermana?
4. ¿Quién es la amiga de su hermana?
5. Y Felipe, ¿qué tiene él?

B. ¿Tiene Felipe mucho interés en la hermana de Lucas?

Las consonantes f, l, m, n, p

The pronunciation of the consonants **f, l, m, n,** and **p** is very similar in both Spanish and English. However, the **p** is not followed by a puff of air as it often is in English. Repeat the following.

f	l	m	n	p
fiesta	la	mucho	nieto	Pepe
favor	Lola	menor	nuevo	papá
familia	Lupe	mayor	no	padre
fácil	abuelo	madre	alumno	piso
	abuela	malo		popular
		moreno		Perú
		cómico		guapo
		amigo		

Trabalenguas

Repeat the following.

Mi hermano menor es Manolo.
Mi abuela no es Lolita.
Mis abuelos no tienen un nieto nuevo.
El apartamento de Pepe tiene dos pisos.
Pepa es peruana. Es una alumna popular.

Refrán

Can you guess what the following proverb means?

Los mejores amigos son los buenos libros.

Cultura y lectura

La familia Garza

Reading Strategy

Using context clues When you read in a foreign language, you will almost always come across some words you do not know. In this reading there are two words you do not know. However, you can guess their meaning from the way they are used in the sentence. Guessing the meaning of words in context (how they are used together with other words) is a very important reading skill in a foreign language.

La familia Garza no es muy grande y no es muy pequeña. Los señores Garza tienen tres hijos—Jorge, Mara y José Luis. Jorge, el menor, tiene ocho años. Mara tiene quince años y José Luis, el mayor, tiene dieciséis años. Mara y José Luis son alumnos en un colegio (instituto) en Lima, la capital de Perú.

Los Garza son de Miraflores, un suburbio bonito de Lima en la costa del Pacífico. Los Garza tienen una casa privada. Su casa tiene siete cuartos. Alrededor de su casa hay un jardín bonito con muchos árboles y muchas flores.

Hoy hay una celebración muy importante en la casa de los Garza. Es el cumpleaños de Mara. Hay una fiesta en su honor. Todos sus parientes—sus primos, sus tíos y sus abuelos—y sus amigos tienen regalos para la quinceañera. La quinceañera es una muchacha muy importante. Hay una torta con quince velas para ella.

¿Comprendes?

A. **Contesten.** *(Answer.)*
1. ¿Cuántos hijos tienen los Garza?
2. ¿Cuántos años tienen sus hijos?
3. ¿Dónde son alumnos Mara y José Luis?
4. ¿De dónde son los Garza?
5. ¿Qué tienen los Garza en Miraflores?
6. ¿Qué hay alrededor de su casa?
7. ¿Qué hay en el jardín?

B. ¿Por qué tienen los parientes de Mara regalos para ella?

C. Today is a very important day for Mara. Why? In the United States, which birthday is a very important birthday for a girl? What is it called?

D. Were you able to guess the meaning of words in context? How do you say *trees* in Spanish? How do you say *flowers?*

PASO 3

Repaso

1. In this unit, I learned the verb **tener.**

tengo	tenemos
tienes	*tenéis*
tiene	tienen

2. I also learned the possessive adjectives.

mi primo	**mi** prima	**mis** primos	**mis** primas
tu primo	**tu** prima	**tus** primos	**tus** primas
su primo	**su** prima	**sus** primos	**sus** primas

BUT

nuestro primo	**nuestra** prima	**nuestros** primos	**nuestras** primas

¡Pongo todo junto!

1 **Todos tenemos.** Completen. *(Complete.)*

1. Yo _____ trece años.
2. Y mi hermana _____ diez años.
3. Nosotros _____ un apartamento en Lima.
4. Nuestra casa _____ seis cuartos.
5. ¿Tú _____ una casa o un apartamento?
6. Tus hermanos y tú, ¿cuántos años _____ ustedes?

2 **¿De quién es?** Contesten. *(Answer.)*

1. ¿Cuántos años tiene tu hermano?
2. ¿Cuántos cuartos tiene su casa (la casa de ustedes)?
3. ¿Quiénes son los hermanos de tu padre?
4. ¿Quién es tu primo o tu prima?
5. ¿Cómo es su gato o su perro?

La Molina, Lima, Perú

Edificios altos, Miraflores, Lima, Perú

PASO 3

¡Te toca a ti!

1 Fotos de un álbum

✓ *Talk about someone's family*

Look at this photo taken from the Gomez' family album. With a classmate describe some of the family members. Take turns and be as original as possible.

Una familia de ascendencia mexicana

Hablar

2 Una fiesta o una celebración

✓ *Compare a family celebration*

Work with a classmate. Pretend one of you is from a Spanish-speaking country and the other is from the United States. Tell one another about a **quinceañera** and a *sweet sixteen*.

PASO 3

3 Mi familia y yo

✓ *Write about yourself and your family*

You hope to be able to spend a couple of weeks during your summer vacation with a family in Argentina. You have to write a letter about yourself and your family to be selected for the visit. Make your description as complete as you possibly can.

Writing Strategy

Ordering details Once again, remember that when you write in a foreign language you have to "stick to" what you know how to say. Even though you may only be able to write a little, you have to give your writing some order. The order often depends upon your topic. In this writing activity, the topic will be a home so you may want to use what is called "spatial ordering." This means that you will describe things as they actually appear, the order in which they appear—from left to right, bottom to top—any order that makes sense and works. First be sure to make yourself a list of Spanish words you know that describe a house or an apartment.

Escribir

4 La casa o el apartamento de mis sueños

Write a description of your dream home. Be as complete as you can.

Assessment

¿Estoy listo(a)?

Palabras

To review words from **Paso 1**, turn to pages 58–59.

1 Completen. (*Complete.*)

1. Mis padres tienen dos hijos. Yo soy Carlos y mi _____ es Ana.
2. Mi padre tiene una hermana. Su hermana es mi _____.
3. Mi tío Alberto tiene un hijo. Su hijo es mi _____.
4–5. Los padres de mis padres son mis _____ y yo soy su _____.

2 Identifiquen. (*Identify.*)

6.　　　　　　　7.　　　　　　　8.

To review words from **Paso 2**, turn to pages 66–67.

9.　　　　　　　10.　　　　　　　11.

Formas

To review the use of **tener**, turn to pages 62 and 70.

3 Escriban una oración nueva. (*Write a new sentence.*)

12. Susana tiene muchos primos.
    Sus amigos _____.
13. Él tiene un perro.
    Tú también _____.
14. Tenemos una casa privada.
    Yo no _____.
15. Ustedes tienen un jardín bonito.
    Nosotros _____.
16. Ella tiene un profesor muy bueno.
    Yo también _____.

4 Completen. *(Complete.)*

17. Yo tengo un hermano. _____ hermano tiene doce años.
18. El amigo de mi hermano es Carlos. _____ amigo Carlos es un alumno muy bueno.
19. Nosotros tenemos un apartamento. _____ apartamento es bastante grande.
20. Tú tienes un perro, ¿no? ¿Es muy divertido _____ perro?
21. Carlos y María, ¿tienen _____ padres un carro nuevo?
22. Yo tengo muchos cursos en la escuela y _____ cursos son interesantes.

To review possessive adjectives, turn to page 72.

Cultura

5 Identifiquen. *(Identify.)*

23. la capital de Perú
24. un suburbio de la capital de Perú
25. una muchacha que hoy celebra sus quince años

To review this cultural information, turn to pages 78–79.

Plaza de Armas. Lima. Perú

PASO 4

Diversiones

Canta con Justo
Mi familia

Tengo un cuadro	Yo quiero estar
de mi familia	siempre con ellos estar
ellos sonríen	bueno es tener un hogar
con alegría	en donde reine la paz
lindos momentos	yo quiero estar
increíbles recuerdos	siempre con ellos estar
que hoy hay en mí.	como olvidar
	excelentes momentos
	que mi familia me da.

Teatro

Make gestures, such as brushing your teeth or washing your hair, and have classmates shout out the name of the room in the house where you would do what you are acting out. Try to be as imaginative as possible. This "charade" game can be done as a team competition as well.

Juego **Un pariente** Unscramble the letters to reveal the names of relatives. Then unscramble the circled letters to reveal the mystery relative.

1. B U A L E O Ⓞ _ _ _ _ _
2. D A M R E _ _ Ⓞ _ _
3. R I A P M Ⓞ _ _ _ _
4. T I E N O _ _ Ⓞ _ _
5. O N I R B O S _ _ _ Ⓞ _ _ _

_ _ _ _ _

Rompecabezas

Act out with expression. Try to figure out what expression and tone of voice are appropriate when role-playing both Leonora and her father.

Leonora	Papá, ¿el perrito?
Papá	Pero, ¿qué perrito, mi hija? ¡Tienes tres!
Leonora	Sí, sí. Tenemos tres.
Papá	Tres perritos son muchos, mi hija.
Leonora	Sí, papá. Pero nuestros perros son adorables, ¿no?
Papá	¿Nuestros perros? ¿Son mis perros también?
Leonora	¡Cómo no, papá! Son tus perros también.
Papá	OK, mi hija. Nuestros perros son adorables.

PASO 4

 ## Manos a la obra

1. **Un árbol genealógico** Draw a family tree. It can be your own family, someone else's family, a famous family, or even a make-believe family. After you draw your family tree, label all the family members. Then work with a classmate and say as much as you can about **el árbol genealógico.**

2. **Un álbum familiar** Get some old family photos. Make a family album. Then either say or write as much as you can about the photos in your family album.

3. **La casa de mis sueños** Draw a picture of the house or apartment you wrote about on page 83. Then tell some things about it.

Investigaciones

Perú The geography of Peru is fascinating. Find out some information about the three major geographical areas or regions of Peru.

 ### Spanish Online

For more information about Peru, go to the Glencoe Spanish Web site: spanish.glencoe.com.

Machu Picchu

Entrevista

¿Tienes una familia grande o pequeña?

¿Cuántas personas hay en tu familia?

¿Cuándo es tu cumpleaños?

¿Cuántos años tienes?

¿Tiene tu familia una casa privada o un apartamento?

¿Cuántos cuartos tiene?

¿Tienen ustedes un gato o un perro?

Si tienen un gato o un perro, ¿cómo es?

Sinónimos y antónimos Use this *vocabulary book* to practice your vocabulary through the use of synonyms and antonyms.

Step 1 **Fold** a sheet of notebook paper in half like a *hot dog.*

Step 2 On one side, **cut** every third line. This usually results in ten tabs. Do this with two sheets of paper to make two books.

Step 3 **Label** the tops of the *vocabulary books* with the word **Sinónimos** on one and **Antónimos** on the other. As you learn new vocabulary in each unit, try to categorize words in this manner. Remember also to think of words you have previously learned to fill in your books.

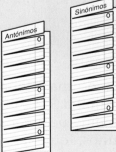

PASO 4

Más cultura y lectura

Distintos tipos de casas

Hay muchos tipos de casas en el mundo hispanohablante.

◀ La familia Chancay es de un pueblo pequeño de los Andes en Perú. Los Andes son montañas muy altas en la América del Sur. Aquí tienen ustedes una fotografía de una casa típica de la región andina. Es de piedra con techo de paja.

▲ Los Toledo no tienen una casa privada. Ellos tienen un departamento en un edificio alto en San Isidro. San Isidro es otro suburbio muy bonito de Lima, la capital. Su departamento es muy bonito y muy moderno, ¿no? El edificio es bastante alto. De su departamento hay vistas muy bonitas.

▲ Aquí tenemos una fotografía de la casa de la familia Sosa. Ellos son de un pueblo muy pequeño en la región de Iquitos. Iquitos es un puerto del río Amazonas en Perú. Es una zona de junglas tropicales. La casa de los Sosa es una casa lacustre—una casa sobre palos[1].

[1] palos *stilts*

¿Comprendes?

Identifiquen. *(Identify.)*
1. un suburbio bonito de Lima
2. un apartamento en Perú
3. unas montañas altas en la América del Sur
4. una casa típica de la región andina
5. un río muy largo de la América del Sur
6. una casa sobre palos en una región tropical

Conexiones
Las Bellas Artes

El arte y la historia

Art and history are often closely connected. Looking at a beautiful painting brings us much enjoyment. It can also teach us a great deal about the period in which it was produced. A portrait, for example, shows us how people looked and dressed at the time.

Today many families keep a photo album. Prior to the invention of photography, many families had a portrait painted. This was particularly true of the royal families—**las familias reales.**

Here are some very basic words associated with art.

el cuadro

el retrato

la escultora

la estatua

la pintura

la pintora

la escultura

el caballete

el pintor

el escultor

PASO 4

CONEXIONES
Las Bellas Artes (continuado)

Diego Velázquez—el famoso pintor español

Muchas familias tienen un álbum de fotografías de los miembros de su familia. ¡Qué adorable es la foto de un bebé— sobre todo (especialmente) si el bebé es un hijo, sobrino o nieto!

Pero antes de la invención de la cámara en los 1800, no hay fotografías. Si no hay fotos, no hay álbum de familia.

¿Qué hay? Pues, muchas familias, sobre todo las familias reales, tienen retratos.

Aquí tenemos el retrato del Rey Felipe IV de España. Es del famoso pintor español del siglo XVII, Diego Velázquez.

Y aquí tenemos un cuadro muy famoso de Velázquez—*Las Meninas*. En el cuadro tenemos la hija del Rey con sus damas y su perro; en el espejo[1], el reflejo de la Reina y del Rey; delante de[2] su caballete, el pintor mismo, Diego Velázquez.

[1]espejo *mirror* [2]delante de *in front of*

El *Museo* del Prado. Madrid. España

Investigaciones

Velázquez If art interests you, find out some more about the famous Spanish painter Diego Velázquez and his works.

Spanish Online

For more information about Spanish art, go to the Glencoe Spanish Web site: **spanish.glencoe.com**.

¿Comprendes?

A. **Busquen.** *(Look at the painting* Las Meninas *and find the following people.)*
  1. el artista
  2. la hija del Rey
  3. las meninas o damas de la princesa
  4. el perro de la princesa
  5. el padre de la princesa, el Rey
  6. la madre de la princesa, la Reina

B. Velázquez has excellent ways of showing dimension. Give examples of what he does in this painting.

C. Discuss what you learn about the clothing of the seventeenth century when you look at these paintings.

¡Hablo como un pro!

Tell all you can about the following illustration.

Vocabulario

Identifying family members

la familia	la madre	el/la sobrino(a)
los parientes	la madrastra	el/la primo(a)
el/la abuelo(a)	el/la hijo(a)	el perro (perrito)
el/la nieto(a)	el/la hermano(a)	el gato
el padre	el/la hermanastro(a)	
el padrastro	el/la tío(a)	

Talking about family affairs or events

el cumpleaños	la vela	tener... años
el regalo	la fiesta	
la torta, el pastel	la quinceañera	

Identifying rooms of the house

la sala	el cuarto (de dormir), la
el comedor	recámara, el dormitorio
la cocina	el balcón
el cuarto de baño	la terraza

Talking about a home

la casa	el jardín
el apartamento	el carro
el edificio	el garaje
el piso	privado(a)
la planta baja	

Other useful expressions

¿cuántos(as)?	menor
mucho(a)	mayor
poco(a)	todo(a)
viejo(a)	hay

Unidad

3

En casa y en clase

Objetivos

In this unit you will learn to:

- talk about what you and others do at home
- talk about going to school
- talk about some school activities
- talk about parties
- count from 100 to 1000
- describe where you and others go
- describe where you and others are
- discuss some differences between schools in the United States and schools in Spanish-speaking countries

¡Vamos a la escuela con nuestros amigos!

¡Qué bien!

CALLE LAS DAMAS

Palabras En casa

Mamá prepara la comida en la cocina.

Más números
100	ciento, cien
200	doscientos
300	trescientos
400	cuatrocientos
500	quinientos
600	seiscientos
700	setecientos
800	ochocientos
900	novecientos
1000	mil

Nota

Ciento is shortened to **cien** before any word that is not a number.
  cien pesos
  ciento ochenta pesos

¿Qué toma la familia?

El desayuno.

el desayuno

La familia toma el desayuno.
Toma el desayuno en la cocina.

La familia está en el comedor.
La familia cena en el comedor.

¿Cuándo va la familia a la sala?

¿Cuándo? Después de la cena.

Después de la cena, la familia va a la sala.

mirar

estudiar

hablar

Mamá mira la televisión.
Mira su emisión favorita.
Mi hermana habla por teléfono.

Mi hermano prepara su lección de español.
Él estudia mucho.

A veces la familia da una fiesta.
Guadalupe celebra su cumpleaños.
Durante la fiesta ella baila.
Su primo canta.

Paso 1: Palabras

PASO 1

¿Qué palabra necesito?

1 Historieta En casa

Contesten. (*Answer.*)

1. ¿Está en casa la familia Amaral?
2. ¿Quién prepara la comida? ¿Mamá o papá?
3. ¿Dónde prepara la comida?
4. ¿Dónde cena la familia?
5. Después de la cena, ¿adónde va la familia?
6. ¿Qué mira papá?
7. ¿Mira su emisión favorita en la televisión?

San Miguel de Allende, México

2 Historieta José Luis

Contesten. (*Answer.*)

1. Después de la cena, ¿prepara José Luis su lección de español?
2. ¿Prepara su lección en su cuarto de dormir?
3. Después, ¿habla por teléfono?
4. ¿Habla con su amiga?
5. ¿Habla con su amiga de sus cursos?
6. ¿Habla también de sus planes para el viernes?

¡Felices 15 Años!

3 Historieta Una fiesta Contesten según se indica. (*Answer as indicated.*)

1. ¿Qué da la familia de Anita? (una fiesta)
2. ¿La familia da la fiesta en honor de quién? (Anita)
3. ¿A quiénes invita la familia a la fiesta? (a sus parientes y a sus amigos)
4. ¿Qué celebra la familia? (el cumpleaños de Anita)
5. ¿Cuántos años tiene Anita? (quince)
6. ¿Qué tienen sus amigos y parientes para la quinceañera? (regalos)
7. ¿Quién canta durante la fiesta? (su tía)
8. ¿Baila su tía también? (no, su primo)

¿Qué? Sigan el modelo. *(Follow the model.)*

    Mamá prepara la comida. →
    ¿Qué prepara mamá?

1. Mamá mira la televisión.
2. Papá mira la tele.
3. José estudia matemáticas.
4. Elena prepara su lección.
5. Carlos celebra su cumpleaños.

 Una familia española The Suárez family is from Madrid. Look at these illustrations of the Suárez family at home. Tell what they do. You may also want to describe them.

 ¿Dónde? Tell what someone is doing. Class members will have to guess where he or she does it.

    Jorge baila. →
    ¿Baila Jorge en la fiesta?

PASO 1

Formas — Los verbos en -ar—formas singulares

Talking about what people do

1. Many verbs or action words in Spanish belong to a family called a conjugation. The first conjugation verbs have an infinitive (*to speak, to prepare*) that ends in **-ar**. All regular **-ar** verbs have the same endings. Note that the endings change with each subject.

	mirar	hablar	preparar	endings
yo	miro	hablo	preparo	-o
tú	miras	hablas	preparas	-as
él ella Ud.	mira	habla	prepara	-a

2. Because the ending changes, you do not always have to use the subject in Spanish. The ending tells you who does the action.

You use the ending **-o** when you talk *about* yourself.

You use the ending **-as** when you talk *to* a friend.

You use the ending **-a** when you talk *about* someone.

¿Cómo lo digo?

7 Historieta En casa Contesten según se indica. (*Answer as indicated.*)

1. ¿Quién prepara la comida? (papá)
2. ¿Dónde prepara la comida? (en la cocina)
3. ¿Dónde cena la familia? (en el comedor)
4. ¿Qué mira mamá? (la televisión)
5. ¿Dónde mira la televisión? (en la sala)
6. ¿Cuándo mira la televisión? (después de la cena)
7. ¿Cuándo prepara Carlos su lección de español? (después de la cena)

Papá prepara una tortilla española. Málaga, España

8 **Hablo por teléfono.** Practiquen la conversación.
(Practice the conversation.)

9 **Historieta** **¡Hola!** Contesten.
(Answer based on the conversation.)

1. ¿Habla Roberto por teléfono?
2. ¿Mira él la televisión?
3. ¿Con quién habla?
4. ¿Es Teresa la profesora?
5. ¿Es Teresa una amiga de Roberto?
6. ¿Estudia Teresa?
7. ¿Estudia Roberto?

10 **Historieta** **Yo** Contesten. *(Answer about yourself.)*

1. ¿Hablas inglés?
2. ¿Hablas inglés y español?
3. ¿Hablas inglés o español en casa?
4. ¿Qué hablas en la clase de español?
5. ¿Estudias mucho en la escuela?
6. ¿Preparas tu lección de español en casa?
7. ¿Preparas tu lección después de la cena?
8. Después, ¿miras la televisión?
9. ¿Miras la televisión en la sala?

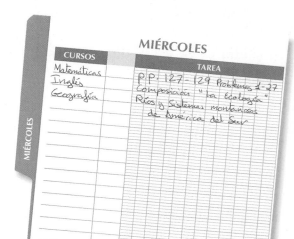

11 **Perdón, ¿qué?** Sigan el modelo. *(Follow the model.)*

Preparo la comida. →
Perdón, ¿qué preparas?

1. Preparo mi lección.
2. Estudio matemáticas.
3. Hablo italiano.

4. Miro mi emisión favorita.
5. Tomo el desayuno.

12 **Historieta** **Una fiesta** Completen. *(Complete.)*

Hoy es el cumpleaños de Catalina. Ella __1__ (celebrar) sus quince años. Catalina __2__ (invitar) a sus amigos y a sus parientes a la fiesta. Su mamá __3__ (preparar) una comida para la fiesta.

Yo soy una amiga de Catalina. Durante la fiesta yo __4__ (bailar). Yo __5__ (bailar) mucho pero no __6__ (cantar). Yo no __7__ (cantar) porque no tengo una voz bonita.

Y tú, ¿__8__ (cantar) y __9__ (bailar) cuando vas a una fiesta?

13 **Juego** **¿Quién?** Throw a ball to someone in the class. Ask him or her a question with **tú.** He or she catches the ball and answers your question with **Yo no.** Then he or she throws the ball to a third person who gives the name of a person who does what you ask.

Los verbos ir, dar, estar—formas singulares

Talking about people's activities

The verbs **ir** *(to go)*, **dar** *(to give)*, and **estar** *(to be)* are irregular verbs because they have a different **yo** form. All other forms are the same as those of a regular **-ar** verb.

yo	voy	doy	estoy
tú	vas	das	estás
él			
ella	va	da	está
Ud.			

Nota

You use **estar** to express how you feel.
¿Cómo estás?
Estoy bien, gracias.

¿Cómo lo digo?

14 **A la fiesta** Practiquen la conversación. *(Practice the conversation.)*

—¿Vas a la fiesta de Tomás?

—Sí, voy. Tú vas también, ¿no?

—Claro que voy. Tomás siempre da una fiesta buena.

El *colegio* San José. Estepona. España

15 **Yo** Contesten. *(Answer about yourself.)*

1. ¿Estás en la escuela ahora?
2. ¿Estás en la clase de español?
3. ¿En qué clase estás?
4. Después de las clases, ¿vas a casa?
5. ¿Vas a casa con tus hermanos?
6. ¿Vas a casa con tus amigos?
7. Cuando estás en casa, ¿vas a la sala?
8. Cuando estás en la sala, ¿miras la televisión?

16 **Perdón, ¿cuándo vas?**

Sigan el modelo. *(Follow the model.)*

Voy a la cafetería después de la clase de español. →
Perdón, ¿cuándo vas a la cafetería?

1. Voy a casa después de las clases.
2. Voy a la sala después de la cena.
3. Estoy en casa los domingos.
4. Doy una fiesta el viernes.

17 **R o m p e c a b e z a s**

Palabras nuevas Change one letter in each word to form a new word.

1. voy
2. mala
3. todas
4. su
5. en

*For more practice using words and forms from **Paso 1**, do Activity 5 on page H6 at the end of this book.*

Palabras   A la escuela 🎧

en el bus escolar   **a pie**   **en carro**

¿Adónde van los alumnos?

Van a la escuela.

Los alumnos van a la escuela.
No van en el bus escolar.
Van a pie.

Los alumnos llevan uniforme
    a la escuela.
Los alumnos entran en la escuela.

Los alumnos están en la clase de español.
El profesor habla.
Los alumnos escuchan cuando el profesor habla.
Ellos prestan atención.

un CD

un DVD

un video

Algunos alumnos escuchan un CD.
Otros miran un video.

Los alumnos sacan notas buenas.

una nota buena

una nota mala

Las alumnas toman el almuerzo
en la cafetería.

Un alumno tiene una pregunta.
Levanta la mano.
El profesor contesta (a) la pregunta.
Los alumnos toman apuntes.

Nota

La mano is a funny
word. It ends in **o**
but takes **la**.

la mano

tomar apuntes

¿Qué palabra necesito?

1 **Historieta** A la **escuela**

Contesten. *(Answer.)*

1. ¿Van los alumnos a la escuela?
2. ¿Algunos van a pie?
3. ¿Van otros en carro?
4. ¿Toman algunos el bus escolar?
5. ¿Entran los alumnos en la escuela?
6. ¿Llevan uniforme cuando van a la escuela?

Toman el bus escolar,
Quito, Ecuador

2 **Historieta** En clase Contesten según se indica.
(Answer as indicated.)

1. ¿En qué clase están los alumnos? (la clase de español)
2. ¿Quién habla? (el profesor)
3. ¿Quiénes escuchan? (los alumnos)
4. ¿Prestan atención cuando el profesor habla? (sí)
5. ¿Qué escuchan? (un CD)
6. ¿Qué miran? (un video)
7. ¿Hablan mucho los alumnos en la clase de español? (sí)
8. ¿Qué contestan? (muchas preguntas)

Los alumnos están en la cafetería,
Santurce, Puerto Rico

3 En la **escuela** ¿Sí o no? *(True or false?)*

1. El profesor levanta la mano cuando tiene una pregunta.
2. Los alumnos escuchan cuando el profesor habla.
3. Los alumnos hablan cuando el profesor habla.
4. Los alumnos estudian mucho y sacan notas buenas.
5. Cuando estudian mucho sacan notas malas.
6. Los alumnos cenan en la cafetería de la escuela.

4 **Perdón.** Sigan el modelo. *(Follow the model.)*

> **Van a la escuela.** →
> **Perdón. ¿Adónde van?**

1. Van a la clase de español.
2. Van a la cafetería.
3. Van a casa.
4. Van a la fiesta.

Las alumnas van a la escuela.
San Andrés, Colombia

5 **¿Una clase típica?** Look at all that's taking place in this classroom. Describe it in your own words.

PASO 2

 **Formas**   Los verbos en **-ar**—formas plurales: **ir, dar, estar**
Describing people's activities

1. Now study the plural forms of regular **-ar** verbs.

	mirar	hablar	tomar	endings
nosotros(as)	miramos	hablamos	tomamos	-amos
ellos ellas Uds.	miran	hablan	toman	-an

You use **-amos** when you talk *about* yourself and someone else.

You use **-an** when you talk *about* or *to* two or more people.

Nota

In many parts of Spain, **vosotros(as)** is used instead of **ustedes** (abbreviated **Uds.**) when speaking to two or more friends or relatives.
vosotros habláis

2. The verbs **ir, dar,** and **estar** have the same plural endings as a regular **-ar** verb.

nosotros	vamos	damos	estamos
ellos ellas Uds.	van	dan	están

¿Cómo lo digo?

6 **Historieta** Los alumnos también
Sigan el modelo. *(Follow the model.)*

> **La profesora va a la escuela en carro.** →
> **Los alumnos van a la escuela en carro también.**

1. La profesora entra en la escuela.
2. La profesora habla.
3. La profesora escucha.
4. La profesora contesta muchas preguntas.
5. La profesora prepara su lección.
6. La profesora toma el almuerzo en la cafetería.

7 **Historieta** **En casa** Contesten.
(Answer about yourself and a friend.)

1. Cuando ustedes están en casa, ¿miran la televisión?
2. ¿Miran la televisión antes o después de la cena?
3. ¿Van ustedes a la sala?
4. ¿Escuchan ustedes CDs también?
5. ¿Preparan su lección de español?
6. ¿Estudian ustedes mucho?

8 **Y ustedes, ¿qué?**
Sigan el modelo. *(Follow the model.)*

> **hablar** →
> —**¿Qué hablan ustedes?**
> —**Hablamos español.**

1. preparar
2. mirar
3. escuchar
4. estudiar
5. celebrar
6. llevar
7. tomar

8,95 €/unidad

9 **Historieta** **En un colegio en Ecuador**
Completen. *(Complete.)*

Julio __1__ (ser) ecuatoriano. Él __2__ (estudiar) en un colegio en Quito. Los alumnos de su colegio __3__ (llevar) uniforme. Uno de los amigos de Julio __4__ (hablar):

—Sí, nosotros __5__ (llevar) uniforme al colegio. ¿No __6__ (llevar) ustedes uniforme cuando __7__ (ir) a la escuela?

Los amigos de Julio __8__ (tomar) muchos cursos. En algunos cursos los profesores __9__ (dar) muchos exámenes. Algunos cursos __10__ (ser) fáciles y otros __11__ (ser) difíciles.

Un amigo __12__ (preguntar):

—¡Oye, Julio! ¿En qué cursos __13__ (sacar) tú notas buenas y en qué cursos __14__ (sacar) notas malas?

Julio __15__ (contestar):

—Si yo __16__ (estudiar) mucho, __17__ (sacar) notas altas. Si no __18__ (estudiar) mucho, __19__ (sacar) notas bajas. Y ustedes, ¿__20__ (estudiar) mucho o no?

Los alumnos llevan uniforme.
Quito, Ecuador

PASO 2

10 **Una clase** Ask a classmate about one of his or her classes. Then he or she will ask about one of your classes. You may want to use some of the following words.

estudiar **tomar** grande hablar

prestar atención

¿quién? bueno(a) ¿cuándo? ¿qué?

pequeño(a) ir mirar malo(a) ser

 ## La contracción al
Expressing direction

1. The preposition **a** means *to*. **A** contracts with **el** to form one word—**al**. **A** does not contract with **la**, **las**, or **los**.

Voy a la escuela.	**Voy al colegio.**
Vamos a la fiesta.	**Voy al dormitorio.**

2. The preposition **a** is also used when a specific person or persons follows a verb. It is called the "personal a" and it has no English equivalent.

Miro la televisión.	**Miro a mi hermano.**
Escucho el CD.	**Escucho al profesor.**

El *recreo*, Estepona, España

¿Cómo lo digo?

11 **¿Adónde vas?** Contesten según el modelo.
(Answer according to the model.)

el colegio →
Voy al colegio.

1. el dormitorio
2. el café
3. el cuarto de dormir
4. el garaje
5. la escuela
6. la clase de español
7. la fiesta
8. la cafetería
9. la sala

12 **Voy a...** Preparen una conversación.
(Prepare a conversation based on each illustration.)

—**¿Adónde vas?**
—**¿Quién? ¿Yo?**
—**Sí, tú.**
—**Pues, voy al colegio.**

1.   2.   3.

13 **¿Qué o a quién?** Contesten. *(Answer.)*

1. ¿Miras el video?
2. ¿Miras a la profesora?
3. ¿Miras al muchacho?
4. ¿Miras a las muchachas?
5. ¿Escuchas el CD?
6. ¿Escuchas a tus padres?
7. ¿Escuchas a los profesores?
8. ¿Escuchas al profesor de español?

*For more practice using words and forms from **Paso 2**, do Activity 6 on page H7 at the end of this book.*

Andas bien. ¡Adelante!

Conversación

¿Vas a una fiesta?

Julio	Hola, Ricardo. ¿Qué tal? ¿Cómo estás?
Ricardo	Bien, Julio, ¿Y tú?
Julio	Bien. Oye, ¿adónde vas el viernes?
Ricardo	Voy a casa de Lupita.
Julio	¿A casa de Lupita? ¡Ay, verdad! Ella da una fiesta.
Ricardo	Sí. Tú vas también, ¿no?
Julio	Sí, claro. ¿Por qué no vamos juntos?

¿Comprendes?

A. Contesten. *(Answer.)*

1. ¿Quiénes hablan?
2. ¿Adónde va Ricardo el viernes?
3. ¿Qué da Lupita?
4. ¿Va Julio también?
5. ¿Van juntos los dos amigos?

B. Do you think Julio had forgotten about the party? Why?

Pronunciación

La consonante t

The **t** in Spanish is pronounced with the tip of the tongue pressed against the upper teeth. It is not followed by a puff of air. Repeat the following.

ta	te	ti	to	tu
taco	Teresa	tímido	toma	tú
canta	interesante	tiempo	tomate	estudia
está	teléfono	tiene	alto	estupendo
presta		latín		

Trabalenguas

Repeat the following.

> **Tú tienes un gato tímido.**
> **Tú tomas apuntes en latín.**
> **Teresa invita a Tito a la fiesta.**

Refrán

Can you guess what the following proverb means?

En boca cerrada no entran moscas.

Cultura y lectura
Un muchacho español

Reading Strategy

Looking for clues When you are reading, you may come across a word you are not familiar with. Sometimes that word is followed by another word that tells you something more about it and helps clarify its meaning. Look for examples of this as you read this selection.

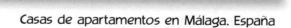

Casas de apartamentos en Málaga, España

Miguel es un muchacho malagueño. Su familia tiene un piso (un apartamento) muy bonito en Málaga en el sur de España.

Por la mañana Miguel toma el desayuno en casa con su familia. Su desayuno favorito es churros y chocolate. Después del desayuno, Miguel va a la escuela.

Miguel tiene catorce años y es alumno en el colegio San José. Los alumnos de su colegio llevan uniforme. Su colegio es una escuela privada. En España y en Latinoamérica muchos alumnos van a escuelas privadas. En el colegio los alumnos toman unos ocho cursos. Son muchos, ¿no?

Miguel y sus amigos toman el almuerzo en la cafetería o cantina de la escuela. Después de las clases van a un café donde hablan de sus amigos, de sus profesores y de sus clases. En el café toman un refresco, una soda o un sándwich. Después van a casa. En casa Miguel cena con su familia. Después va a su dormitorio. En su dormitorio prepara sus lecciones. Luego va a la sala donde mira su emisión favorita en la tele.

¿Comprendes?

Churros y chocolate

A. Contesten. *(Answer.)*
1. ¿Quién es un muchacho malagueño?
2. ¿Dónde tiene su familia un piso?
3. ¿Dónde toma Miguel el desayuno?
4. ¿Cuál es su desayuno favorito?
5. ¿Cuántos años tiene Miguel?
6. ¿Qué llevan Miguel y los otros alumnos a su escuela?
7. ¿Qué tipo de escuela es su colegio?
8. ¿Toman los alumnos muchos cursos?

B. Escojan. *(Choose the correct completion.)*
1. Miguel y sus amigos toman el almuerzo _____.
   a. en casa   **b.** en clase   **c.** en la cafetería
2. Después de las clases van _____.
   a. al colegio   **b.** al café   **c.** a casa
3. En el café toman _____.
   a. el bus   **b.** el desayuno   **c.** un refresco
4. Miguel cena _____.
   a. en casa   **b.** en la escuela   **c.** en el café
5. Él prepara sus lecciones _____.
   a. en la sala   **b.** en clase   **c.** en su dormitorio

C. Den la palabra. *(Give another word.)*
1. un apartamento en España
2. la cantina
3. un sándwich o una soda

D. Comparen. *(Compare some things you learned about schools in Spain and Latin America with schools in the United States.)*

Repaso

1. In this unit, I learned the present tense of regular **-ar** verbs.

mirar

yo	miro		nosotros	miramos
tú	miras		vosotros	*miráis*
él, ella, Ud.	mira		ellos, ellas, Uds.	miran

hablar

yo	hablo		nosotros	hablamos
tú	hablas		vosotros	*habláis*
él, ella, Ud.	habla		ellos, ellas, Uds.	hablan

2. I also learned the verbs **ir, dar,** and **estar.** They have the same endings as a regular **-ar** verb in all forms except **yo.**

yo   voy   doy   estoy

3. The preposition **a** contracts with **el** to form the word **al.**

Voy al café.

Escucho al profesor.

Los amigos hablan en el Parque Forestal, Santiago de Chile

¡Pongo todo junto!

1 **Todos** Escriban. *(Rewrite each sentence with the new subject.)*

1. Ella mira su emisión favorita.
   Ellas
2. Tú hablas español.
   Yo
3. Tomamos apuntes.
   Teresa
4. No preparo la cena.
   Tú
5. Ustedes cantan.
   Nosotros

2 **Yo** Contesten. *(Answer.)*

1. ¿Adónde vas después de las clases?
2. ¿Estás en la clase de español o en casa?
3. ¿Das una fiesta a veces?

3 **¿Adónde y a quién?** Completen. *(Complete.)*

1. Voy _____ escuela.
2. Escucho _____ profesor.
3. Vamos _____ laboratorio de biología.
4. Él invita _____ amigos.
5. Ellos van _____ dormitorio.

Las alumnas van a casa. Argentina

4 **Juego** **Más información** Play a game called "adding information." One student will say something. Then another student will add something to it. Use the model as a guide.

—**Él saca notas malas.**

—**Sí, él saca notas malas. No estudia.**

5

Use your manipulatives to practice the verbs you learned in this unit.

PASO 3

¡Te toca a ti!

 Hablar

1 En casa

✓ *Talk about what you do at home*

Work with a classmate. Tell one another some of the typical things you do at home. Compare your activities and tell what you both do.

La Torre del Oro. Sevilla, España

 Hablar

2 Diferencias

 ✓ *Talk about school activities*

Your school is going to have an exchange student from Sevilla. Based on what you have learned about schools in the Spanish-speaking world, tell some things the exchange student will find that are different. Also tell what he or she will find that is similar.

 Hablar

 3 A la escuela

 ✓ *Talk about going to school*

With a classmate, look at this illustration of students going to school. Take turns saying as much as you can about it.

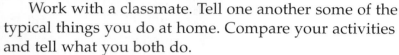

4 La vida *escolar*

✓ *Write about school life*

Your Spanish friend wants to know what a typical school day is like. In a short e-mail, tell him or her all you can about a typical day in school.

To :	julio_torres@colegiomirabal.es
From :	ann_stevens@wilsonmiddle.edu
Subject :	¡Hola!
Date :	25 de enero

Add/Edit Attachments   Send

Writing Strategy

Preparing for an interview An interview is one way to gather information for a story or a report. A good interviewer should prepare questions ahead of time. The best interview questions are open-ended. Open-ended questions cannot be answered with "yes" or "no." They give the person being interviewed more opportunity to "open up" and speak freely.

Escribir

5 Guadalupe Álvaro

It is the beginning of a new school year. Your first assignment for the school newspaper is to write an article about a new exchange student, Guadalupe Álvaro. Guadalupe is from Quito, Ecuador. You decide to interview Guadalupe before writing your article. To prepare for the interview, write down as many questions as you can. Ask her about her personal life, her school life in Quito, her friends, etc. After you have prepared your questions, conduct the interview with a partner who plays the role of Guadalupe. Write down your partner's answers to your questions. Then organize your notes and write your article.

Quito, Ecuador

Assessment

¿Estoy listo(a)?

Palabras

*To review words from **Paso 1**, turn to pages 98–99.*

1 Completen. *(Complete.)*

1. Mamá o papá prepara _____ en la cocina.
2. _____ la cena, todos van a la sala.
3. En la sala miramos la _____.
4. Mi hermano _____ por teléfono con su amiga.
5–6. Hoy Alicia _____ su cumpleaños y su familia _____ una fiesta.

*To review words from **Paso 2**, turn to pages 106–107.*

2 Contesten. *(Answer.)*

7. ¿Qué llevan los alumnos a la escuela?
8. ¿Cómo van a la escuela?
9. ¿Quiénes prestan atención cuando el profesor habla?
10. ¿Qué notas sacan los alumnos buenos?
11. ¿Dónde toman el almuerzo los alumnos?

Formas

*To review the use of **-ar** verbs, turn to pages 102 and 110.*

3 Escojan. *(Choose.)*

12. Yo _____ español.
    a. hablo   **b.** habla   **c.** hablamos
13. Nosotros _____ mucho.
    a. estudia   **b.** estudio   **c.** estudiamos
14. Tú _____ la televisión.
    a. miras   **b.** miran   **c.** miro
15. Él _____ a la escuela.
    a. van   **b.** vas   **c.** va
16. Ustedes _____ muy bien.
    a. bailas   **b.** baila   **c.** bailan
17. Yo _____ el desayuno en casa.
    a. toma   **b.** tomo   **c.** tomamos

Alumnos ecuatorianos. Quito

4 Contesten. *(Answer.)*

    18. ¿Vas a la escuela?

    19. ¿En qué clase estás ahora?

To review the use of **ir, dar,** and **estar,** turn to pages 104 and 110.

5 Completen. *(Complete.)*

    20. Voy _____ escuela a pie.

    21. José es español y va _____ colegio San José.

    22. Escuchamos _____ profesor.

To review the use of the personal a, turn to page 112.

Cultura

6 ¿Sí o no? *(True or false?)*

    23. Un malagueño es de Madrid, España.

    24. Muchos alumnos en España y en Latinoamérica van a escuelas privadas.

    25. Muchos alumnos en España llevan uniforme a la escuela.

To review this cultural information, turn to pages 116–117.

Plaza de Cibeles. Madrid. España

Diversiones

Canta con Justo
La Bamba

Pa - ra bai-lar la bam - ba, pa - ra bai-lar la bam-ba se ne-ce-si - ta u - na po - ca de

gra - cia, Ay u - na po - ca de gra-cia y o-tra co-si - ta Ay a - rri-ba Ay a - rri - ba

Ay a - rri - ba Ay a - rri - ba Ay a-rri - ba Y - he por ti se - ré, por ti se - ré.____

Chorus

Bam - ba___bam - ba   Bam - ba___bam - ba   Bam - ba___bam - ba   Bam - ba bam - ba

Yo no soy marinero
Ay yo no soy marinero, soy capitán
Soy capitán, soy capitán

Bamba, bamba
Bamba, bamba
Bamba, bamba

En mi casa me dicen,
En mi casa me dicen
el inocente
porque tengo muchachas
Ay porque tengo muchachas
de quince a veinte
Ay arriba arriba
ay arriba ay arriba ay arriba y he
por ti seré, por ti seré.

a ver como todo el mundo cuenta
    en español
10-9-8-7-6-5-4-3-2-1-0

Teatro

Dramatize something and call on someone to tell what you are doing. Take turns. You may wish to act out the following.

hablar   mirar   cantar

escuchar   bailar   estudiar

celebrar

 ## Manos a la obra

Un álbum Take some photos of your Spanish class. Write a caption for each photo. Make a collage with your photos. The collage can be used for a bulletin board.

Juego Cada uno en su sitio Tell where each of the following might take place. **¡Cuidado!** Some might happen in more than one place.

cenar con la familia   preparar la comida   tomar el desayuno   mirar un video

escuchar a la profesora   mirar una emisión favorita   bailar

dar una fiesta   hablar por teléfono   llevar uniforme

EN CASA	EN LA ESCUELA

Entrevista

¿Cómo vas a la escuela?

¿Dónde tomas el desayuno? ¿En casa o en la escuela?

¿Cómo es tu clase de español?

¿Dónde tomas el almuerzo?

¿De qué hablas con tus amigos?

¿Vas a casa o a un café después de las clases? Después de la cena, ¿estudias o miras la tele?

¿Qué miras en la televisión?

¿Escuchas CDs?

¿Qué tipo de música escuchas?

Rompecabezas

Las palabras partidas Join two pieces to form a word. When you have finished, you should have ten words. Do not use any piece more than once.

_____ _____

_____ _____

_____ _____

_____ _____

_____ _____

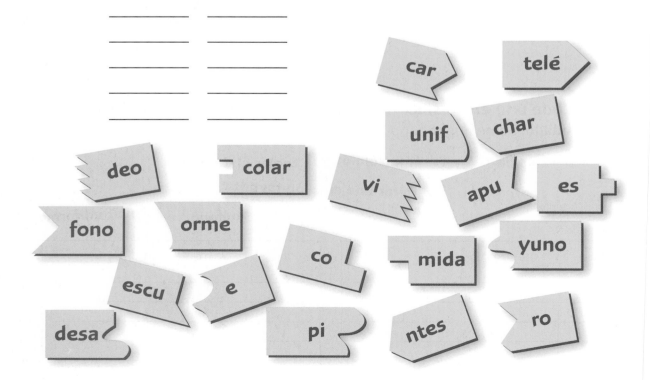

car   telé

unif   char

deo   colar

vi   apu   es

fono   orme

co   yuno

mida

escu   e

desa   pi   ntes   ro

Investigaciones

Un héroe o una heroína Select an important person or hero from either Spain or Latin America and find out some information about him or her.

Spanish Online

For more information about important people from Spain or Latin America, go to the Glencoe Spanish Web site: **spanish.glencoe.com**.

PLEGABLES™
Study Organizer

Preguntas Use this *tab book* to practice asking and answering questions.

Step 1 **Fold** a sheet of paper (8½″ x 11″) like a *hot dog* but fold it so that one side is one inch longer than the other.

Step 2 On the shorter side only, cut five equal tabs. On the front of each tab, write a question word you have learned. For example, you may wish to write the following.

Step 3 On the bottom edge, write any sentence you would like.

Step 4 Under each flap, write the word from your sentence that answers the question on the front of the flap.

Más cultura y lectura

Escuelas con los nombres de héroes

Muchas escuelas en Estados Unidos tienen o llevan el nombre de un héroe o de una persona importante. Aquí hay unos ejemplos.

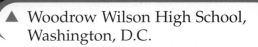

▲ Woodrow Wilson High School, Washington, D.C.

▲ George Washington University, Washington, D.C.

▲ Lincoln Center of the Arts public middle school, Milwaukee, Wisconsin

En España y en Latinoamérica muchas escuelas también llevan el nombre de un héroe o de una persona famosa.

▲ Algunas escuelas en Puerto Rico llevan el nombre de Luis Muñoz Marín, un gobernador importante de la isla.

▲ Aquí tenemos una fotografía de Simón Bolívar, el gran héroe latinoamericano. Simón Bolívar es el libertador de los países del norte del continente sudamericano. Él lucha[1] contra España por la independencia. Hay escuelas en Venezuela y en Colombia que llevan su nombre.

▲ Aquí tenemos una fotografía del liceo Gabriela Mistral en Puntarenas, Chile. Gabriela Mistral (1889–1957) es una poeta chilena muy famosa. Es también maestra[2] en varias escuelas primarias en Chile. En 1945 ella gana[3] el Premio Nóbel de Literatura.

[1]lucha *fights*   [2]maestra *teacher*   [3]gana *wins*

¿Comprendes?

Identifiquen. (*Identify.*)

1. el primer presidente de Estados Unidos
2. un político famoso de Puerto Rico
3. una poeta famosa de Chile
4. un americano famoso que lucha por la igualdad racial

CONEXIONES
La tecnología

La computadora

Computers have changed the world. Today they are commonplace in our homes, schools, and businesses. You may want to familiarize yourself with some computer jargon in Spanish.

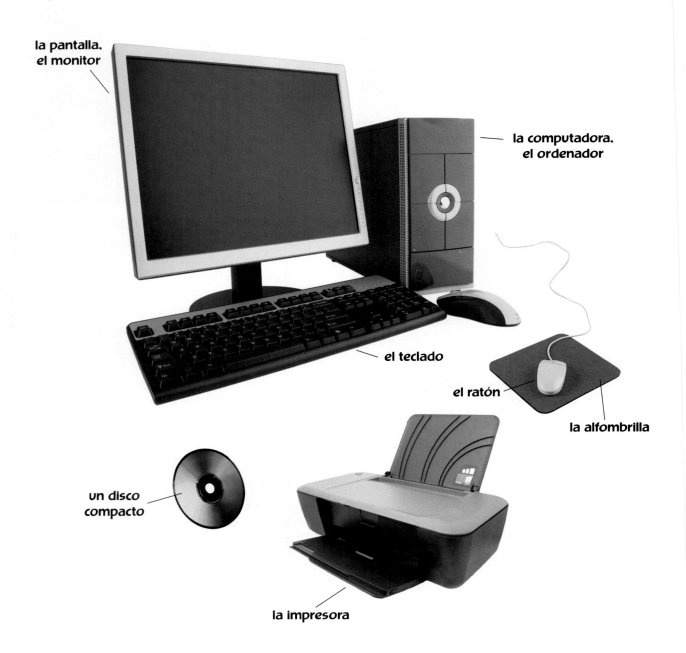

la pantalla, el monitor

la computadora, el ordenador

el teclado

el ratón

la alfombrilla

un disco compacto

la impresora

¡Conecta la computadora!

Una computadora procesa datos. El hardware es la computadora y todo el equipo[1] conectado con la computadora. El software es el conjunto de programas de la computadora. Un programa es un grupo o una serie de instrucciones que preparan para la computadora. Con el programa, la computadora continúa a funcionar en orden lógico y determinado.

El internet—¡Conecta al mundo!

Con el Internet hay acceso al mundo entero. Hay información sobre la historia, la economía, el arte, la música y muchas otras áreas de interés. Cuando navegas por la red[2], es posible conectar con los centros de noticias. Es posible enviar correo[3] electrónico y conversar con amigos en otras partes del mundo. Y hay la posibilidad de crear una página Web. Sí, ¡el mundo entero a la mano en una pantalla!

[1]equipo *equipment*   [2]red *Net*   [3]correo *mail*

¿Comprendes?

A. **Pareen.** (*Match the words.*)

1. data	**a.** el disco compacto
2. terminal	**b.** el Internet
3. compact disc	**c.** navegar por la red
4. Web page	**d.** los datos
5. Internet	**e.** el correo electrónico
6. e-mail	**f.** la terminal
7. to surf the Net	**g.** la página Web

B. **Una página Web** Look at the monitor on page 130. If you have access to the Internet either at home or at school, go to **spanish.glencoe.com ¡a practicar el español!**

¡Hablo como un pro!

Tell all you can about the following illustration.

Vocabulario

Talking about home activities

el desayuno	la emisión	mirar
el almuerzo	el teléfono	hablar
la cena	preparar	ir
la comida	tomar	dar
la televisión	cenar	estar

Talking about a party

invitar	bailar
celebrar	cantar

Getting to school

la escuela	en carro
el uniforme	ir
el bus escolar	llevar
a pie	entrar

Discussing classroom activities

un CD	prestar atención
un video	tomar apuntes
un DVD	levantar la mano
estar en clase	contestar (a) la pregunta
estudiar	sacar notas (buenas,
escuchar	malas)

Other useful expressions

después de	¿qué?
a veces	¿cuándo?
durante	¿adónde?

Unidad 4

De compras

Objetivos

In this unit you will learn to:

- ％ identify and describe school supplies
- ％ count from 1000 to 2,000,000
- ％ identify and describe articles of clothing
- ％ state color and size preferences
- ％ tell what you are going to do and what you have to do
- ％ express amazement
- ％ tell what belongs to you and to others
- ％ talk about clothing preferences in Spanish-speaking countries

¡Qué día más fantástico!

artesana

Palabras En la papelería 🎧

la papelería

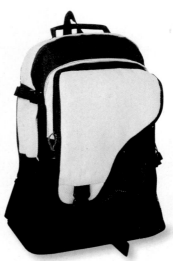

la mochila

un cuaderno,
un bloc

una carpeta

una hoja
de papel

un libro

una calculadora

las tijeras

un bolígrafo,
una pluma

un marcador

un lápiz, dos lápices

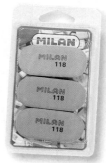

una goma (de borrar),
un borrador

José necesita materiales escolares.
Tiene que ir a la papelería.

José está en la papelería.
Necesita un cuaderno y un bolígrafo.
Busca los cuadernos.

José compra el cuaderno.
El cuaderno cuesta ochenta pesos.

José va a pagar.
Tiene que ir a la caja.
José paga en la caja.

Cuando va a la escuela, José lleva sus
materiales escolares en una mochila.

Más números

1000	mil
2000	dos mil
2002	dos mil dos
2500	dos mil quinientos
3000	tres mil
3015	tres mil quince
3650	tres mil seiscientos cincuenta
1200	mil doscientos
1492	mil cuatrocientos noventa y dos
1814	mil ochocientos catorce
1898	mil ochocientos noventa y ocho
1,000,000	un millón
2,000,000	dos millones

¿Qué palabra necesito?

1 Materiales que necesitamos

¿Sí o no? *(True or false?)*

1. Para la clase de inglés, necesitamos una calculadora.
2. Muchos alumnos necesitan una goma de borrar para la clase de matemáticas.
3. Necesito un libro de historia para mi clase de estudios sociales.
4. Necesitamos un marcador para muchas clases.
5. Necesitamos muchas hojas de papel, un bolígrafo y un libro de literatura para la clase de inglés.

Una papelería. Málaga. España

2 Historieta En la papelería
Contesten con **sí.** *(Answer with sí.)*

1. ¿Necesita la muchacha materiales escolares?
2. ¿Tiene que ir a la papelería?
3. ¿Entra en la papelería?
4. ¿Busca una calculadora?
5. ¿Habla la muchacha con la dependienta?
6. ¿Cuesta ochenta euros la calculadora?
7. ¿Paga la muchacha en la caja?

3 Preguntas Hagan preguntas.
(Make up questions.)

¿Dónde?   ¿Adónde?   ¿Quién?

¿Cuándo?   ¿Cuánto?   ¿Qué?

1. Paco va a comprar un bolígrafo *hoy*.
2. Paco tiene que ir *a la papelería*.
3. Él busca *un bolígrafo* en la papelería.
4. *La dependienta* habla con Paco.
5. El bolígrafo cuesta *ocho euros*.
6. *Paco* compra el bolígrafo.
7. Él paga *en la caja*.

4 **En la papelería** Work with a classmate. You're buying the following school supplies. Take turns being the customer and the salesperson.

22 €

11 €

27,50 €

0,20 €

3,30 €

0,25 €

0,35 €

5 **Juego** **¿Qué es?** Play a guessing game. Your partner will hide a school supply behind his or her back. Guess what he or she is hiding. Use **tienes.** Take turns.

6 **R o m p e c a b e z a s**

Los materiales escolares Fill in the missing letter in each word. Then unscramble these letters to reveal the name of a school supply.

1. l á p i c e _
2. l _ b r o
3. m o c h i l _
4. c a r p e _ a
5. h o _ a
6. b o l í g _ a f o
7. p a p _ l

_ _ _ _ _ _ _

Formas

Ir a, tener que + **el infinitivo**
Telling what you are going to do
and what you have to do

1. The expression **ir a** followed by the infinitive means
to be going to. It is used to express what is going to
happen in the near future.

> María **va a celebrar** sus quince años.
> Sus amigos **van a comprar** un regalo.

2. **Tener que** + the infinitive means *to have to.*

> Tomás **tiene que comprar** una calculadora.
> **Tiene que ir** a la papelería.

¿Cómo lo digo?

7 **Historieta** Una fiesta

Contesten con **sí.** *(Answer with sí.)*

1. ¿Vas a dar una fiesta?
2. ¿Vas a dar una fiesta para Alberto?
3. ¿Él va a celebrar sus trece años?
4. ¿Vas a invitar a sus amigos a la fiesta?
5. ¿Van a comprar regalos sus amigos?
6. ¿Van a dar los regalos a Alberto?
7. Durante la fiesta, ¿ustedes van a bailar?
8. ¿Van a tomar un refresco?

8 **Historieta** **A la papelería**

Contesten según se indica. *(Answer as indicated.)*

1. ¿Qué tienes que tener para la clase de matemáticas? (una calculadora)
2. ¿Adónde tienes que ir? (a la papelería)
3. ¿Qué tienes que buscar? (la calculadora)
4. ¿Y qué más tienes que comprar? (una goma de borrar)
5. ¿Dónde tienes que pagar? (en la caja)

9 **¡Tenemos tanto que hacer!**

Sigan el modelo. *(Follow the model.)*

> **mirar la televisión / ir a la papelería** ⟶
> **No vamos a mirar la televisión porque tenemos que ir a la papelería.**

1. escuchar un CD / estudiar
2. hablar por teléfono / mirar una emisión importante
3. tomar seis cursos / sacar notas buenas
4. tomar apuntes / escuchar al profesor
5. ir a la fiesta / estudiar para un examen

Una papelería, Guanajuato, México

La muchacha tiene que estudiar, Lima, Perú

10 **No voy a...** Tell a classmate some things you're not going to do tomorrow because you have to do something else. Tell what you have to do. Your classmate will let you know if he or she is in the same situation.

*For more practice using words and forms from **Paso 1**, do Activity 7 on page H8 at the end of this book.*

Palabras En la tienda de ropa 🎧

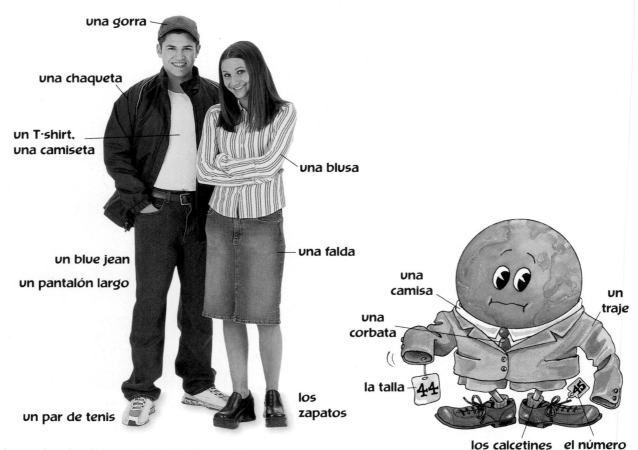

una gorra

una chaqueta

un T-shirt,
una camiseta

una blusa

un blue jean
un pantalón largo

una falda

una camisa

una corbata

un traje

la talla — 44

un par de tenis

los zapatos

la talla

los calcetines   el número

El muchacho lleva un T-shirt y un jean.
La muchacha lleva una blusa, una falda y zapatos.

Los colores

¿De qué color es?

verde   blanco(a)   rosado(a)   rojo(a)

negro(a)   azul   amarillo(a)   gris

Alicia está en la tienda de ropa.
Ella habla con la dependienta.

La dependienta trabaja en la tienda.

Ángel compra un par de zapatos.
Habla con el dependiente.

una camisa de mangas cortas

una camisa de mangas largas

La blusa de mangas cortas es barata.
No cuesta mucho. Cuesta poco.
Hoy hay una liquidación.
Los precios son muy bajos.

La blusa de mangas largas es cara.
Cuesta mucho.

¿Qué palabra necesito?

1 **¿Qué es y cuánto cuesta?**
Identifiquen. *(Identify and give price in euros.)*

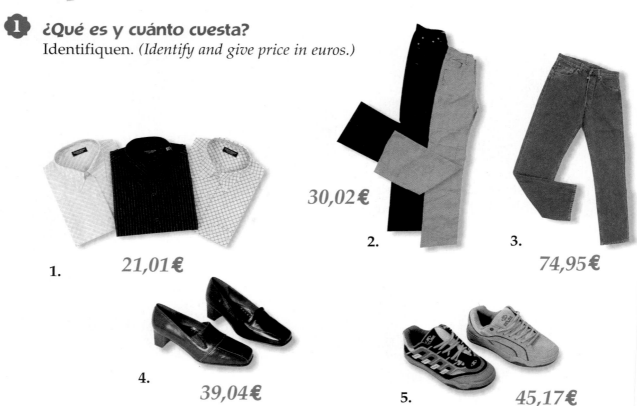

30,02€

2.

3.

1. 21,01€

74,95€

4.

39,04€

5. 45,17€

2 **Historieta** **En la tienda de ropa**
Contesten según se indica. *(Answer as indicated.)*

1. ¿Qué tiene que comprar Eduardo? (un regalo)
2. ¿Para quién es el regalo? (su padre)
3. ¿Qué busca para su padre? (una camisa)
4. ¿Con quién habla Eduardo? (el dependiente)
5. ¿Dónde trabaja el dependiente? (en la tienda de ropa)
6. ¿Qué talla usa el padre de Eduardo? (treinta y ocho)
7. ¿Qué tiene el dependiente? (muchas camisas en su talla)
8. ¿Qué mira Eduardo? (una camisa azul de mangas cortas)
9. ¿Compra Eduardo la camisa? (sí)
10. ¿Es muy cara? (no, bastante barata)

3 **¿De qué color es?**
Completen. *(Complete with the color.)*

1. Tomás compra un
pantalón _____.

2. Ana busca una
blusa _____.

3. Emilia mira una
camisa _____.

4. Silvia compra una
chaqueta _____.

5. Su amiga va a comprar
una falda _____.

4 **Juego** **¿Quién es?** Work with a classmate.
One of you describes what someone in the
class is wearing. The other has to guess who
it is. Take turns.

5 **Mi ropa favorita** Work with a classmate.
Discuss your favorite clothing. See if you are
on the same wavelength.

6 **Comparaciones** Many clothing sizes are
different in the European countries from
those in the United States. Look at this
comparative chart. What sizes would you
use if you were shopping in Spain?

CONVERSION DE TALLAS

Ropa de señora — Vestidos y abrigos						
Estados Unidos	6	8	10	12	14	16
España	36	38	40	42	44	46
Sudamérica	34	36	38	40	42	44
Ropa de señora — Blusas y jersey						
Estados Unidos	30	32	34	36	38	40
España	38	40	42	44	46	48
Sudamérica	38	40	42	44	46	48
Ropa de caballeros — Trajes						
Estados Unidos	34	36	38	40	42	44
España	44	46	48	50	52	54
Sudamérica	44	46	48	50	52	54
Calzado — señoras						
Estados Unidos	4	5	6	7	8	9
España	34/35	35/36	36/37	38/39	39/40	41/42
Sudamérica	2	3	4	5	6	7
Calzado — caballeros						
Estados Unidos	8	8½	9	9½	10	10½
España	41	42	43	43	44	45
Sudamérica	6	6½	7	7½	8	8½

Formas

Los colores
Talking about colors

1. Colors agree with the noun they modify the same as any other adjective. Review the following.

el traje blanco	la camisa blanca
los trajes blancos	las camisas blancas
el traje verde	la camisa verde
los trajes verdes	las camisas verdes
el traje azul	la camisa azul
los trajes azules	las camisas azules

Escaparate de una tienda de ropa, Puerto Banús, Marbella, España

2. You express some colors by referring to an object of that color. They do not agree with the noun they modify.

zapatos
(de color) **marrón**

una falda
(de color) **verde olivo**

dos camisas
(de color) **violeta**

un lápiz
(de color) **naranja**

Note that you can say **de color** or omit it.

SIMBOLISMO

BLANCO
Es símbolo de la pureza, la limpieza y la inocencia.

AZUL
Es símbolo de la tranquilidad (la paz). Se relaciona con el cielo y el mar y representa la confianza.

VERDE
Simboliza la naturaleza y se relaciona con la productividad y los espacios limpios.

ROJO
Es el color de la alegría, el amor y la pasión. También simboliza las emergencias.

AMARILLO
Es el color de la vitalidad y la luminosidad. Significa fortuna, independencia y luz.

¿Cómo lo digo?

7 **Mis colores favoritos** Completen.
(Complete with your favorite colors.)

1. una camisa _____
2. una camiseta _____
3. una gorra _____
4. zapatos _____
5. calcetines _____
6. un pantalón _____
7. una chaqueta _____

 ¡Qué... más... !
Expressing amazement

To express *what a* in Spanish, you use **qué** with **más**.

¡Qué tienda más elegante!
¡Qué corbata más bonita!

¿Cómo lo digo?

8 **¡Increíble!** Sigan el modelo.
 (Follow the model.)

> **clase / grande** →
> **¡Qué clase más grande!**

1. clase / inteligente
2. profesor / interesante
3. cursos / difíciles
4. casa / bonita
5. amigo / bueno
6. camisa / cara
7. tienda / elegante

Escaparate de una tienda de ropa,
Calle Serrano, Madrid, España

PASO 2

 ## La contracción del

Talking about what belongs to you and to others

1. You have already learned that the preposition **a** contracts with **el** to form one word—**al.**

2. The preposition **de,** which can mean *of, from,* or *about,* also contracts with **el** to form one word—**del.**

   > **¿Cuál es el precio del pantalón?**
   > **Los alumnos hablan del profesor.**
   > **Ella es del centro del estado de Florida.**

3. You also use **de** to indicate possession or ownership.

   > **Es la casa de la familia Ruiz.**
   > **Son los libros de los profesores.**

¿Cómo lo digo?

9 **Historieta** **En la tienda de ropa**

Contesten con **sí.** (*Answer with* sí.)

1. ¿Está Susana en la tienda de ropa?
2. ¿Habla ella del cumpleaños de su padre?
3. ¿Habla del regalo que va a dar a su padre?
4. ¿Busca un pantalón corto para su padre?
5. ¿Habla del precio con el dependiente?
6. ¿Es el precio del pantalón corto bastante alto?

Una tienda de ropa, Isabela, Puerto Rico

10 **Historieta** **Un muchacho americano**

Contesten con **sí.** (*Answer with* sí.)

1. ¿Es Roberto de la Ciudad de Nueva York?
2. ¿Habla Roberto del curso de matemáticas?
3. ¿Habla también del profesor?
4. ¿Usa Roberto la calculadora del profesor?
5. Después de sus clases, ¿habla Roberto con sus amigos?
6. ¿Hablan de la escuela?
7. ¿Hablan de los cursos que toman?
8. ¿Hablan de la fiesta del Club de español?

11 **¿Quién lleva qué?** Work in small groups. Take turns describing what someone in your group is wearing.

UN POCO MÁS *For more practice using words and forms from **Paso 2**, do Activity 8 on page H9 at the end of this book.*

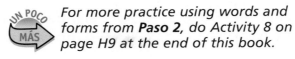

Andas bien. ¡Adelante!

Conversación

Alejandro busca ropa nueva.

Dependiente Buenos días. ¿Qué deseas?
Alejandro Un blue jean, por favor.
Dependiente Y, ¿qué talla usas?
Alejandro Treinta y dos.
Dependiente Tengo muchos jeans. Un momentito. Voy a buscar un treinta y dos.
(Alejandro tries on the jeans.)
Dependiente ¿Está bien?
Alejandro Perfecto. ¿Cuánto es, por favor?
Dependiente Mil quinientos pesos.
Alejandro Y necesito una camisa.
Dependiente ¿Una camisa? ¿De qué color?
Alejandro Una camisa blanca o azul— de mangas cortas, por favor.
Dependiente Hoy tienes mucha suerte. Tenemos una liquidación y los precios son muy bajos.

¿Comprendes?

A. Contesten. *(Answer.)*
1. ¿Dónde está Alejandro?
2. ¿Con quién habla?
3. ¿Qué desea Alejandro?
4. ¿Qué talla usa?
5. ¿Tiene muchos jeans el dependiente?
6. ¿Cuál es el precio del blue jean?
7. ¿Qué más necesita Alejandro?
8. ¿Qué color necesita?
9. ¿Hay una liquidación hoy?
10. ¿Cómo son los precios?

B. Vocabulario en contexto
1. ¿Qué significa **suerte?**
2. ¿Qué significa **liquidación?**

Pronunciación

La consonante d

The pronunciation of **d** in Spanish varies according to its position in the word. When a word begins with **d** (initial position) or follows the consonants **l, n,** or **r,** the tongue gently strikes the back of the upper front teeth. Repeat the following.

da	de	di	do	du
da	desayuno	día	domingo	duda
falda	dependiente	diciembre	todo	durante
tienda	verde	difícil	cuando	

When **d** appears within the word between vowels (medial position), **d** is extremely soft. Your tongue should strike the lower part of your upper teeth, almost between the upper and lower teeth. Repeat the following.

da	de	di	do	du
nada	modelo	estudio	sábado	educación
privada	cuaderno	adiós		
ensalada				

When a word ends in **d** (final position), **d** is either extremely soft or omitted completely—not pronounced. Repeat the following.

nacionalidad   ciudad

Trabalenguas

Repeat the following.

Diego da el CD a Donato en la ciudad.
La falda verde está en la tienda.
La ensalada verde es de David.

Refrán

Can you guess what the following proverb means?

Más vale tarde que nunca.

Cultura y lectura

La ropa que llevan los jóvenes

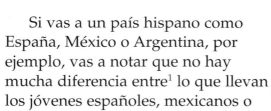

Reading Strategy

Using visuals Visuals can help us understand what we are reading. Visuals often illustrate the content of the reading selection. Before starting to read, look at the photographs that accompany the selection. What do you think the reading will be about?

Si vas a un país hispano como España, México o Argentina, por ejemplo, vas a notar que no hay mucha diferencia entre¹ lo que llevan los jóvenes españoles, mexicanos o argentinos y lo que llevamos nosotros. En cuanto a² la moda o los estilos, los gustos³ de los jóvenes son muy parecidos o similares.

La ropa favorita de los jóvenes hispanos, ¿qué es? Pues, es un blue jean con una camiseta, un par de tenis y a veces una gorra. Pero hay una diferencia importante. Cuando los jóvenes van a la escuela, no llevan su ropa favorita. Tienen que llevar uniforme.

¹ entre *between*   ² En cuanto a *As for*   ³ gustos *likes, tastes*

Escaparate de una tienda de departamentos.
Plaza del Callao, Madrid, España

¿Sí o no? *(True or false?)*

1. Hay mucha diferencia entre lo que lleva un joven español y un joven argentino.
2. El blue jean es muy popular entre los jóvenes de muchos países.
3. La ropa que llevamos en EE.UU. es muy parecida o similar a la ropa que llevan los jóvenes en los países hispanos.
4. En muchas escuelas de EE.UU. los alumnos tienen que llevar uniforme.

Repaso

1. In this unit, I learned the expression **tener que**. Tener que followed by an infinitive means *to have to*.

> **Tengo que trabajar.**
> **Los alumnos tienen que ir a la escuela en uniforme.**

2. The expression **ir a** + the infinitive means *to be going to*.

> **Voy a llevar** un blue jean a la fiesta.
> **Van a comprar** un regalo para su padre.

3. The preposition **de** contracts with **el** to form one word—**del**.

> **¿Cuál es el precio del pantalón?**
> **Hablan del curso de español.**

4. **¡Qué... más... !** means *What a . . . !*

> **¡Qué traje más bonito!**
> **¡Qué tienda más elegante!**

Escaparate de una tienda de moda.
Barcelona, España

¡Pongo todo junto!

1 **No, porque...** Sigan el modelo. *(Follow the model.)*

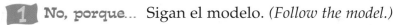

> **Yo / ir a la fiesta / trabajar** →
> **Yo no voy a ir a la fiesta porque tengo que trabajar.**

1. Él / mirar la tele / estudiar
2. Ellos / ir a la tienda / ir a la escuela
3. Tú / hablar inglés / hablar español
4. Nosotros / llevar un blue jean / llevar un traje

2 **¿De qué, de quién y de dónde?**
Completen. *(Complete with* de.*)*

1. Hablan _____ cursos que toman.
2. Es el libro _____ profesor.
3. Es una fotografía _____ hermano _____ amiga de Felipe.
4. Ellos son _____ barrio de Salamanca.

3 **Sigan el modelo.** *(Follow the model.)*

> **casa bonita** →
> **Adela, ¡qué casa más bonita tienes!**

1. traje elegante
2. libro interesante
3. fotografía bonita
4. carro grande

4

Work with a partner. Use your manipulatives to make sentences.

¡Qué libros más interesantes!

¡Te toca a ti!

Hablar

1 **Un *look* nuevo**

 ✓ *State your color and style preferences in clothes*

You and your partner have decided that you are going to change your style of clothing. Discuss what the "new you" is going to look like.

Hablar

2 **Regalos**

 ✓ *Shop for clothing*

 You have just spent a few weeks in Peru and you want to buy some gifts for family and friends back home. Make a list of what you want to buy. With a classmate, take turns being the customer and the salesperson as you buy the items on your list.

Un centro comercial, Lima, Perú

Hablar

3 **En la papelería**

 ✓ *Shop for school supplies with a classmate*

Take turns asking questions about what the boy has to buy.

Escribir

4 Necesito ropa.

✓ *Order clothing from a catalogue*

You need some items from the catalogue. Write a letter stating which items you need, what color, size, etc.

Writing Strategy

Planning It is important to have a plan before you begin to write. Think about what you want to say and how to make it interesting. Think about the vocabulary you'll need and perhaps even make a list of words and expressions you would like to use.

Escribir

5 El *look*

Write a note to an Argentine friend describing the type of clothing your friends wear to school. Tell what types of clothes and colors *are "in"* (**estar de moda**).

Unos amigos en la Plaza de Mayo. Buenos Aires, Argentina

Assessment

¿Estoy listo(a)?

Palabras

1 Identifiquen. *(Identify.)*

> To review words from **Paso 1,** turn to pages 136–137.

1.   2.   3.

4.   5.

2 Identifiquen. *(Identify.)*

> To review words from **Paso 2,** turn to pages 142–143.

6.   7.   8.

3 Completen. *(Complete.)*

9. La muchacha _____ un blue jean y una camiseta.
10. La camisa no cuesta mucho. Es bastante _____.
11. Rubén compra un par de _____, número veintiocho.
12. Él paga en la _____.
13. El _____ trabaja en la tienda.

Formas

 4 Contesten. *(Answer.)*
   14. ¿No vas a ir a la fiesta?
   15. ¿Tienes que trabajar?

To review **ir a** and **tener que,** turn to page 140.

5 Completen. *(Complete with something that makes sense.)*
16–17. Ellos no van a _____ porque tienen que _____.

6 Completen. *(Complete with the appropriate color.)*

   18. dos faldas _____

   19. una camisa _____

   20. zapatos _____

To review colors, turn to pages 142 and 146.

7 Sigan el modelo. *(Follow the model.)*
   Es el libro _____ profesor. (interesante) →
   Es el libro del profesor. ¡Qué libro más interesante!
21–22. Es la casa _____ familia Suárez. (grande)
23–24. Es la clase _____ profesor Ureña. (fantástica)

To review the contraction **del** and the expression **¡Qué ___ más ___!,** turn to pages 147–148.

Cultura

 8 Contesten. *(Answer.)*
   25. ¿Qué llevan los jóvenes en los países hispanos?

To review this cultural information, turn to pages 152–153.

Ciudad Universitaria, Santo Domingo

Diversiones

Canta con Justo
De colores

De_____ co-lo_____res,   de co- lo-res se vis-ten los cam-pos en la pri-ma-ve-ra._____

De_____ co-lo_____res,   de co- lo-res son los pa-ja - ri-tos que vie-nen de a-fue-ra._____

De_____ co-lo_____res,   de co- lo-res es el ar-co i-ris que ve-mos lu - cir_____

y por e - so los gran-des a - mo - res de mu-chos co — lo - res me gus-tan a

mí.   y por e - so los gran-des   a - mo - res de mu-chos co — lo - res me gus-tan.

De colores, sí—de
   blanco y negro y rojo y azul y castaño.
Son colores, son colores de gente que ríe
   y estrecha la mano—
Son colores, son colores de gente que
   sabe de la libertad
y por eso los grandes amores de muchos
   colores me gustan a mí.
y por eso los grandes amores de muchos
   colores me gustan a mí.

De colores son esos paisajes que viste la
   aurora—
De colores, de colores son las maravillas
   que el sol atesora—
De colores, de colores es el arco iris que
   vemos lucir
y por eso los grandes amores de muchos
   colores me gustan a mí.
y por eso los grandes amores de muchos
   colores me gustan a mí.

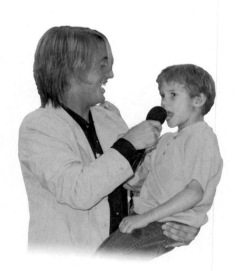

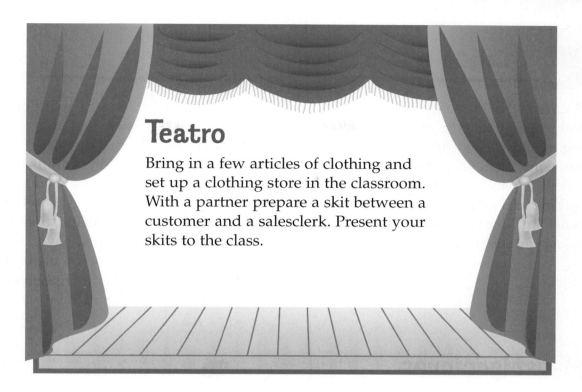

Teatro

Bring in a few articles of clothing and set up a clothing store in the classroom. With a partner prepare a skit between a customer and a salesclerk. Present your skits to the class.

Juego ¿Qué hay en la mochila?

Pass around a backpack. As each of you gets the backpack, put a school supply in it. Tell what you put in it—**Ahora en la mochila hay** (*whatever you put in*). See if you can also name all the things that are already in the backpack. Note that the game gets more complicated as it progresses.

Rompecabezas

Palabras nuevas Change one letter in each of the following words to form a new word.

1. caja
2. piso
3. con
4. llevo
5. ropa
6. cola

PASO 4

 ## Manos a la obra

1. El catálogo Prepare a page for a clothing catalogue by drawing or cutting out articles of clothing from a magazine. Paste them on a board or on a sheet of paper. Label each article of clothing and give the colors and sizes it comes in. Give the price and, if possible, a brief description of it.

2. Muñecas Cut out a large paper doll from cardboard to use to make an image of yourself. Use whatever materials you want to "dress yourself" in your favorite clothing. Draw your face or use materials to represent what you look like. Use your imagination in creating yourself. When you have finished your "self-image," on the back of your **muñeca,** write a description of who you are and what you are wearing.

Investigaciones

Un personaje latino famoso Oscar de la Renta is a world-famous fashion designer from the Dominican Republic. In spite of his fame in the elegant world of fashion, de la Renta is known for the charitable work he does for the underprivileged in his native country. Do some research to learn more about Oscar de la Renta.

 ### Spanish Online

For more information about Oscar de la Renta and the Dominican Republic, go to the Glencoe Spanish Web site: spanish.glencoe.com.

El gran diseñador dominicano
Oscar de la Renta

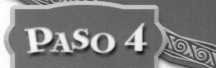

Entrevista

¿Qué materiales escolares usas mucho?
¿Dónde compras los materiales escolares?
¿Qué llevas cuando vas a la escuela?
¿Qué llevas cuando no estás en la escuela?
¿Dónde compras tu ropa?

Descripciones Use this *miniature matchbook* to help you communicate in an interesting and more descriptive way.

Step 1 **Fold** a sheet of paper (8½" x 11") in half like a *hot dog*.

Step 2 **Cut** the sheet in half along the fold line.

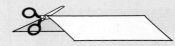

Step 3 **Fold** the two long strips in half like *hot dogs,* leaving one side ½" shorter than the other side.

Step 4 **Fold** the ½" tab over the shorter side on each strip.

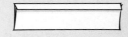

Step 5 **Cut** each of the two strips in half forming four halves. Then cut each half into thirds, making twelve miniature matchbooks.

Step 6 **Glue** the twelve small matchbooks inside a *hamburger* fold (three rows of four each).

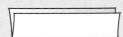

Step 7 On the front of each matchbook, write a subject you are going to tell or write about, for example, **la escuela**. Open up the tab and list any words you think you could use to make your discussion more interesting. You can add topics and words as you continue with your study of Spanish. If you glue several sections together, this **plegable** will "grow."

Más cultura y lectura

La ropa indígena

En muchos países de Latinoamérica hay mucha población india o indígena. La ropa que llevan los indígenas es muy interesante y muy bonita.

▶ En Guatemala, por ejemplo, la ropa cambia o varía de un pueblo[1] a otro. El traje que lleva una señora de la región de Huehuetenango no es el mismo traje que lleva una señora de Chichicastenango.

▶ Las indígenas de Guatemala no llevan sombrero. Pero las indígenas de Perú, sí. Ellas llevan sombrero.

[1] pueblo *village, town*

Las indígenas del famoso pueblo de Otavalo en Ecuador llevan dos faldas de lana[2] oscura y una blusa brillante. Los señores de Otavalo llevan un pantalón blanco, una camisa blanca y un poncho azul. Ellos llevan trenzas[3] también.

[2] lana *wool*   [3] trenzas *braids*

Otavalo, Ecuador

¿Comprendes?

A. Poblaciones indígenas Name the three countries mentioned that have large indigenous populations. Other Latin American countries with large indigenous populations are Bolivia and Mexico.

B. La ropa indígena There are some articles of clothing made by the indigenous people that keep their Spanish name in English. Look at the photographs to find out what they are.

el sarape

los huaraches

el poncho

CONEXIONES
Las matemáticas

Las finanzas

Whether we like it or not, we always have to take into account our finances—the way we spend our money. If we don't have enough money to buy a certain outfit or article of clothing, for example, we probably shouldn't buy it. We have to budget our money so that we do not overspend. It's also a good idea to try to save some money, even if we do it just a little bit at a time. Let's learn some vocabulary in Spanish that relates to our finances.

trabajar y ganar dinero

gastar dinero

ahorrar dinero

depositar dinero en el banco

tener una cuenta de ahorros

preparar un presupuesto

Un presupuesto

No es una buena idea gastar todo el dinero que tienes. Tienes que preparar un presupuesto. Si no tienes un presupuesto, es muy fácil gastar todo el dinero. Aquí tenemos un presupuesto típico.

El total o monto de los gastos tiene que ser menos que la cantidad del dinero que tienes. Si no, no tienes un buen presupuesto.

$$A - B = C$$
$$100 \quad 80 \quad 20$$

A—el total del dinero que tienes por una semana, un mes, un año
B—el total de tus gastos
C—el resto, el dinero que tienes para tus ahorros

Gastos	
materiales escolares	50 pesos
ropa	170 pesos
refrescos	90 pesos
regalos para amigos, parientes	100 pesos
diversiones – cine, conciertos	117 pesos
videos, CDs	210 pesos

¿Comprendes?

Preparen un presupuesto.
(Prepare your budget. If you don't have one, make one up.)

¡Hablo como un pro!

Tell all you can about the following illustration.

Vocabulario

Identifying school supplies

los materiales escolares	el marcador	el libro
la mochila	la goma, el borrador	la hoja de papel
el lápiz, los lápices	el cuaderno, el bloc	la calculadora
el bolígrafo, la pluma	la carpeta	las tijeras

Identifying articles of clothing

la ropa	el blue jean, los blue jeans	la gorra
el pantalón	la falda	los calcetines
la camisa	la blusa	los zapatos
la corbata	la chaqueta	los tenis, el par de tenis
el T-shirt, la camiseta	el traje	

Identifying colors

¿De qué color es?	amarillo(a)	de color marrón
blanco(a)	verde	de color violeta
negro(a)	rosado(a)	de color verde
gris	rojo(a)	olivo
azul		de color naranja

Identifying some types of stores

la papelería
la tienda de ropa

Describing clothes

de manga larga (corta)
la talla
el número

Shopping

el/la dependiente(a)	necesitar
el/la empleado(a)	buscar
la caja	comprar
el precio	pagar
caro(a)	usar
barato(a)	trabajar
bajo	
la liquidación	

Other useful expressions

¿Qué desea Ud.?
¿Qué talla usa Ud.?
¿Qué número usa Ud.?
¿Cuánto es?
Cuesta mucho (poco).

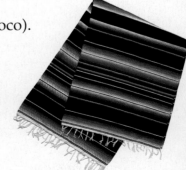

Unidad

5

En el café y en el mercado

Objetivos

In this unit you will learn to:

- ❡ order food or a beverage at a café
- ❡ identify some foods
- ❡ shop for food
- ❡ talk about what you and others do
- ❡ talk about foods of the Spanish-speaking world
- ❡ talk about differences between eating habits in the United States and in the Spanish-speaking world

¡Qué jugo más delicioso!

MERCADO MUNICIPAL DE ABASTOS

Palabras   En el café 🎧

una mesa ocupada

una silla

el mesero, el camarero

el menú

una mesa libre

Marta va al café.
Ella ve una mesa libre.
Marta espera a su amigo Luis.
Luis llega.

Marta lee el menú.
Luis lee el menú también.

Nota

When you are reading, try to guess the meaning of unfamiliar words. Sometimes other words in the sentence provide the context or setting and will help you understand words you do not know.

Elena estudia español en la escuela. Aprende el español. Ella lee un menú en español. Comprende el menú porque aprende el español en la escuela. Ella comprende, habla, lee y escribe en español. Recibe o saca notas muy buenas en español.

Para beber

los refrescos

una gaseosa

una cola

un café

un té helado

Para comer

una ensalada

el pan

un sándwich (bocadillo) de jamón y queso

una hamburguesa

papas fritas, patatas fritas

un helado de vainilla

el postre

una sopa

la cuenta

Sí, señores. ¿Qué desean Uds.?

Tengo sed. Una cola para mí.

Y yo tengo hambre. Un sándwich de jamón y queso, por favor.

El mesero escribe la orden.

Isabel bebe una cola.
Mario Unimundo come un sándwich.

¿Qué palabra necesito?

1 Historieta Al café

Contesten. (*Answer.*)

1. ¿Adónde va Antonio?
2. ¿Busca una mesa libre?
3. ¿Qué ve?
4. ¿Espera Antonio a su amiga?
5. ¿Llega su amiga Alicia?
6. ¿Lee Antonio el menú?
7. ¿Lee Alicia el menú?
8. ¿Tiene Antonio hambre o sed?
9. ¿Qué bebe o come él?
10. ¿Tiene Alicia hambre o sed?
11. ¿Qué bebe o come ella?

Varios cafés en Lima, Perú

2 ¿Qué come o bebe?

Sigan el modelo. (*Follow the model.*)

José bebe una cola.

José come un sándwich.

 **1.**

 **2.**

 3.

 **4.**

 **5.**

 **6.**

3 **Historieta** **En el café** Contesten según se indica.
(Answer as indicated.)

1. ¿Quién trabaja en el café? (el mesero)
2. ¿Con quién habla él? (con su cliente)
3. ¿Qué lee el cliente? (el menú)
4. ¿Qué desea el cliente? (una hamburguesa y una cola)
5. ¿Escribe la orden el mesero? (sí)
6. ¿Qué come el cliente? (una hamburguesa)
7. Y, ¿qué bebe? (una cola)
8. ¿Qué paga el cliente? (la cuenta)

4 **Historieta** **En la escuela**

Contesten. *(Answer.)*

1. ¿Estudia Teresa el español en la escuela?
2. ¿Aprende ella el español?
3. ¿Comprende cuando el profesor habla?
4. ¿Escribe Teresa en español?
5. ¿Lee Teresa en español?
6. ¿Recibe ella una nota buena en español?

La niña aprende a leer y a escribir. México

5 **Al café** Work in small groups. You are in a café in Ronda. One of you will be the server. Have a conversation from the time you enter the café until you leave.

Una plaza. Ronda. España

Formas
Los verbos en -er e -ir en el singular
Talking about what you do

1. You have already learned the regular **-ar** verbs in Spanish. You are now going to learn regular **-er** and **-ir** verbs. The infinitive of second conjugation verbs ends in **-er** and the infinitive of third conjugation verbs ends in **-ir.** The singular endings for **-er** and **-ir** verbs are the same.

	comer	leer	escribir	endings
	com-	le-	escrib-	
yo	como	leo	escribo	-o
tú	comes	lees	escribes	-es
él ella Ud.	come	lee	escribe	-e

2. The forms of the verb **ver** are the same.

veo	ves	ve

Un café al aire libre, Málaga, España

¿Cómo lo digo?

 6 **Vamos a un café.** Practiquen la conversación.
(Practice the conversation.)

7 **En el café** Contesten.

(Answer based on the conversation.)

1. ¿Tiene Julia hambre?
2. ¿Desea comer algo?
3. ¿Adónde van Carlos y Julia?
4. ¿Lee Julia el menú en español?
5. ¿Comprende el menú?
6. ¿Qué come Julia?
7. Y Carlos, ¿come o no?
8. ¿Qué bebe Carlos?
9. ¿Bebe mucha soda?

8 **Historieta** En la escuela

Contesten. *(Answer about yourself.)*

1. ¿Aprendes el español en la escuela?
2. ¿Comprendes cuando el profesor habla?
3. ¿Lees en español?
4. ¿Escribes también?
5. A veces, ¿ves un video en la clase de español?
6. ¿Comprendes el video?
7. ¿Recibes notas buenas en español?
8. ¿Comprendes, hablas, lees y escribes el español?

El alumno escribe en su cuaderno.
Santiago de Chile

 **9** **¿Qué comes?** Sigan el modelo. *(Follow the model.)*

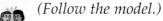

¿Qué comes cuando tienes hambre? →
Como una hamburguesa.

 1.

 2.

 3.

 4.

 5.

 For more practice using words and forms from Paso 1, do Activity 9 on page H10 at the end of this book.

10 **Historieta** **En el café**

Completen. *(Complete.)*

Yo __1__ (ir) al café y __2__ (ver) una mesa libre. Hay un menú en la mesa. Yo __3__ (leer) el menú. Ah, yo __4__ (ver) a mi amigo Fernando. Él __5__ (entrar) en el café.

Fernando __6__ (leer) el menú también. Él __7__ (decidir) lo que va a comer. Fernando __8__ (comer) una hamburguesa con papas fritas. Y yo __9__ (comer) un bocadillo de jamón y queso. Él __10__ (beber) una cola y yo también __11__ (beber) una cola.

Y tú, ¿qué __12__ (comer) y __13__ (beber) cuando __14__ (ir) a un café?

Un café en la Plaza Mayor. Madrid, España

11 **El curso de inglés** Have a discussion with a classmate about your English class. Tell as much as you can about what you do and learn. You may want to use some of the following words.

aprender   leer   recibir

escribir   comprender

12 **Juego** **Preguntas y más preguntas**

Throw a ball to someone in the class. Ask him or her a question with **tú** using one of the verbs below. He or she catches the ball and answers your question with **yo no.** He or she then throws the ball to a third person who catches it and gives the name of a person who does what you ask. Use the following words in the game: **ver, leer, comer, comprender, recibir.**

Palabras En el mercado 🎧

las frutas
los tomates
los plátanos
las manzanas
las naranjas

las legumbres, los vegetales
la lechuga
las habichuelas, los frijoles
las zanahorias
el maíz
las judías verdes, los ejotes
las papas, las patatas
los guisantes

el mercado

En el mercado venden frutas y vegetales.
Todo está muy fresco.

la carne

los mariscos

el pescado

el pollo

los huevos

La señora es de Argentina.
Vive en Buenos Aires.
Por la mañana va de compras.

el supermercado

un bote (una lata) de atún

un paquete de arroz

una bolsa de papas fritas

una botella de agua mineral

un envase de leche

productos congelados

PASO 2

¿Qué palabra necesito?

 1 **Historieta** **Al mercado**

Contesten con **sí.** (*Answer with* sí.)

1. ¿Venden frutas y vegetales en el mercado?
2. ¿Venden carne y pescado también?
3. ¿Va de compras la señora Dávila?
4. ¿Va al mercado de San Miguel?
5. ¿Ve ella muchos vegetales frescos?
6. ¿Compra ella lechuga?
7. ¿Compra tomates también?
8. ¿Están a dos euros el kilo los tomates?
9. ¿Va a preparar la señora una ensalada?
10. ¿Necesita ella algo más?

Vegetales y tomates. Mercado municipal. Málaga, España

2 **Historieta** **En el supermercado**

Completen. (*Complete.*)

El __1__ es muy grande y moderno. En el __2__ venden todo tipo de comestibles. Venden vegetales __3__ y vegetales congelados. Hoy el señor Salas va al supermercado. Él tiene que comprar muchas cosas. Aquí tenemos su lista.

un __4__ de atún (porque el señor va a preparar una ensalada de atún)

una lechuga y dos __5__ de tomates (porque el señor va a preparar una ensalada)

medio kilo de __6__ picada (porque el señor va a preparar una hamburguesa)

un __7__ de papas fritas congeladas (porque el señor no quiere preparar las papas)

tres __8__ de cola (porque el señor tiene que beber algo con sus comidas)

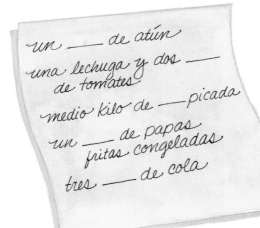

un ___ de atún
una lechuga y dos ___ de tomates
medio kilo de ___ picada
un ___ de papas fritas congeladas
tres ___ de cola

3 **¿El desayuno, el almuerzo o la cena?**

Escojan. *(Choose.)*

1. **a.** En la cena comemos pan tostado con mermelada.
   b. En el desayuno comemos cereales, huevos y frutas.

2. **a.** En el desayuno comemos un bocadillo de pollo con papas fritas y una ensalada de lechuga y tomate.
   b. En la cena comemos carne o pescado, papas o arroz y un vegetal.

3. **a.** En el almuerzo comemos un bocadillo de jamón y queso y después un helado.
   b. En el desayuno comemos helado y fruta.

4 **Juego** **Una competencia** Compete with a classmate. See which one of you can make up the most expressions using the following words.

un kilo   una bolsa   una lata

un paquete   una botella

Un mercado del altiplano, Ecuador

5 **Juego** **¿Vegetal o fruta?** One of you will go to the front of the room and call out foods. If it's a vegetable, your classmates will raise their right hand. If it's a fruit, they will raise their left hand. If it's something other than a fruit or vegetable, they will clap their hands.

Formas

Los verbos en -er e -ir en el plural
Talking about what you and others do

1. Study the following plural forms of **-er** and **-ir** verbs. You will note that there is a difference in the **nosotros(as)** form.

-er verbs

	comer com-	leer le-	endings
nosotros(as)	comemos	leemos	-emos
ellos ellas Uds.	comen	leen	-en

-ir verbs

	vivir viv-	escribir escrib-	endings
nosotros(as)	vivimos	escribimos	-imos
ellos ellas Uds.	viven	escriben	-en

2. Remember that in Spain people use the **vosotros(as)** form when talking to two or more friends.

   vosotros(as)   *coméis*   *vivís*

3. Note the plural forms of the verb **ver.**

   vemos   *veis*   **ven**

¿Lees el menú?
¿Qué comes?

Restaurante El Paseo

Sopas

	1.25
Sopa de Pollo	2.10
Caldo Gallego	1.25
Frijoles Negros	

Ensaladas

Ensalada de Lechuga y Tomate	1.50
Ensalada de Aguacata (en temporada)	1.75
Ensalada Mixta (por persona)	2.95
Ensalada de Espárragos	4.25

Huevos

Tortilla de Queso	2.95
Tortilla de Camarones	5.50
Tortilla de Chorizo	3.95
Tortilla de Petit-Pois ó de Papa ó de Plátano	2.95
Tortilla de Jamón	3.25
Tortilla Combinación (2)	3.50
Dos Huevos Fritos ó Revueltos con Jamón o Bacon y Papas	2.25
Dos Huevos Fritos o Revueltos con Papas	1.75
Dos Huevos con Tostadas	1.75

Postres

FLAN "EL PUB"	1.75

ESPECIALIDADES DE LA CASA

FLAN	1.25
NATILLA	1.25
PUDIN DIPLOMATICO	1.25

Servidos con Dulce en Conservas

PASTEL DE MANZANA (A la Moda 50¢ Extra)	1.25
HELADOS Fresa, Vainilla, Chocolate	1.25

¿Cómo lo digo?

6 **Historieta** **En nuestra clase**
Lean. *(Read the following.)*

  Nosotros vivimos en Madrid. En nuestra escuela aprendemos el inglés. Para nosotros, el inglés no es muy fácil. Pero prestamos mucha atención y comprendemos cuando nuestro profesor de inglés habla. En clase leemos también. Escribimos un poco, no mucho. A veces vemos un DVD. Nuestra clase de inglés es interesante. Aprendemos mucho y recibimos notas buenas.

Madrid, España

7 **Historieta** **La clase de inglés** Contesten.
(Answer based on the information in Activity 6.)

1. ¿Dónde viven los jóvenes?
2. ¿Qué aprenden en la escuela?
3. ¿Cómo es la clase de inglés?
4. ¿Prestan ellos mucha atención al profesor?
5. ¿Comprenden cuando su profesor habla?
6. ¿Leen en inglés también?
7. ¿Escriben mucho?
8. ¿Qué ven a veces?
9. ¿Aprenden mucho o poco?
10. ¿Qué notas reciben ellos en inglés?

8 **Comemos** Sigan los modelos. *(Follow the models.)*

 muchas frutas →

—¿Comen ustedes muchas frutas?

—Sí, (No, no) comemos muchas frutas.

más fruta o vegetales →

—¿Comen ustedes más fruta o vegetales?

—Comemos más frutas (vegetales).

1. muchas legumbres
2. muchos mariscos
3. muchos huevos
4. mucho pollo
5. más carne o pescado
6. más carne o pollo
7. más papas o arroz
8. más arroz o maíz

¿Vas a comer una paella?

9 **Historieta** **Nosotros** Contesten.
(Answer about yourself and some friends.)

1. ¿Dónde viven ustedes?
2. ¿Viven ustedes en una casa o en un apartamento?
3. ¿Qué aprenden ustedes en la escuela?
4. ¿En qué clase leen ustedes mucho?
5. ¿En qué clase escriben ustedes mucho?
6. ¿Qué tipo de notas reciben ustedes?
7. ¿Comen ustedes en la cafetería de la escuela?
8. ¿Qué comen ustedes en la cafetería?

Málaga, España

10 **En la escuela y después en el café**

Completen. *(Complete.)*

aprender

1. En la escuela yo _____ el español pero mi primo Luis no _____ el español. Él _____ el francés. ¿Qué _____ tú? ¿El español o el francés? Luis y yo _____ matemáticas. Ustedes también _____ matemáticas, ¿no?

recibir

2. Yo _____ notas buenas y mi primo también _____ notas buenas. Nosotros _____ notas muy altas en inglés y en español. ¿En qué cursos _____ ustedes notas altas?

comer

3. Cuando yo voy al café _____ un bocadillo de jamón y queso pero mi primo, no. Él siempre _____ una hamburguesa con papas fritas. Nosotros no _____ la misma cosa. Y tú, ¿qué _____ cuando vas a un café? ¿_____ lo que _____ yo o lo que _____ mi primo?

Una clase de álgebra en una escuela secundaria. Cuba

UN POCO MÁS

*For more practice using words and forms from **Paso 2**, do Activity 10 on page H11 at the end of this book.*

Andas bien. ¡Adelante!

Conversación

En el café

Felipe	Carmen, ¿ves una mesa libre?
Carmen	Sí, Felipe, allí hay una. ¡Vamos! ¡Hay mucha gente!
Felipe	¿Tienes hambre?
Carmen	Sí, un poco. Voy a comer algo.
Felipe	Yo también.
Carmen	¿Qué comes? ¿Una vez más tu hamburguesa famosa?
Felipe	No. Voy a comer un bocadillo de jamón y queso. ¿Y tú?
Carmen	Una ensalada de atún.
Mesero	¡Buenas tardes! ¿Qué desean ustedes?
Carmen	Una ensalada de atún y un bocadillo de jamón y queso, por favor.
Mesero	Y, ¿para beber?
Carmen	Para mí, una cola.
Felipe	Una cola para mí también.
Mesero	Dos colas. Gracias.

¿Comprendes?

Contesten. *(Answer.)*

1. ¿Dónde están Carmen y Felipe?
2. ¿Ve Carmen una mesa libre?
3. ¿Hay mucha gente en el café?
4. ¿Tiene Carmen hambre?

5. ¿Qué come siempre Felipe?
6. ¿Qué va a comer hoy?
7. Y Carmen, ¿qué come?
8. ¿Qué beben los dos?

Pronunciación

Las consonantes **b, v**

There is no difference in pronunciation between a **b** and a **v** in Spanish. The **b** or **v** sound is somewhat softer than the sound of an English *b*. When making this sound, the lips barely touch. Repeat the following.

ba	be	bi	bo	bu
bajo	bebé	bicicleta	recibo	bueno
bastante	escribe	bien	botella	bus
trabaja	recibe	biología	bote	aburrido

va	ve	vi	vo	vu
vamos	verano	vive	vosotros	vuelo
nueva	venezolano	vivimos	huevo	
vainilla	vende			

Trabalenguas

Repeat the following.

El joven vive en la avenida Bolívar en Bogotá.
Bárbara trabaja los sábados en el laboratorio de biología.
La joven ve la bicicleta nueva en la televisión.
Bárbara bebe una botella de soda en el bus.
En el verano vamos a visitar a nuestros abuelos.
No nieva en Venezuela donde vivimos.

Refrán

Can you guess what the following proverb means?

Cuatro ojos ven más que dos.

Cultura y lectura
Comida mexicana y española

Reading Strategy

Using previous knowledge Before you read a selection, look at the title. Think of what you already know about the topic, in this case, Mexican food. Have you ever been to a Mexican restaurant or seen frozen Mexican dinners in the supermarket? If you think about some Mexican foods you have seen, it will help you understand the reading.

Los sándwiches, o las «tortas», son populares en México.

Como vivimos en Estados Unidos, tenemos muchos restaurantes mexicanos. Los restaurantes mexicanos son muy populares. Cuando deciden comer en un restaurante y no en casa, muchas familias americanas comen en un restaurante mexicano.

Muchas comidas mexicanas llevan tortillas. Una tortilla es un tipo de panqueque. Algunas tortillas son de maíz. Otras son de harina[1]. Los mexicanos preparan muchas cosas diferentes con las tortillas.

[1] harina *flour*

Las señoras preparan tortillas. México

Un taco es una tortilla frita rellena de² carne picada o pollo con tomate, lechuga y queso.

Una enchilada es una tortilla blanda enrollada³. Lleva carne, pollo o queso. Muchos platos mexicanos van acompañados de arroz y frijoles.

Aquí ven ustedes otra tortilla. Es una tortilla española. Es muy diferente, ¿no? Es una tortilla de huevos con papas, o en España, patatas, y cebolla⁴. Una tortilla española es deliciosa. Tienes que comer una buena tortilla «a la española».

² rellena de *stuffed with*
³ enrollada *rolled up*
⁴ cebolla *onion*

¿Comprendes?

A. Contesten. *(Answer.)*
1. ¿Dónde viven ustedes?
2. En EE.UU., ¿hay muchos restaurantes mexicanos?
3. ¿Dónde comen muchas familias cuando no van a comer en casa?
4. ¿De qué van acompañados muchos platos mexicanos?
5. ¿De qué es una tortilla española?
6. ¿Hay mucha diferencia entre una tortilla mexicana y una tortilla española?

B. Describan. *(Describe the following.)*
1. un taco
2. una enchilada
3. una tortilla mexicana
4. una tortilla española

PASO 3

Repaso

1. In this unit, I learned regular **-er** (second conjugation) and **-ir** (third conjugation) verbs.

2. All forms of **-er** and **-ir** verbs are the same, except **nosotros** (and **vosotros**).

comer

como	**comemos**
comes	*coméis*
come	**comen**

vivir

vivo	**vivimos**
vives	*vivís*
vive	**viven**

Un café en la Plaza de San Francisco,
La Habana, Cuba

¡Pongo todo junto!

 1 **Contesten.** *(Answer.)*

1. ¿Qué venden en el mercado?
2. ¿Qué comen ustedes en el almuerzo?
3. ¿Dónde viven ustedes?
4. ¿Qué aprendes en la escuela?
5. ¿Leen y escriben ustedes mucho?
6. ¿Comprenden los alumnos cuando el profesor habla?
7. Tú, ¿en qué cursos recibes notas buenas?
8. ¿Recibe una quinceañera muchos regalos?

La señora vende frutas y legumbres.
Quito, Ecuador

 2 **Completen.** *(Complete.)*

En el café los clientes __1__ (ver) al mesero. Ellos __2__ (hablar) con el mesero. Los clientes __3__ (leer) el menú. El mesero __4__ (escribir) la orden en una hoja de papel o en un bloc pequeño. Y tú, ¿__5__ (leer) el menú cuando __6__ (ir) a un café? ¿__7__ (Comprender) tú el menú cuando __8__ (leer)?

El señor vende ajo.
Estepona, España

¡Te toca a ti!

Un joven vende pescado, Perú

1 En el mercado

✓ *Talk about shopping for food*

You're at a market in San Isidro, Perú. Make a list of items you have to buy. With a classmate, take turns being the vendor and customer as you shop for the items on your list.

Hablar

2 ¿Qué comes?

✓ *Talk about eating habits*

Work with a classmate. Find out what each of you eats for different meals.

Hablar

3 En el café

✓ *Order things at a café*

Work in groups of three or four. You're all friends from Sevilla, España. After school you go to a café where you talk about lots of things—school, teachers, friends, etc. One of you will be the server. You have to interrupt once in a while to take orders and serve.

En un café, Sevilla, España

Escribir

4 El menú

 ✓ *Plan a menu*

Write a menu in Spanish for your school cafeteria.

Café Luna

sándwich	14 pesos
tamal	10 pesos
enchilada	11 pesos
café	2 pesos
limonada	3 pesos

Writing Strategy

Ordering ideas You can order ideas in a variety of ways when writing. Therefore, you must be aware of the purpose of your writing in order to choose the best way to organize your material. When describing an event, it is logical to put the events in the order in which they happen. Using a sensible and logical approach helps readers develop a picture in their minds.

Escribir

5 ¿Qué preparas?

Your class is planning a Spanish meal. Describe the trip you take with your classmates to the local market or supermarket to buy the ingredients. Tell what you buy, whom you buy it from, and how much everything costs.

Málaga, España

PASO 3

Assessment

¿Estoy listo(a)?

Palabras

1 Completen. *(Complete.)*

1. La mesa está _____. No está ocupada.
2. El _____ trabaja en el café.
3. La muchacha lee el _____ y decide lo que va a comer.
4. El muchacho va a _____ una gaseosa.
5. Él come un _____ de vainilla y su amiga come un _____ de chocolate.
6. Después de comer en el café, José paga la _____.

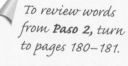

To review words from **Paso 1,** turn to pages 172–173.

2 Identifiquen. *(Identify.)*

7.	8.	9.

To review words from **Paso 2,** turn to pages 180–181.

10.	11.	12.

3 Contesten. *(Answer.)*

13. ¿A cuánto están los tomates?
14. ¿Algo más?

Formas

4 Completen. *(Complete.)*

15. Nosotros _____ en Estados Unidos. (vivir)
16. Los alumnos _____ en la cafetería. (comer)
17. Yo _____ cuando él habla. (comprender)
18–19. Nosotros _____ y _____ mucho. (leer, escribir)
20. ¿Tú _____ muchos regalos? (recibir)
21. Ustedes _____ en una casa grande. (vivir)
22. Ella _____ frutas y vegetales en el mercado. (vender)

To review -er and -ir verbs, turn to pages 176 and 184.

Cultura

5 Identifiquen. *(Identify.)*

23. un tipo de panqueque de maíz o de harina
24. una tortilla de huevos con patatas y cebolla
25. una tortilla enrollada que tiene carne, pollo o queso

To review this cultural information, turn to pages 190–191.

Las señoras preparan tortillas. Guatemala

Diversiones

Canta con Justo
Te toca a ti, me toca a mí

Es - toy a- quí sen-ta - do en un café, ba-jo un sol de pri - ma-ve - ra.

Cuan-do en-tre la gen - te pue-do ver a Ma - rí - a que vie-ne a mi me - sa Ca-ma - re-ro, yo de-se-o o-tro ca-

fé Mi a - mi-ga es-ta tar-de tie-ne sed. Por fa-vor, e-lla quie-re a-gua fre-sca y un sa-bro- so pe-da-zo de pas-tel.

Te to-ca a ti, me to - ca a mí. ¿Quién pa-ga la cuen-ta? Qui-zá po - de - mos com-par- tir y ya no hay pro-

ble-ma Te to-ca a ti, me to - ca a mí. ¿Quién pa-ga la cuen-ta? Qui-zá po - de-mos com-par-tir y ya no hay pro - ble-ma.

Me gusta escribir en el café
En las tardes de verano
Tomar mi desayuno y comprender
Que vivir es un bello regalo...

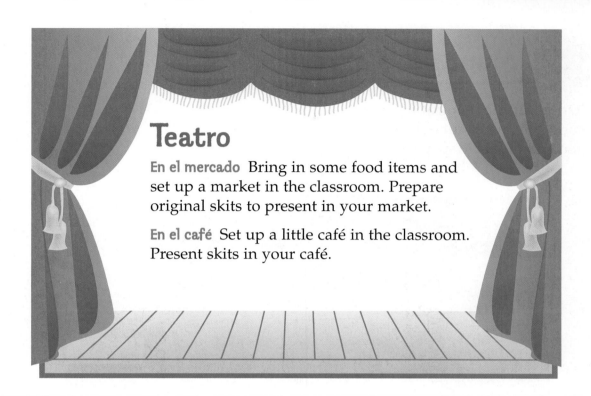

Teatro

En el mercado Bring in some food items and set up a market in the classroom. Prepare original skits to present in your market.

En el café Set up a little café in the classroom. Present skits in your café.

Juego Cada uno a su sitio Look at the following words and decide in which category they belong. Sometimes you will find that a word will fit in more than one place.

EL CAFÉ	LA ESCUELA	LA CASA	LA ROPA
_____	_____	_____	_____
_____	_____	_____	_____
_____	_____	_____	_____
_____	_____	_____	_____

el menú la cocina la terraza el uniforme

la sala

el perro la televisión la alumna

los calcetines el comedor las tijeras

el mesero la cafetería el cuarto de baño la computadora

la camisa los zapatos la falda

la gorra

Manos a la obra

Un anuncio Look at this food ad. Use it as a model. Draw or cut out some food items. Prepare a food ad for a newspaper or supermarket brochure.

Leche entera, semidesnatada o desnatada RAM, envase de 1 L,

EL CARRO ESTRELLA
0,59 €

CALIDAD MEJOR PRECIO

HUEVOS
Frescos Medianos

EL CARRO ESTRELLA
1,05 €

Huevos clase M, envase de 12 unidades,

CALIDAD HIPERCOR. PRECIOS HIPERBUENOS

Investigaciones

Ethnic foods vary a great deal from region to region. What people eat and use in their cooking is often influenced by what is available where they live. Latin America covers a vast area in both North and South America. Pick a country or area of a country and learn about a typical dish from that region. Write a description of it.

Spanish Online

For more information about food in the Spanish-speaking world, go to the Glencoe Spanish Web site: spanish.glencoe.com.

Use your manipulatives to play "verb games" with your classmates.

Rompecabezas

¿Dónde trabaja? Can you figure out where each person works?

1. el camarero
2. la profesora
3. la dependienta
4. el artista

a. un museo
b. el café
c. la escuela
d. la tienda

PLEGABLES™
Study Organizer

Dibujar y escribir Use this *single picture frame* book to help you illustrate the stories you write.

Step 1 **Fold** a sheet of paper (8½" x 11") in half like a *hamburger*.

Step 2 **Open** the *hamburger* and gently roll one side of the *hamburger* toward the valley. Try not to crease the roll.

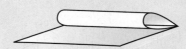

Step 3 **Cut** a rectangle out of the middle of the rolled side of paper, leaving a ½" border and forming a frame.

Step 4 **Fold** another sheet of paper (8½" x 11") in half like a *hamburger*.

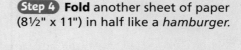

Step 5 **Apply** glue to the picture frame and place inside the *hamburger* fold.

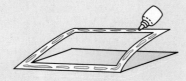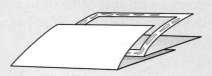

Variation:
• Place a picture behind the frame and glue the edges of the frame to the other side of the *hamburger* fold. This locks the picture in place.
• Cut out only three sides of the rolled rectangle. This forms a window with a cover that opens and closes.

PASO 4

Más cultura y lectura

Mercados y supermercados del mundo hispano

Los mercados en el mundo hispano son muy variados. También son muy interesantes.

▲ Aquí vemos un mercado típico en Valencia, España. Mucha gente va de compras en un mercado como el mercado en la foto. En el mercado venden productos muy frescos.

▲ Y aquí tenemos un mercado indígena en Ecuador. Hay muchos mercados como el mercado de Otavalo en muchos países latinoamericanos.

▶ El supermercado en Lima, Perú es muy grande y moderno, ¿no? En el supermercado venden comestibles frescos y congelados.

▲ Una bodega es una tienda donde venden comida. A veces es una tienda grande, pero muchas veces es una tienda bastante pequeña. La bodega (*grocery store* en inglés) tiene varios nombres en español. En México y en los países de Centroamérica es una tienda de abarrotes. En el Caribe es un colmado como el colmado que vemos aquí en la esquina[1] de una calle[2] de Santo Domingo.

[1] esquina *corner*   [2] calle *street*

▲ Aquí ven ustedes un hipermercado en Estepona, España. Los hipermercados son muy grandes. Están frecuentemente en un centro comercial. En los hipermercados venden de todo—comestibles, ropa, materiales escolares, computadoras, bicicletas. ¡Todo!

¿Comprendes?

Pretend you're talking to a friend who is not studying Spanish. In English, describe the following types of markets that one finds in Spain and/or in Latin America.

1. un mercado municipal
2. un mercado indígena
3. una bodega o una tienda de abarrotes
4. un supermercado
5. un hipermercado

Conexiones
Las matemáticas

El sistema métrico

When you travel through many of the Spanish-speaking countries, you will have to make some mathematical conversions. This is definitely true when you buy food. In most of the Spanish-speaking world, the metric system rather than the English system is used for weights and measures. Let's take a look at some of these metric measures.

Leche esterilizada 1,5l

0,89 €

El litro te sale a 0,59 €

**Entrecot de ternera
El kg**

11,99 €

**Queso curado mini GRAN CAPITÁN
Por piezas, el kg**

8,65 €

**Arroz Basmati
500 grs.**

1,65 €

**Café molido mezcla o natural
MARCILLA, o filtro,
paquete de 250 g.**

1,11 €

Pesos y medidas[1]

Pesos

Las medidas tradicionales para peso en Estados Unidos son la onza, la libra y la tonelada. En el sistema métrico decimal, las medidas para peso están basadas en el kilogramo o kilo.

En un kilo hay mil (1.000) gramos. El kilo equivale a 2,2 libras. Una libra es un poco menos de medio kilo o quinientos (500) gramos.

Líquidos

En Estados Unidos las medidas para líquidos son la pinta, el cuarto y el galón. En el sistema métrico es el litro. Un litro contiene un poco más que[2] un cuarto.

[1] Pesos y medidas *Weights and measures*

[2] un poco más que *a little more than*

¿Comprendes?

Look at the food items on page 204 and answer.

1. ¿Cuál es el precio de un litro de leche?
2. ¿Cuántas botellas de leche vas a comprar si necesitas más o menos un galón?
3. ¿Cuánto cuesta un kilo de ternera?
4. ¿Cuánto cuesta un paquete de café?
5. ¿Cuántos paquetes de café vas a comprar si necesitas un kilo?

¡Hablo como un pro!

Tell all you can about the following illustration.

Vocabulario

Getting along in a café

el café	la orden	comer
la mesa	la cuenta	beber
la silla	libre	esperar
el/la mesero(a), el/la	ocupado(a)	llegar
camarero(a)	ver	¿Qué desean ustedes?
el menú	leer	

Identifying snacks and beverages

los refrescos	el pan	la ensalada
una cola	la sopa	el postre
una gaseosa	el bocadillo, el sándwich	el helado de vainilla, de
el café	el jamón	chocolate
la leche	el queso	
el agua mineral	la hamburguesa	
un té helado	las papas (patatas) fritas	

Shopping for food

el mercado	una botella	fresco(a)
el supermercado	un envase	vender
un bote, una lata	un kilo	¿A cuánto está(n)?
un paquete	medio(a)	algo más
una bolsa	congelado(a)	nada más

Identifying foods and meals

las legumbres, los vegetales	el maíz	los mariscos
la lechuga	las frutas	el pescado
las papas, las patatas	las manzanas	el pollo
las judías verdes, los ejotes	las naranjas	el huevo
las habichuelas, los frijoles	los plátanos	el atún
los guisantes	los tomates	el arroz
las zanahorias	la carne	

Other useful expressions

por la mañana	tener hambre	escribir
ir de compras	aprender	recibir
tener sed	comprender	vivir

Unidad

6 Los deportes

Objetivos

In this unit you will learn to:

- %o talk about sports
- %o talk about what you begin to, want to, and prefer to do
- %o talk about people's activities
- %o express what interests, bores, or pleases you
- %o discuss the role of sports in the Spanish-speaking world

Marla
Deportes y Regalos

Palabras   El fútbol 🎧

- la cabeza
- el brazo
- la mano izquierda
- el equipo
- la mano derecha
- la rodilla
- la pierna
- el pie
- el jugador
- la jugadora

el estadio

- el tablero indicador
- 2do. TIEMPO
- el tanto
- el espectador, la espectadora
- la portería
- el portero

el campo de fútbol

Hoy hay un partido.
El Real Madrid juega contra el Barcelona.

Los jugadores juegan al fútbol.
Un jugador lanza el balón.
Lanza el balón con el pie.
El portero guarda la portería.

El segundo tiempo empieza.
Los dos equipos vuelven al campo.
El tanto queda empatado a cero.

El portero no puede bloquear
   (parar) el balón.
El balón entra en la portería.
López mete un gol.
Él marca un tanto.

El Real Madrid gana el partido.
El Barcelona pierde.
Los espectadores no duermen
   durante el partido.

¿Qué palabra necesito?

1 **Un partido de fútbol** Completen según se indica.
(Answer as indicated.)

1. Diego lanza el balón con _____.

2. Él no lanza el balón con _____.

3. También lanza el balón con _____.

4. Pero no lanza el balón con _____.

5. Diego es un jugador muy bueno porque tiene _____ fuertes.

2 **Historieta El fútbol** Contesten según se indica.
(Answer as indicated.)

1. ¿Cuántos jugadores hay en el equipo de fútbol? (once)
2. ¿Cuántos tiempos hay en un partido de fútbol? (dos)
3. ¿Quién guarda la portería? (el portero)
4. ¿Cuándo mete un gol el jugador? (cuando el balón entra en la portería)
5. ¿Qué marca un jugador cuando el balón entra en la portería? (un tanto)
6. En el estadio, ¿qué indica el tablero? (el tanto)
7. ¿Cuándo queda empatado el tanto? (cuando los dos equipos tienen el mismo tanto)

3 **Historieta** **Un partido de fútbol**

Contesten. *(Answer.)*

1. ¿Cuántos equipos de fútbol hay en el campo de fútbol?
2. ¿Cuántos jugadores hay en cada equipo?
3. ¿Qué tiempo empieza, el primero o el segundo?
4. ¿Vuelven los jugadores al campo cuando empieza el segundo tiempo?
5. ¿Tiene un jugador el balón?
6. ¿Lanza el balón con el pie o con la mano?
7. ¿Para el balón el portero o entra el balón en la portería?
8. ¿Mete el jugador un gol?
9. ¿Marca un tanto?
10. ¿Queda empatado el tanto?
11. ¿Quién gana, el Valencia o el Liverpool?
12. ¿Qué equipo pierde?
13. ¿Siempre pierde?

El estadio de Mestalla, Valencia, España

4 **Un partido de fútbol** Work with a classmate. Take turns asking and answering each other's questions about the illustration below.

🏰 Formas

Verbos de cambio radical e → ie
Telling what you begin to, want to, or prefer to do

1. Some verbs in Spanish are called stem-changing verbs. The verbs **empezar, querer, perder,** and **preferir** are examples of stem-changing verbs. All forms, except the **nosotros** (and **vosotros**) forms, change the **e** of the infinitive to **ie.** The endings of these verbs are the same as those of a regular verb.

	empezar	querer	preferir
yo	empiezo	quiero	prefiero
tú	empiezas	quieres	prefieres
él, ella, Ud.	empieza	quiere	prefiere
nosotros(as)	empezamos	queremos	preferimos
vosotros(as)	empezáis	queréis	preferís
ellos, ellas, Uds.	empiezan	quieren	prefieren

2. The verbs **empezar, querer,** and **preferir** are often followed by an infinitive.

> **Prefieren ganar. No quieren perder.**

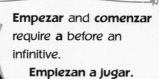

Nota

Empezar and **comenzar** require **a** before an infinitive.

Empiezan a jugar.
Comienzan a jugar.

Los muchachos juegan fútbol en Tortuguero, Costa Rica.

¿Cómo lo digo?

5 **Historieta** **Queremos ganar.**

Contesten. *(Answer.)*

1. ¿Empiezan ustedes a jugar?
2. ¿Empiezan ustedes a jugar a las tres?
3. ¿Quieren ustedes ganar el partido?
4. ¿Quieren ustedes marcar un tanto?
5. ¿Pierden ustedes a veces o ganan siempre?
6. ¿Prefieren ustedes jugar en el parque o en la calle?

Papá y su hijo juegan fútbol.
Plaza Catedral, Cádiz, España

6 **Historieta** **El partido continúa.**

Formen oraciones según el modelo.
(Form sentences according to the model.)

> **el segundo tiempo / empezar ⟶**
> **El segundo tiempo empieza.**

1. los jugadores / empezar a jugar
2. los dos equipos / querer ganar
3. ellos / preferir marcar muchos tantos
4. Sánchez / querer meter un gol
5. el portero / querer parar el balón
6. el equipo de Sánchez / no perder

7 **Historieta** **¿Un(a) aficionado(a) a los deportes?**

Contesten. *(Answer about yourself.)*

1. ¿Prefieres jugar al béisbol o al fútbol?
2. ¿Prefieres jugar con un grupo de amigos o con un equipo formal?
3. ¿Prefieres jugar en el partido o prefieres mirar el partido?
4. ¿Prefieres ser jugador(a) o espectador(a)?
5. ¿Siempre quieres ganar?
6. ¿Pierdes a veces?

Estadio Morumbi en São Paulo, Brasil

Verbos de cambio radical o → ue
Describing more activities

1. The verbs **volver** (*to return to a place*), **devolver** (*to return a thing*), **poder** (*to be able to*), and **dormir** (*to sleep*) are also stem-changing verbs. The **o** of the stem changes to **ue** in all forms except **nosotros** (and **vosotros**). The endings are the same as those of the regular verbs. Study the following forms.

	volver	poder	dormir
yo	**vuelvo**	**puedo**	**duermo**
tú	**vuelves**	**puedes**	**duermes**
él, ella, Ud.	**vuelve**	**puede**	**duerme**
nosotros(as)	volvemos	podemos	dormimos
vosotros(as)	*volvéis*	*podéis*	*dormís*
ellos, ellas, Uds.	**vuelven**	**pueden**	**duermen**

2. The **u** in the verb **jugar** changes to **ue** in all forms except **nosotros** (and **vosotros**).

jugar   **juego, juegas, juega, jugamos,** *jugáis,* **juegan**

> **Nota**
> **Jugar** is sometimes followed by **a** when a sport is mentioned. Both of the following are acceptable:
> **Juegan al fútbol.**
> **Juegan fútbol.**

Es Increíble Lo Que Puede Hacer Con Más Espacio.

¿Cómo lo digo?

8 **¿Qué juegan?** Practiquen la conversación.
(Practice the conversation.)

9 **Historieta ¿Qué quieren jugar?**

Contesten. *(Answer based on the conversation.)*

1. ¿Quiénes juegan mucho al fútbol?
2. ¿A qué juegan Tomás y Elena?
3. ¿Pueden los jugadores usar las manos cuando juegan al fútbol?
4. ¿Con qué tienen que lanzar el balón?
5. ¿Quieren jugar Tomás y Elena?
6. ¿Prefieren jugar o mirar?

 10 **Historieta** **Un partido de fútbol** Contesten. (*Answer.*)

1. ¿Juegan ustedes (al) fútbol?
2. ¿Juegan con unos amigos o con el equipo de su escuela?
3. ¿Vuelven ustedes al campo cuando empieza el segundo tiempo?
4. ¿Pueden ustedes usar las manos cuando juegan (al) fútbol?
5. ¿Tienen ustedes que lanzar el balón con los pies o el brazo?
6. ¿Duermen ustedes bien después de jugar (al) fútbol?

Los niños juegan al fútbol, Casares, España

11 **Historieta** **En la clase de español**

Contesten. (*Answer.*)
1. ¿Juegas al Bingo en la clase de español?
2. ¿Puedes hablar inglés en la clase de español?
3. ¿Qué lengua puedes o tienes que hablar en la clase de español?
4. ¿Duermes en la clase de español?
5. ¿Devuelve el/la profesor(a) los exámenes pronto?

PASO 1

12 Historieta **Sí, pero ahora no puede.**
Completen. *(Complete.)*

Yo __1__ (jugar) mucho al fútbol y Diana
__2__ (jugar) mucho también, pero ahora
ella no __3__ (poder).

—Diana, ¿por qué no __4__ (poder)
jugar ahora?

—No __5__ (poder) porque __6__
(querer) ir a casa.

Sí, Diana __7__ (querer) ir a casa porque
ella __8__ (tener) un amigo que __9__
(volver) hoy de Puerto Rico y ella __10__
(querer) estar en casa. Pero mañana todos
nosotros __11__ (ir) a jugar. Y el amigo
puertorriqueño de Diana __12__ (poder)
jugar también. Su amigo __13__ (jugar)
muy bien.

Los futbolistas celebran después de un partido.

13 **Quiero pero no puedo.** A classmate will ask you if you want to
do something or go somewhere. Tell him or her that you want to
but you can't because you have to do something else. Tell what it is
you have to do. Take turns asking and answering the questions.

14 **¿Es así o no?** Choose one of the illustrations below and make a statement
about it. Your partner will look at the other illustration and agree with your
statement or correct you if his or her picture is different.

*For more practice using words and
forms from **Paso 1,** do Activity 11 on
page H12 at the end of this book.*

Palabras   El béisbol 🎧

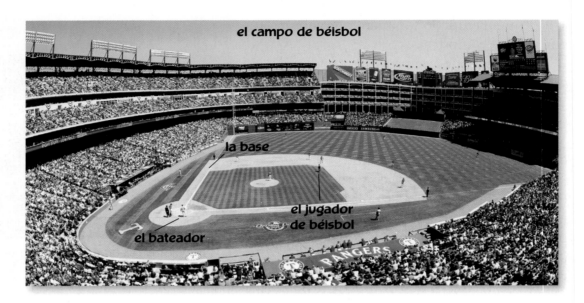

el campo de béisbol

la base

el jugador de béisbol

el bateador

el pícher, el lanzador

la pelota

El pícher lanza la pelota.

el cátcher, el receptor

El cátcher devuelve la pelota.

atrapar

la jardinera

el guante

el bate

el platillo

La jugadora atrapa la pelota.
Atrapa la pelota con el guante.

correr

El bateador batea.
Batea un jonrón.
El jugador corre de una base a otra.

En un juego de béisbol hay nueve entradas.
Si después de la novena entrada el tanto
queda empatado, el partido continúa.

El básquetbol, El baloncesto

pasar el balón

Son campeones.
Ganan un trofeo.

driblar con
el balón

la cancha de básquetbol

el balón

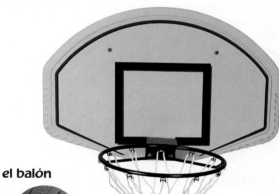

el cesto,
la canasta

meter el balón
en el cesto

encestar

tirar el balón

PASO 2

¿Qué palabra necesito?

1 ¿Qué deporte es? Escojan. *(Choose.)*

1. El jugador lanza el balón con el pie.
2. Hay cinco jugadores en el equipo.
3. Hay nueve entradas en el partido.
4. El jugador corre de una base a otra.
5. El portero para o bloquea el balón.
6. El jugador tira el balón y encesta.

Una cancha de pelota. Copán. Honduras

2 Historieta **El béisbol** Escojan. *(Choose.)*

1. Juegan (al) béisbol en _____ de béisbol.
   a. un campo   **b.** una pelota   **c.** una base
2. El pícher _____ la pelota.
   a. lanza   **b.** encesta   **c.** batea
3. El jardinero atrapa la pelota en _____.
   a. una portería   **b.** un cesto   **c.** un guante
4. El jugador _____ de una base a otra.
   a. tira   **b.** devuelve   **c.** corre
5. En un partido de béisbol hay _____ entradas.
   a. dos   **b.** nueve   **c.** once

3 Historieta **El baloncesto** Contesten. *(Answer.)*

1. ¿Es el baloncesto un deporte de equipo o un deporte individual?
2. ¿Hay cinco o nueve jugadores en un equipo de baloncesto?
3. Durante un partido de baloncesto, ¿los jugadores driblan con el balón o lanzan el balón con el pie?
4. ¿El jugador tira el balón en el cesto o en la portería?
5. ¿El encestado (canasto) vale dos puntos o seis puntos?

4 Historieta Los campeones

Contesten. *(Answer.)*

1. ¿Juegan muy bien los Leones?
2. ¿Tienen un equipo muy bueno?
3. ¿Ganan o pierden muchos partidos?
4. ¿Son campeones?
5. ¿Ganan un trofeo?
6. ¿Duermen los espectadores cuando miran un partido de los Leones?

Jugadores de baloncesto en España

5 Juego ¿Qué deporte es?
Work with a classmate. Give him or her some information about a sport. He or she has to guess what sport you're talking about. Take turns.

6 Juego ¡Adivina quién es!
Think of your favorite sports hero. Tell a classmate something about him or her. Your classmate will ask you three questions about your hero before guessing who it is. Then reverse roles and you guess who your classmate's hero is.

7 Pobre Mario
Work with a partner. One of you can be Mario and the other, María. Mario is confused. He wants to do everything but he always makes mistakes. Mario will explain what he wants to do and María tells him why he cannot.

Quiero jugar baloncesto.

Quiero jugar béisbol.

Quiero jugar fútbol.

¡Ay, Mario!

PASO 2

Formas

Los verbos interesar, aburrir, gustar
Expressing what interests, bores, or pleases you

1. The verbs **interesar** and **aburrir** function the same in English and in Spanish. Study the following examples.

¿Te aburre el béisbol?   *Does baseball bore you?*
No, el béisbol me interesa.   *No, baseball interests me.*

¿Te aburren los deportes?   *Do sports bore you?*
No, los deportes me interesan.   *No, sports interest me.*

2. The verb **gustar** in Spanish works (functions) the same as **interesar** and **aburrir. Gustar** conveys the meaning *to like,* but its true meaning is *to please.* The Spanish way of saying *I like baseball* is *Baseball pleases me.*

¿Te aburre el béisbol? No, no. Me interesa.
¿Te gusta el béisbol? Sí, me gusta mucho el béisbol.
¿Te gustan los deportes en general? Sí, me gustan.

El colegio San José, Estepona, España

3. **Gustar** is often used with an infinitive to tell what you like to do.

¿Te gusta ganar? Sí. No me gusta perder.
¿Te gusta comer?

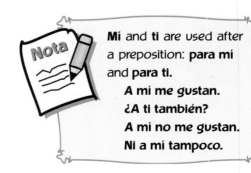

> **Nota**
>
> **Mí** and **ti** are used after a preposition: **para mí** and **para ti.**
>
> **A mí me gustan.**
> **¿A ti también?**
> **A mí no me gustan.**
> **Ni a mí tampoco.**

¿Cómo lo digo?

8 **¿Qué cursos te interesan y qué cursos te aburren?** Contesten. *(Answer.)*

1. ¿Te interesa la historia?
2. ¿Te interesa la geografía?
3. ¿Te interesa la biología?
4. ¿Te interesa la educación física?
5. ¿Te interesan las matemáticas?
6. ¿Te interesan las ciencias?

¿Es una clase interesante?
Santiago de Chile

9 **¿Te interesan o te aburren?**

 Sigan el modelo. *(Follow the model.)*

> **las ciencias** →
> **Las ciencias me interesan. No me aburren.**

1. las matemáticas
2. los estudios sociales
3. mis cursos
4. los deportes

10 **¿Te interesa o te aburre?**

Contesten. *(Answer.)*

1. ¿Te interesa o te aburre el béisbol?
2. ¿Te interesa o te aburre el arte?
3. ¿Te interesan o te aburren los partidos de fútbol?
4. ¿Te interesan o te aburren las emisiones deportivas?

11 **Los deportes** Contesten. *(Answer.)*

1. ¿Te gusta el fútbol?
2. ¿Te gusta el béisbol?
3. ¿Te gusta el voleibol?
4. ¿Te gusta más el béisbol o el fútbol?
5. ¿Te gusta más el voleibol o el básquetbol?
6. ¿Te gusta el golf?
7. ¿Te gusta el tenis?

¿Quieres un helado? Plasencia, España

12 **Los alimentos** Contesten. *(Answer.)*

1. ¿Te gusta la ensalada?
2. ¿Te gusta un sándwich de jamón y queso?
3. ¿Te gusta el pescado?
4. ¿Te gusta el helado?
5. ¿Te gusta la torta?
6. ¿Te gustan las frutas?
7. ¿Te gustan los tomates?
8. ¿Te gustan las hamburguesas?
9. ¿Te gustan los mariscos?

13 **¿Te gusta la ropa?**

Sigan el modelo. *(Follow the model.)*

—¿Te gusta la gorra? →
—Sí, a mí me gusta.

1.

2.

3.

4.

5.

6.

  14 ¿Qué te gusta hacer?

Contesten. *(Answer.)*

1. ¿Te gusta cantar?
2. ¿Te gusta bailar?
3. ¿Te gusta comer?
4. ¿Te gusta leer?
5. ¿Te gusta más hablar o escuchar?
6. ¿Te gusta más jugar o ser espectador(a)?

 15 **Gustos** Work with a classmate. Tell one another some things you like and don't like. Let one another know when you agree. Following are some categories you may want to explore.

ropa comida deportes cursos actividades

Los niños juegan baloncesto. Quetzalan, México

 UN POCO MÁS *For more practice using words and forms from **Paso 2**, do Activity 12 on page H13 at the end of this book.*

 Andas bien. ¡Adelante!

Conversación
Un partido de fútbol

¿Comprendes?

Contesten. *(Answer.)*

1. ¿Va a jugar fútbol Madela?
2. ¿Quiere jugar Alicia?
3. ¿Cuándo van a jugar?
4. ¿Puede jugar la amiga de Alicia?
5. Si juega Alicia, ¿cuántas jugadoras tienen?
6. ¿Cuándo puede jugar la amiga de Alicia?
7. Y, ¿quién juega hoy?

Las consonantes s, c, z

The consonant **s** is pronounced the same as the *s* in *sing*. Repeat the following.

sa	se	si	so	su
sala	base	sí	peso	su
pasa	serio	simpático	piso	Susana
saca	seis	siete	sopa	supermercado
mesa	mesero		sobrino	

The consonant **c** in combination with **e** or **i** (**ce, ci**) is pronounced the same as an **s** in all areas of Latin America. In many parts of Spain, **ce** and **ci** are pronounced like the *th* in English. Likewise, the pronunciation of **z** in combination with **a, o, u** (**za, zo, zu**) is the same as an **s** throughout Latin America and as a *th* in most areas of Spain. Repeat the following.

za	ce	ci	zo	zu
cabeza	cero	cinco	zona	zumo
empieza	encesta	ciudad	almuerzo	Zúñiga
lanza	cena		venezolano	Venezuela

Trabalenguas

Repeat the following.

> González enseña en la sala de clase.
> El sobrino de Susana es serio y sincero.
> La ciudad de Zaragoza tiene cinco zonas.
> Toma el almuerzo a las doce y diez en la cocina.

Refrán

Can you guess what the following proverb means?

Perro que ladra no muerde.

RUFO

¡Guao! ¡Guao!

PASO 3

Cultura y lectura

Los deportes en el mundo hispano

El Valencia contra el Manchester

El fútbol

El fútbol es un deporte muy popular en todos los países hispanos. Los equipos nacionales tienen millones de aficionados[1], pero el fútbol que juegan en los países hispanos no es el fútbol que jugamos nosotros. El fútbol americano no es muy popular. El fútbol que juegan es lo que llamamos «soccer». Los jugadores no pueden tocar el balón con las manos ni con los brazos. Tienen que usar la cabeza, el pie o las piernas.

Dos jóvenes juegan béisbol en un parque de la Habana. Cuba.

El béisbol

El béisbol es popular en algunos países hispanos, pero no en todos. El béisbol tiene muchos aficionados en Cuba, Puerto Rico, la República Dominicana, Venezuela, Nicaragua, México y Panamá.

Muchos jugadores de béisbol de las Grandes Ligas son latinos. Entre 1919 y hoy, más de cien jugadores latinos juegan en la Serie mundial[2].

El pueblo pequeño de San Pedro de Macorís en la República Dominicana produce más jugadores de las Grandes Ligas que cualquier otro[3] pueblo o ciudad del mundo.

[1] aficionados *fans*   [2] Serie mundial *World Series*   [3] cualquier otro *any other*

La golfista Nancy López

El golf y el tenis

El golf y el tenis son otros deportes que gozan de[4] mucha popularidad en los países hispanos. ¿Puedes nombrar algunos jugadores latinos de golf o de tenis?

[4] gozan de *enjoy*

La tenista argentina Gabriela Sabatini

¿Comprendes?

A. Contesten. *(Answer.)*

1. ¿Cuál es un deporte popular en todos los países de habla española?
2. ¿Tienen muchos aficionados los equipos nacionales?
3. ¿Eres muy aficionado(a) al fútbol?
4. ¿Te gusta mucho el fútbol?
5. El fútbol que juegan en los países hispanos, ¿es como el fútbol americano o no?
6. ¿Qué no pueden usar los jugadores de fútbol cuando lanzan el balón?

B. Busquen. *(Find the following information.)*

1. países hispanos donde es muy popular el béisbol
2. desde 1919 el número de jugadores latinos de béisbol que juegan en la Serie mundial
3. un pueblo que produce muchos buenos jugadores de béisbol

C. Give a major difference between the football played in the United States and the football played in the Spanish-speaking countries.

Repaso

1. In this unit, I learned stem-changing verbs e → ie, o → ue.
   Stem-changing verbs with **e** change to **ie** in all forms except
   nosotros (and **vosotros**); **o** changes to **ue**.

querer (e → ie)		poder (o → ue)	
quiero	queremos	puedo	podemos
quieres	*queréis*	puedes	*podéis*
quiere	quieren	puede	pueden

2. The verb **gustar** *(to like)* functions the same in Spanish
   as the verbs **interesar** and **aburrir**.

   Me interesan los deportes. ¿Te interesan a ti?
   No me aburren los deportes. ¿Te aburren a ti?
   Me gustan mucho los deportes. Y, ¿a ti te gustan?

   Nota

   Mí and **ti** are used
   following a preposition.
   **A mí me gustan
   los deportes.
   ¿Y a ti también?**

Un estadio de fútbol.
Barcelona, España

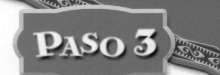

¡Pongo todo junto!

1 ¡A jugar!   Completen. *(Complete.)*

1. Ellos _____ fútbol. (jugar)
2. Y nosotros _____ béisbol. (jugar)
3. ¿Qué _____ ustedes jugar? (preferir)
4. ¿Tú _____ jugar con nosotros? (poder)
5. Si yo _____, nuestro equipo gana. Nosotros no _____. (jugar, perder)
6. ¿A qué hora _____ el partido? (empezar)

2   Intereses y gustos
Sigan el modelo. *(Follow the model.)*

los deportes ⟶

¿Te aburren los deportes?
Sí, me aburren.

¿Te interesan los deportes?
Sí, me interesan.

¿Te gustan mucho
los deportes? Sí, me
gustan mucho.

1. el béisbol y el básquetbol
2. el fútbol
3. la televisión
4. las emisiones deportivas
5. los cursos

3 **yo practic o**

Work with a partner. Practice your
verbs using your manipulatives.

PASO 3

¡Te toca a ti!

1 Mi(s) deporte(s) favorito(s)

✓ *Discuss a sport or sports you like*

Pick your favorite sport or sports. Get together with a classmate who likes the same sport or sports as you. Take turns describing the sport or sports you like best.

2 Intereses y gustos

✓ *Discuss what does or does not interest you and what you like to do*

Work with a classmate. Share with one another things that interest you and that you like to do.

El polideportivo de Ojén, España

El fútbol femenino es muy popular en Estados Unidos.

3 Un partido de fútbol

✓ *Describe a soccer game*

You are at a soccer match with a friend (your classmate). He or she has never been to a soccer game before and doesn't understand the game. Your friend has a lot of questions. Answer the questions and explain the game. You may want to use some of the following words.

ganar   empezar   lanzar

marcar   jugar

meter   volver   perder

Escribir

4 El béisbol

 ✓ *Write about baseball*

You have a key pal from Ceuta in Africa. He or she e-mails you and tells you he or she doesn't know anything about baseball. E-mail him or her describing important things about a baseball game.

Una calle de Ceuta. África del Norte

Escribir

5 Un reportaje

 ✓ *Describe a sporting event*

You went to a sporting event at your school. Write an article about the event for the "Spanish Corner" in your school newspaper. You can write your report in the present tense.

Writing Strategy

Gathering information If your writing projects deal with a subject you are not familiar with, you may need to gather information before you begin to write. Some of your best sources are the library, the Internet, and people who know something about the topic. Even if you plan to interview people about the topic, it may be necessary to do some research in the library or on the Internet to acquire enough knowledge to prepare good interview questions.

Escribir

6 La Copa mundial

Many of you already know that the World Cup is a soccer championship. Try to give a description of the World Cup as best you can in Spanish. If you are not familiar with it, you will need to do some research. It might be interesting to take what you know or find out about the World Cup and compare it to the World Series in baseball. Gather information about both these champion-ships and write a report in Spanish.

Assessment

¿Estoy listo(a)?

Palabras

To review words from **Paso 1,** turn to pages 210–211.

1 Completen. *(Complete.)*

1–2. El _____ juega en el partido y el _____ mira el partido.

3–4. Dos partes del cuerpo humano son _____ y _____.

5. El portero _____ la portería.

6. Un equipo _____ y el otro pierde.

7–8. El jugador _____ un gol y marca un _____.

2 Identifiquen. *(Identify the player.)*

9.

To review words from **Paso 2,** turn to pages 220–221.

10–11.

3 Identifiquen. *(Identify the sport.)*

12. Corren de una base a otra.

13. Dribla con el balón.

14. Tira el balón y encesta.

15. Lanza el balón con el pie.

Formas

4 Completen. *(Complete.)*
16. Los jugadores _____ al campo. (volver)
17. Nosotros _____ jugar. (querer)
18. Nuestro equipo no _____. (perder)
19. Tú _____ jugar si quieres. (poder)
20. Nosotros _____ bastante bien. (jugar)

To review stem-changing verbs, turn to pages 214 and 216.

5 Completen. *(Complete.)*
21. ¿Te gust__ los deportes? Sí, _____ gust__ mucho.
22. _____ gust__ el pescado pero a ti no _____ gust__.
23. El arte me interes__ pero los deportes me aburr__.

To review verbs like **interesar**, **aburrir**, and **gustar**, turn to page 224.

Cultura

6 Den la información. *(Give the following information.)*
24. el deporte número uno en los países hispanos
25. dos países donde hay muchos aficionados al béisbol

To review this cultural information, turn to pages 230–231.

El canal de Panamá

PASO 4

Diversiones

Canta con Justo
El gran campeón

Para triun- far   hay que   sa - ber.   Pue-des ga - nar   pue-des   per - der.   Si an-das

bien,   o an-das,   mal,   muy bue-no es po-der   lle-gar   y con-ti-nuar   ha-cia el   fi - nal.   La

vi-da es un par-ti-do,   tú tie-nes que ga-nar.   Si quie-res ser un gran cam-peón de-bes co-

rrer   y no pa-rar.   Tus ma-nos,   pier-nas y   tus pies,   tie-nes que u-sar   pa-ra   ju-

gar.   No es im-po-si-ble, fá-cil es   Siem-pre ha-cia ade-lan-te   por la Co-pa mun-dial.

Levanta un brazo y celebra el gol	Para triunfar, hay que saber	Levanta un brazo y celebra el gol
Canta muy fuerte con esta canción	Que puedes ganar, puedes perder	Canta muy fuerte con esta canción
Este trofeo es para el mejor	Si andas bien, o andas mal	Este trofeo es para el mejor
Y nuestro equipo es el gran campeón	Divino es poder llegar	Y nuestro equipo es el gran campeón
Sube tu brazo, luego bájalo	Y continuar hacia el final	Sube tu brazo, luego bájalo
Mueve tu cuerpo, vamos muévelo	La vida es un partido	Mueve tu cuerpo, vamos muévelo
Este trofeo es para el mejor	tú tienes que ganar	Este trofeo es para el mejor
Y nuestro equipo es el gran campeón		Y nuestro equipo es el gran campeón.

Teatro

Stand up and act out the following "plays."

lanzar el balón con el pie

bloquear el balón   lanzar el balón con la cabeza

correr   **pasar el balón**   **batear**

driblar con el balón

atrapar la pelota   tirar el balón

Play this version of **Simón dice.**

Levanta la mano.
Levanta la mano izquierda.
Levanta el brazo derecho.
Levanta la pierna derecha.
Levanta la rodilla izquierda.

PASO 4

 Manos a la obra

Carteles Make a poster indicating in Spanish all the sporting events that will take place in your school next month.

Juego **Los deportes** Work with a classmate. Take turns saying something about a sport. Your classmate will tell what sport you're talking about.

El beisbolista y héroe puertorriqueño
Roberto Clemente

Investigaciones

Look up some information about any one of the following famous Hispanic athletes. You may choose from the list below or write about any others you know.

Béisbol
José Canseco
Bobby Bonilla
Fernando Valenzuela

Tenis
Mary Joe Fernández
Gigi Fernández
Gabriela Sabatini

Fútbol
Claudio Reyna
Carlos Llamosa
Jaime Moreno

Golf
"Chi Chi" Rodríguez
Nancy López
Lee Trevino

 Spanish Online

For more information about sports in the Spanish-speaking world, go to the Glencoe Spanish Web site: **spanish.glencoe.com**.

Entrevista

¿Te gustan los deportes?

¿Cuál es tu deporte favorito?

¿Juegas con un equipo de tu escuela?

¿Con qué equipo juegas?

¿Prefieres jugar o ser espectador(a)?

¿Tiene tu escuela un equipo muy bueno?

¿En qué deporte?

¿Cuántos partidos gana el equipo?

Y, ¿cuántos pierde?

PLEGABLES ™ **Study Organizer**

Mi autobiografía Use this *minibook* organizer to write and illustrate your autobiography. Before you begin to write, think about the many things concerning yourself that you have the ability to write about in Spanish. On the left pages, draw the events of your life in chronological order. On the right, write about your drawings.

Step 1 **Fold** a sheet of paper (8½" x 11") in half like a *hot dog*.

Step 2 **Fold** it in half again like a *hamburger*.

Step 3 Then **fold** in half again, forming eights.

Step 4 **Open** the fold and cut the eight sections apart.

Step 5 **Place** all eight sections in a stack and fold in half like a hamburger.

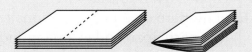

Step 6 **Staple** along the center fold line. Glue the front and back sheets into a construction paper cover.

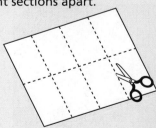

Más cultura y lectura

La Copa mundial

Fernando Hierro y Roberto Carlos da Silva son dos jugadores de fútbol muy buenos. Los dos juegan con el mismo equipo profesional, el Real Madrid. Es un equipo español muy popular e Hierro y da Silva tienen muchos aficionados.

Los dos van a jugar en la Copa mundial[1]. Pero no van a jugar con el mismo equipo. Cada uno va a jugar con un equipo diferente. ¿Cómo es posible? Pues, da Silva juega con el equipo español, el Real Madrid. Pero él no es español. Es del Brasil y en la Copa mundial él tiene que jugar con el equipo de su país. Él va a jugar con el equipo brasileño. Hierro es español y él va a jugar con el equipo de España. Así, los dos compañeros tienen que jugar en equipos contrarios.

▲ Un grupo de aficionados de fútbol en Madrid

Cada cuatro años las estrellas[2] de cada país forman parte de su equipo nacional. Hay treinta y dos equipos nacionales que juegan en la Copa mundial.

[1] Copa mundial *World Cup*
[2] estrellas *stars*

◄ La Copa de la FIFA

▲ España contra Irlanda

¿Comprendes?

Busquen. *(Find the following information.)*
1. con qué equipo juegan Hierro y da Silva
2. la nacionalidad de da Silva
3. la nacionalidad de Hierro
4. con qué equipo tiene que jugar da Silva en la Copa mundial
5. con qué equipo juega Hierro en la Copa mundial
6. el número de equipos nacionales que participan en la Copa mundial

Personajes latinos famosos

◀ Sammy Sosa es un jardinero derecho con los Chicago Cubs. En tres temporadas consecutivas Sosa golpea más de cincuenta jonrones.

¿De dónde es Sammy Sosa? Es de San Pedro de Macorís en la República Dominicana. Es el pueblo que produce más jugadores de las Grandes Ligas que cualquier otro pueblo o ciudad.

Sosa es un jugador popular y es también una persona muy buena. En 1998, él funda la Fundación Sammy Sosa para ayudar[1] a niños necesitados[2] en Chicago y en la República Dominicana. En 1999 la Fundación establece el Centro Médico Sammy Sosa para niños en su pueblo natal, San Pedro de Macorís.

[1] ayudar *to help*   [2] necesitados *needy*

▶ El joven español Sergio García es un jugador de golf muy famoso. Es de Castellón en España. Tiene el apodo[3] «el Niño» porque empieza a jugar cuando es muy joven. Su objetivo es de «ser el mejor[4] del mundo». Como en el caso de Tiger Woods, el padre de Sergio es un entrenador[5].

[3] apodo *nickname*
[4] mejor *best*
[5] entrenador *trainer, coach*

Tell all you knew about Sammy Sosa or Sergio García before you read about them. Then tell what you learned from the reading.

Conexiones
Las ciencias

La anatomía

Staying in good physical shape is important for all athletes. To do so, they have to know how to care for their bodies. They also have to know something about their bones and muscles to avoid injuries. All athletes should have some basic knowledge of anatomy. Anatomy is the branch of science that studies the structure of humans and animals.

Before reading this selection on anatomy, study the diagrams of the human body.

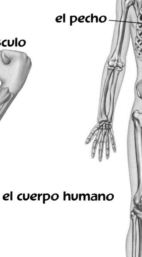

El esqueleto

El esqueleto humano tiene doscientos seis huesos. Hay treinta y dos huesos en cada brazo y treinta y uno en cada pierna. El cuerpo cuenta con más de seiscientos músculos. Algunos músculos están conectados a un hueso. Pueden estar conectados directamente a un hueso o por medio de un tendón.

Además de[1] los músculos esqueléticos, hay muchos músculos internos. El corazón es un ejemplo.

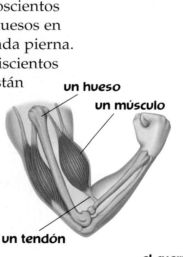

un hueso

un músculo

un tendón

[1] Además de *Besides*

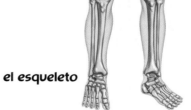

el pecho

el cuerpo humano

el esqueleto

El corazón

El corazón es un órgano muscular. Es el órgano principal de la circulación de la sangre[2]. Está situado más o menos en el centro del pecho.

Los pulmones

Los dos pulmones están situados a cada lado[3] del corazón. El pulmón es el órgano principal del aparato respiratorio. El aire llega a cada pulmón por un bronquio. La sangre llega por la artería pulmonar. La sangre, cuando llega, está cargada de dióxido de carbono. Cuando sale[4] de las venas pulmonares la sangre está purificada.

No hay duda[5] que el cuerpo humano es una máquina[6] extraordinaria.

el corazón

los pulmones

[2] sangre *blood*
[3] a cada lado *on each side*
[4] sale *it leaves*

[5] duda *doubt*
[6] máquina *machine*

¿Comprendes?

A. Busquen. *(Find all the cognates in the reading.)*

B. Busquen. *(Find the following information.)*
1. el número de huesos en cada brazo
2. el número de huesos en cada pierna
3. lo que puede conectar un músculo a un hueso
4. un músculo interno, un órgano vital
5. el órgano principal del aparato respiratorio

¡Hablo como un pro!

Tell all you can about the following illustration.

OSOS 0
TIGRES 1

COLEGIO

Vocabulario

Identifying sports

el deporte   el fútbol   el béisbol   el básquetbol, el baloncesto

Describing a sporting event in general

el estadio	el equipo	jugar	lanzar
el/la espectador(a)	el tablero indicador	empezar	correr
el campo	el tanto	continuar	guardar
la cancha	empatado	indicar	perder
el partido	el/la campeón(ona)	entrar	ganar
el/la jugador(a)	un trofeo	tirar	contra

Describing a football (soccer) game

el fútbol	el/la portero(a)	parar	usar
el balón	la portería	tocar	marcar un tanto
el tiempo	bloquear	poder	meter un gol

Describing a baseball game

el béisbol	el/la cátcher,	la base	el bate
el/la bateador(a)	el/la receptor(a)	un jonrón	el guante
el/la pícher,	el/la jardinero(a)	la entrada	batear
el/la lanzador(a)	el platillo	la pelota	atrapar
			devolver

Describing a basketball game

el básquetbol,	driblar
el baloncesto	pasar
el cesto, la canasta	encestar
el balón	meter

Identifying some parts of the body

el pie	la mano
la pierna	el brazo
la rodilla	la cabeza

Expressing likes and dislikes

gustar
interesar
aburrir

Other useful expressions

derecho(a)	volver
izquierdo(a)	quedar
durante	dormir

«Una moneda de oro»

Francisco Monterde

Introducción

Francisco Monterde es de México. Nace en 1894. Es poeta, dramaturgo y novelista. Es también cuentista. Publica una colección de cuentos[1] en 1943. Sus cuentos presentan un estudio serio de la historia de México.

Aquí tenemos una adaptación del cuento «Una moneda de oro». Es un cuento sencillo[2] y tierno[3]. El autor habla de una pobre familia mexicana del campo.

[1] cuentos *stories* [2] sencillo *simple* [3] tierno *tender*

Literary Companion

«Una moneda de oro» Francisco Monterde

Palabras

el parque

la luna

el dedo

el suelo

una moneda de oro

Es temprano por la noche (8:30).
Hay una moneda en el suelo.

La moneda refleja la luz de la luna.
Un señor halla la moneda.

la luz

La señora enciende la luz.

el agujero

el bolsillo

Ella cose el bolsillo porque
tiene un agujero.

el chaleco

La señora cuelga el chaleco
en la silla.

el mantel

El señor esconde la moneda.
Pone (Mete) la moneda debajo del mantel.

El señor levanta el mantel.
Debajo del mantel hay dinero.
El señor está muy alegre.

un juguete

Es la Navidad.
El señor recoge el juguete.
La niña está dormida.

¿Qué palabra necesito?

1 Escojan. *(Choose.)*

1. El _____ de diciembre es la Navidad.
   a. veinticinco   **b.** veinticuatro
2. Los niños reciben _____ para la Navidad.
   a. sillas   **b.** juguetes
3. Él tiene que coser el bolsillo porque tiene _____.
   a. un agujero   **b.** una moneda

4. El señor no pierde la moneda.
   _____ la moneda.
   a. Busca   **b.** Halla
5. La señora cuelga _____ en la silla.
   a. el chaleco   **b.** el mantel
6. ¿Ellos van a ver la moneda? No.
   Voy a _____ la moneda.
   a. recoger   **b.** esconder
7. En la mano hay cinco _____.
   a. monedas   **b.** dedos

2 Contesten. *(Answer.)*

1. ¿Dónde está el señor? (en el parque)
2. ¿Qué parte del día es? (la noche)
3. ¿Qué halla el señor? (una moneda)

4. ¿Recoge la moneda? (sí)
5. ¿De qué es la moneda? (de oro)
6. ¿Qué refleja la moneda? (la luna)

«Una moneda de oro»

Francisco Monterde

Es una Navidad alegre para el pobre. El pobre es Andrés. No tiene dinero y no tiene trabajo desde el otoño.

Es temprano por la noche. Andrés pasa por el parque. En el suelo ve una moneda que refleja la luz de la luna. —¿Es una moneda de oro?—pregunta Andrés. —Pesa° mucho. ¡Imposible! No puede ser una moneda de oro. Es sólo una medalla.

Andrés sale° del parque y examina la moneda. No, no es una medalla. Es realmente una moneda de oro. Andrés acaricia° la moneda. ¡Es muy agradable su contacto!

Pesa *It weighs*

sale *leaves*
acaricia *caresses*

Con la moneda entre los dedos, mete la mano derecha en el bolsillo de su pantalón. No, no puede meter la moneda en el bolsillo. Tiene miedo° de perder la moneda. Examina el bolsillo. No, no tiene agujeros. No hay problema. Puede meter la moneda en el bolsillo. No va a perder la moneda.

Andrés va a casa a pie. Anda rápido. La moneda de oro salta° en el bolsillo. El pobre Andrés está muy contento.

Luego tiene una duda°. ¿Es falsa la moneda? Andrés tiene una idea. Va a entrar en una tienda. Va a comprar algo. Y va a pagar con la moneda. Si el dependiente acepta la moneda, es buena, ¿no? Y si no acepta la moneda, ¿qué? Andrés reflexiona. No, no va a ir a la tienda. Prefiere ir a casa con la moneda. Su mujer va a estar muy contenta.

Tiene miedo *He is afraid*

salto *jumps around*

duda *doubt*

Su casa es una casa humilde. Tiene sólo dos piezas o cuartos. Cuando llega a casa, su mujer no está. No está porque cada día tiene que ir a entregar° la ropa que cose para ganar° unos pesos.

Andrés enciende una luz. Pone la moneda en la mesa. En unos momentos oye° a su mujer y a su hija. Ellas vuelven a casa. Esconde la moneda debajo del mantel.

entregar *return, deliver*
ganar *to earn*
oye *he hears*

La niña entra. Andrés toma la niña en sus brazos. Luego llega su mujer. Tiene una expresión triste y melancólica. —¿Tienes trabajo?— pregunta ella. —Hoy no puedo comprar pan. No me pagan cuando entrego la costura°.

costura *sewing*

Andrés no contesta. Levanta el mantel. Su mujer ve la moneda. Toma la moneda en las manos. —¿Quién te da la moneda?

—Nadie.° —Andrés habla con su mujer. Explica cómo halla la moneda en el parque.

Nadie *No one*

La niña toma la moneda y empieza a jugar con la moneda. Andrés tiene miedo. No quiere perder la moneda. Puede irse por° un agujero.

irse por *slip through*

Andrés toma la moneda y pone la moneda en uno de los bolsillos de su chaleco. —¿Qué compramos con la moneda?—pregunta Andrés.

—No compramos nada. Tenemos que pagar mucho—suspira su mujer. —Debemos° mucho.

Debemos *We owe*

—Es verdad—contesta Andrés. —Pero hoy es Nochebuena°. Tenemos que celebrar.

Nochebuena *Christmas Eve*

—No—contesta su mujer. —Primero tenemos que pagar el dinero que debemos.

Andrés está un poco malhumorado. Se quita° el chaleco y el saco. Cuelga el chaleco y el saco en la silla.

Se quita *He takes off*

—Bueno, Andrés. Si quieres, puedes ir a comprar algo. Pero tenemos que guardar lo demás°.

guardar lo demás *keep the rest*

Andrés acepta. Se pone° el chaleco y el saco y sale de casa.

Se pone *He puts on*

En la calle Andrés ve a su amigo Pedro.

—¿Adónde vas? ¿Quieres ir a tomar algo?

Andrés acepta. Los amigos pasan un rato en un café pequeño. Beben y hablan. Y luego Andrés sale. Va a la tienda. Sólo va a comprar comida para esta noche. Y un juguete para la niña.

Andrés compra primero la comida. El paquete está listo°. Andrés busca la moneda. Busca en el chaleco. No está. Busca en el saco. No está. Busca en su pantalón. La moneda no está en sus bolsillos. El pobre Andrés está lleno de terror. Tiene que salir de la tienda sin la comida.

Una vez más está en la calle. Vuelve a casa. Llega a la puerta. No quiere entrar. Pero tiene que entrar. Entra y ve a la niña dormida con la cabeza entre los brazos sobre la mesa. Su mujer está cosiendo a su lado.

—La moneda...

—¿Qué?

—No tengo la moneda.

—¿Cómo?

La niña sobresalta°. Abre los ojos. Baja los brazos y bajo la mesa Andrés y su mujer oyen el retintín° de la moneda de oro.

¡Qué contentos están Andrés y su mujer! Recogen la moneda que la niña había escamoteado° del chaleco cuando estaba colgado en la silla. ¿Qué van a comer? No tienen nada, los pobres.

listo ready

sobresalta jumps up
retintín jingle

había escamoteado had secretly taken out

A. **Contesten.** (*Answer.*)
   1. ¿Quién es el pobre?
   2. ¿Por qué no tiene dinero?
   3. ¿Por dónde pasa Andrés?
   4. ¿Qué ve en el suelo?
   5. ¿Es una moneda de oro o es una medalla?

B. **Escojan.** (*Choose.*)
   1. ¿Por qué no debe Andrés meter la moneda en el bolsillo de su pantalón?
      a. Porque el bolsillo tiene un agujero.
      b. Porque puede perder la moneda.
      c. Porque la moneda es muy grande.

2. Cuando Andrés examina el bolsillo, ¿qué decide?
   a. Puede meter la moneda en el bolsillo porque no tiene agujero.
   b. Va a perder la moneda.
   c. La moneda de oro es sólo una medalla.
3. ¿Cómo va Andrés a casa?
   a. Salta.
   b. A pie y rápido.
   c. Con miedo.
4. ¿Qué duda tiene Andrés?
   a. Si tiene que comprar algo.
   b. Si la moneda es falsa o no.
   c. Si su pantalón tiene un agujero.
5. Si compra algo en una tienda, ¿por qué quiere pagar con la moneda?
   a. Si el dependiente acepta la moneda, no es falsa.
   b. Porque la moneda es falsa y Andrés no quiere la moneda.
   c. Porque no tiene dinero.
6. ¿Qué decide Andrés?
   a. Decide que la moneda es falsa.
   b. Decide que no necesita nada.
   c. Decide que no va a la tienda.

C. ¿Sí o no? *(True or false?)*

1. La casa de Andrés es muy humilde.
2. La casa tiene cuatro piezas.
3. Cuando llega Andrés, su mujer cose.
4. Su mujer cose para ganar dinero.
5. Su mujer y su hija vuelven a casa.
6. Su mujer está muy contenta.
7. Cuando Andrés levanta el mantel, su mujer ve la moneda.
8. La niña empieza a jugar con la moneda.
9. Andrés quiere comprar algo para celebrar la Navidad.
10. Su mujer quiere comprar mucho.
11. Por fin Andrés puede ir a la tienda a comprar algo.

D. Contesten. *(Answer.)*

1. ¿A quién ve Andrés en la calle?
2. ¿Adónde van los dos?
3. Luego, ¿adónde va Andrés?
4. ¿Qué va a comprar?
5. ¿Qué busca Andrés?
6. ¿Qué no puede hallar?
7. ¿Qué ve cuando entra en la casa?
8. ¿Dónde está la moneda?

Handbook

La tiendita

FIUGGI

Alta Moda en P

InfoGap

Activity 1

Alumno A

Ask your partner the following questions. Correct answers are in parentheses.

1. ¿Cómo es Juan? (*Juan es feo.*)
2. ¿Cómo es Enrique? (*Enrique es gracioso. / Enrique es cómico.*)
3. ¿Cómo es Sara? (*Sara es seria.*)
4. ¿Cómo es Elena? (*Elena es pelirroja.*)
5. ¿Cómo es Alejandro? (*Alejandro es alto.*)
6. ¿Cómo es María? (*María es baja.*)

Alumno A

Now answer your partner's questions based on the illustrations.

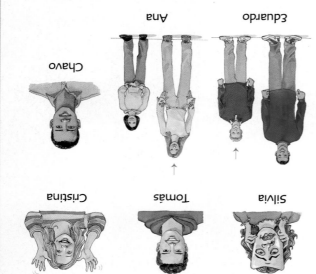

Chavo

Ana

Eduardo

Cristina

Tomás

Silvia

Alumno B

Answer your partner's questions based on the illustrations.

María

Juan

Sara

Elena

Enrique

Alejandro

Alumno B

Now ask your partner the following questions. Correct answers are in parentheses.

1. ¿Cómo es Ana? (*Ana es alta.*)
2. ¿Cómo es Eduardo? (*Eduardo es bajo.*)
3. ¿Cómo es Chavo? (*Chavo es serio.*)
4. ¿Cómo es Silvia? (*Silvia es fea.*)
5. ¿Cómo es Tomás? (*Tomás es guapo.*)
6. ¿Cómo es Cristina? (*Cristina es cómica. / Cristina es graciosa.*)

Activity 2

Alumno A

Ask your partner the following questions. Correct answers are in parentheses.

1. ¿Son amigos Ana y Diego?
   (Sí, Ana y Diego son amigos.)
2. ¿Son muy serios ellos?
   (No, ellos no son muy serios.)
3. ¿Cómo son ellos?
   (Ellos son cómicos. / Ellos son graciosos.)
4. ¿Es Ana morena?
   (No, Ana es rubia.)
5. ¿Cómo es Diego? Es moreno o pelirrojo?
   (Diego es pelirrojo.)

Alumno A

Now answer your partner's questions based on the illustrations.

Alumno B

Answer your partner's questions based on the illustrations.

Alumno B

Now ask your partner the following questions. Correct answers are in parentheses.

1. ¿Son amigos Felipe y Anita?
   (Sí, Felipe y Anita son amigos.)

2. ¿Son ellos de México?
   (No, ellos no son de México.)

3. ¿De dónde son?
   (Son de Estados Unidos.)

4. ¿Cómo es Felipe, alto o bajo?
   (Felipe es alto.)

5. ¿Cómo es Anita, alta o baja?
   (Anita es baja. / Anita no es alta.)

InfoGap

Activity 3

Alumno A

Ask your partner the following questions. Correct answers are in parentheses.

1. ¿Cuántos años tiene Armando?
   (Armando tiene catorce años.)
2. ¿Cuántos años tiene Paco?
   (Paco tiene diecisiete años.)
3. ¿Cuántos años tienes tú?
   (Yo tengo —— años.)
4. ¿Cuántos años tiene el profesor de ciencias? (El profesor de ciencias tiene treinta y seis años.)
5. ¿Cuántos años tiene Susana?
   (Susana tiene veintidós años.)
6. ¿Cuántos años tiene Pepe?
   (Pepe tiene ocho años.)

Alumno A

Use the chart below to answer your partner's questions. Reminder: **tú** is you.

Sofía	15 años
El abuelo	75 años
Alicia	16
Tú	?
Teresa	9 años
Juan	13 años

Alumno B

Use the chart below to answer your partner's questions. Reminder: **tú** is you.

Armando	14 años
Paco	17 años
Tú	?
El profesor de ciencias	36 años
Susana	22 años
Pepe	8 años

Alumno B

Ask your partner the following questions. Correct answers are in parentheses.

1. ¿Cuántos años tiene Sofía?
   (Sofía tiene quince años.)
2. ¿Cuántos años tiene el abuelo?
   (El abuelo tiene setenta y cinco años.)
3. ¿Cuántos años tiene Alicia?
   (Alicia tiene dieciséis años.)
4. ¿Cuántos años tienes tú?
   (Yo tengo _____ años.)
5. ¿Cuántos años tiene Teresa?
   (Teresa tiene nueve años.)
6. ¿Cuántos años tiene Juan?
   (Juan tiene trece años.)

Alumno A

Ask your partner the following questions. Correct answers are in parentheses.

1. ¿Es la terraza? *(No, es la sala.)*
2. ¿Es un garaje? *(No, es un edificio alto.)*
3. ¿Es un jardín? *(No, es un regalo.)*
4. ¿Es un piso? *(No, es una torta. / Es un pastel.)*
5. ¿Es un apartamento? *(No, es una casa.)*
6. ¿Es la cocina? *(No, es el cuarto de dormir/la recámara/el dormitorio.)*

Alumno A

Now answer your partner's questions based on the illustrations.

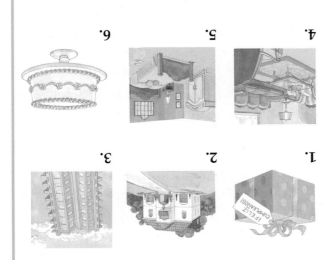

1.   2.   3.

4.   5.   6.

Alumno B

Answer your partner's questions based on the illustrations.

1.   2.   3.

4.   5.   6.

Alumno B

Now ask your partner the following questions. Correct answers are in parentheses.

1. ¿Es una torta? *(No, es un regalo.)*
2. ¿Es un apartamento? *(No, es una casa.)*
3. ¿Es un edificio alto? *(Sí, es un edificio alto.)*
4. ¿Es el comedor? *(No, es la sala.)*
5. ¿Es el cuarto de baño? *(No, es el cuarto de dormir/la recámara/el dormitorio.)*
6. ¿Es una vela? *(No, es una torta. / Es un pastel.)*

Activity 5

Alumno A

Now answer your partner's questions based on the illustrations.

Alumno A

Ask your partner the following questions. Correct answers are in parentheses.

1. ¿Está la familia en el comedor? (No, la familia no está en el comedor. / No, la familia está en la sala.)

2. ¿Habla Mamá por teléfono? (No, Mamá no habla por teléfono. / No, Mamá mira la televisión.)

3. ¿Quién habla por teléfono? (Elena habla por teléfono.)

4. ¿Habla Elena con Tomás? (No, Elena no habla con Tomás.)

5. ¿Estudia Tomás? (Sí, Tomás estudia.)

6. ¿Dónde está Tomás? (Tomás está en la sala.)

Alumno B

Answer your partner's questions based on the illustration.

Alumno B

Now ask your partner the following questions. Correct answers are in parentheses.

1. ¿Dónde está Sara? (Sara está en el cuarto de dormir/la recámara/el dormitorio.)

2. ¿Habla por teléfono Sara? (No, Sara no habla por teléfono. / No, Sara estudia.)

3. ¿Dónde prepara la cena Papá? (Papá prepara la cena en la cocina.)

4. ¿Dónde está el hermano? (El hermano está en la sala.)

5. ¿Toma el desayuno el hermano? (No, el hermano no toma el desayuno. / No, el hermano canta y baila.)

6. ¿Quién está en el comedor? (Mamá está en el comedor. / El gato está en el comedor.)

Activity 6

Alumno A
Now answer your partner's questions based on the photo.

Alumno A
Ask your partner the following questions. Correct answers are in parentheses.

1. ¿Dónde están los alumnos?
   (Los alumnos están en la escuela.)
2. ¿Llevan uniforme los alumnos?
   (Sí, los alumnos llevan uniforme.)
3. ¿Quién tiene una pregunta?
   (Un alumno tiene una pregunta.)
4. ¿Escuchan CDs los alumnos?
   (No, los alumnos no escuchan CDs. / No, los alumnos escuchan al profesor.)
5. ¿Toman apuntes algunos alumnos?
   (Sí, algunos alumnos toman apuntes.)
6. ¿Quiénes prestan atención?
   (Los alumnos prestan atención.)

Alumno B
Now answer your partner's questions based on the photo.

Alumno B
Now ask your partner the following questions. Correct answers are in parentheses.

1. ¿Son alumnos los amigos?
   (Sí, los amigos son alumnos.)
2. ¿Son alumnos en la misma escuela?
   (Sí, son alumnos en la misma escuela.)
3. ¿Qué llevan a la escuela?
   (Llevan uniforme a la escuela.)
4. ¿Entran en la escuela los alumnos?
   (Sí, los alumnos entran en la escuela.)
5. ¿Están en la clase de español los alumnos? (No, los alumnos no están en la clase de español.)
6. ¿Sacan notas buenas los alumnos?
   (Sí, los alumnos sacan notas buenas. / No, los alumnos sacan notas malas.)

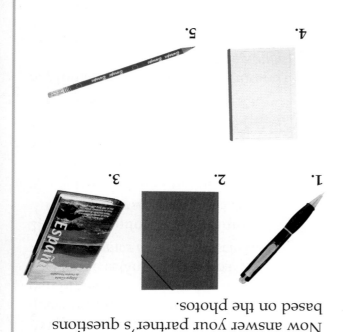

Alumno A

Now answer your partner's questions based on the photos.

Alumno A

Ask your partner the following questions. Correct answers are in parentheses.

1. ¿Buscas un libro?
   (No, busco una calculadora.)
2. ¿Necesitas un bloc?
   (No, necesito tijeras.)
3. ¿Compras un libro?
   (No, compro un marcador.)
4. ¿Buscas una carpeta?
   (No, busco una goma.)
5. ¿Llevas una pluma?
   (No, llevo una mochila.)

Alumno B

Answer your partner's questions based on the photos.

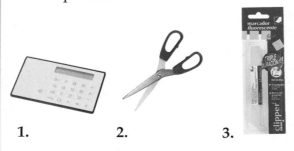

Alumno B

Now ask your partner the following questions. Correct answers are in parentheses.

1. ¿Buscas una calculadora? (No, busco una pluma. / No, busco un bolígrafo.)
2. ¿Necesitas tijeras?
   (No, necesito una carpeta.)
3. ¿Compras un marcador?
   (No, compro un libro.)
4. ¿Buscas una goma?
   (No, busco una hoja de papel.)
5. ¿Necesitas una pluma?
   (No, necesito un lápiz.)

Activity 8

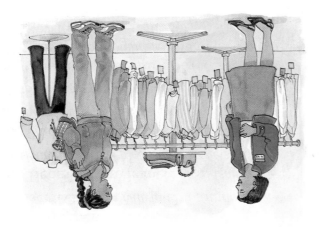

Alumno A

Ask your partner the following questions. Correct answers are in parentheses.

1. ¿Dónde está Ángel, en una tienda o en la escuela?
   (Ángel está en una tienda.)
2. ¿Qué necesita Ángel?
   (Ángel necesita un par de tenis.)
3. ¿Con quién habla Ángel?
   (Ángel habla con el dependiente.)
4. ¿Qué mira Ángel?
   (Ángel mira un par de tenis.)
5. ¿Lleva zapatos o un par de tenis Ángel?
   (Ángel lleva un par de tenis.)

Alumno A

Now answer your partner's questions based on the illustration.

Alumno B

Answer your partner's questions based on the illustration.

Alumno B

Now ask your partner the following questions. Correct answers are in parentheses.

1. ¿Dónde está Alicia?
   (Alicia está en la tienda de ropa.)

2. ¿Con quién habla Alicia?
   (Alicia habla con la dependienta.)

3. ¿Qué lleva Alicia, una falda o blue jeans?
   (Alicia lleva blue jeans.)

4. ¿Qué lleva la dependienta, una gorra o una chaqueta?
   (La dependienta lleva una chaqueta.)

5. ¿De qué color es la chaqueta?
   (La chaqueta es roja.)

Activity 9

Alumno A

Ask your partner the following questions. Correct answers are in parentheses.

1. ¿Con quién está Isabel?
   (Isabel está con Mario Unimundo.)
2. ¿Tiene hambre Isabel? (No, Isabel no tiene hambre. / No, Isabel tiene sed.)
3. ¿Qué bebe Isabel? (Isabel bebe una cola.)
4. ¿Tiene hambre Mario? (Sí, Mario tiene hambre.)
5. ¿Qué come Unimundo? (Unimundo come un sándwich/un bocadillo.)

Alumno A

Now answer your partner's questions based on the photo.

Alumno B

Answer your partner's questions based on the illustration.

Alumno B

Now ask your partner the following questions. Correct answers are in parentheses.

1. ¿Dónde están Isabel y Mario?
   (Isabel y Mario están en un café.)
2. ¿Qué lee Isabel? (Isabel lee el menú.)
3. ¿Con quién hablan Isabel y Mario?
   (Isabel y Mario hablan con el mesero.)
4. ¿Qué escribe el mesero?
   (El mesero escribe la orden.)
5. ¿Es simpático el mesero?
   (Sí, el mesero es simpático.)

Activity 10

Alumno A

Ask your partner the following questions. Correct answers are in parentheses.

1. ¿Qué vende usted, zanahorias o papas? (*Vendo zanahorias.*)
2. ¿Qué ven en el mercado los señores, lechuga o guisantes? (*Los señores ven lechuga en el mercado.*)
3. ¿Qué compras, maíz o judías verdes? (*Compro maíz.*)
4. ¿Qué comes, plátanos o tomates? (*Como plátanos.*)
5. ¿Qué ve la cliente, naranjas o manzanas? (*La cliente ve naranjas.*)

Alumno A

Now answer your partner's questions based on the photos.

5.

4.

1.

2.

3.

Alumno B

Answer your partner's questions based on the photos.

1. 2. 3. 4. 5.

Alumno B

Now ask your partner the following questions. Correct answers are in parentheses.

1. ¿Qué venden los señores, carne o arroz? (*Los señores venden carne.*)
2. ¿Qué comen ustedes, papas fritas o mariscos? (*Comemos mariscos.*)
3. ¿Qué compra la señora, productos congelados o pescado? (*La señora compra pescado.*)
4. ¿Qué comes, pollo o atún? (*Como pollo.*)
5. ¿Qué ve usted en el mercado, leche o huevos? (*Veo huevos.*)

InfoGap

Activity 11

Unidad 6, Paso 1, pages 210–219

Alumno A

Ask your partner the following questions. Correct answers are in parentheses.

1. ¿Qué juega Antonio?
   (Antonio juega [al] fútbol.)
2. ¿Qué quiere el portero?
   (El portero quiere bloquear el balón.)
3. ¿Qué prefieren Luisa y Carlos?
   (Luisa y Carlos prefieren el fútbol.)
4. ¿Prefieres ser espectador(a) o jugador(a)?
   (Yo prefiero ser ______.)
5. ¿Qué lanza la jugadora?
   (La jugadora lanza el balón.)

Alumno A

Now use the chart below to answer your partner's questions. Reminder: **tú** is you.

Los equipos	al campo
Tú	?
Los jugadores	marcar muchos tantos
Marco	ser espectador
Tomás y Sara	fútbol

Alumno B

Use the chart below to answer your partner's questions. Reminder: **tú** is you.

Antonio	fútbol
El portero	bloquear el balón
Luisa y Carlos	el fútbol
Tú	?
La jugadora	el balón

Alumno B

Now ask your partner the following questions. Correct answers are in parentheses.

1. ¿Adónde vuelven los equipos?
   (Los equipos vuelven al campo.)
2. ¿Prefieres ser espectador(a) o jugador(a)? *(Yo prefiero ser ______.)*
3. ¿Qué quieren los jugadores? *(Los jugadores quieren marcar muchos tantos.)*
4. ¿Qué prefiere Marco?
   (Marco prefiere ser espectador.)
5. ¿Qué juegan Tomás y Sara?
   (Tomás y Sara juegan [al] fútbol.)

Alumno A

Now answer your partner's questions based on the illustration.

Alumno A

Ask your partner the following questions. Correct answers are in parentheses.

1. ¿Qué deporte es?
   (*Es el básquetbol. / Es el baloncesto.*)
2. ¿Quiénes están en la cancha de básquetbol, los espectadores o los jugadores? (*Los jugadores están en la cancha de básquetbol.*)
3. ¿Driblan los jugadores con el balón?
   (*No, los jugadores no driblan con el balón.*)
4. ¿Ganan o pierden el partido los jugadores? (*Los jugadores ganan.*)
5. ¿Qué ganan? (*Ganan un trofeo.*)

Alumno B

Answer your partner's questions based on the illustration.

Alumno B

Now ask your partner the following questions. Correct answers are in parentheses.

1. ¿Qué deporte es? (*Es el béisbol.*)
2. ¿Adónde vuelven los jugadores, al campo o a casa?
   (*Los jugadores vuelven al campo.*)
3. ¿Queda empatado el tanto?
   (*Sí, el tanto queda empatado.*)
4. ¿Qué continúa, el tanto o el partido?
   (*El partido continúa.*)
5. ¿Hay muchos espectadores?
   (*Sí, hay muchos espectadores.*)

Verb Charts

Regular Verbs				
INFINITIVO	**hablar** *to speak*	**comer** *to eat*		**vivir** *to live*
PRESENTE	hablo	como		vivo
	hablas	comes		vives
	habla	come		vive
	hablamos	comemos		vivimos
	habláis	*coméis*		*vivís*
	hablan	comen		viven

Stem-Changing Verbs*			
INFINITIVO	**empezar¹ (e ⟶ ie)** *to begin*	**perder² (e ⟶ ie)** *to lose*	**preferir (e ⟶ ie)** *to prefer*
PRESENTE	empiezo	pierdo	prefiero
	empiezas	pierdes	prefieres
	empieza	pierde	prefiere
	empezamos	perdemos	preferimos
	empezáis	*perdéis*	*preferís*
	empiezan	pierden	prefieren

Stem-Changing Verbs			
INFINITIVO	**volver³ (o ⟶ ue)** *to return*	**dormir (o ⟶ ue)** *to sleep*	
PRESENTE	vuelvo	duermo	
	vuelves	duermes	
	vuelve	duerme	
	volvemos	dormimos	
	volvéis	*dormís*	
	vuelven	duermen	

*Note that the **u** in **jugar** *(to play)* changes to **ue.**

juego   juegas   juega   jugamos   jugáis   juegan

¹ *Comenzar is similar.*

² *Querer and entender are similar.*

³ *Devolver and poder are similar.*

Verb Charts

Irregular Verbs			
INFINITIVO	**dar** *to give*	**estar** *to be*	**ir** *to go*
PRESENTE	doy das da damos *dais* dan	estoy estás está estamos *estáis* están	voy vas va vamos *vais* van
INFINITIVO	**ser** *to be*	**tener** *to have*	**ver** *to see*
PRESENTE	soy eres es somos *sois* son	tengo tienes tiene tenemos *tenéis* tienen	veo ves ve vemos *veis* ven

Plaza de Cibeles, Madrid, España

Spanish-English Dictionary

*This Spanish-English Dictionary contains all productive and receptive vocabulary from the text. The bold numbers following each productive entry indicate the unit and vocabulary section in which the word is introduced. For example, **3.2** means that the word was taught in **Unidad 3, Paso 2. BV** refers to the preliminary **Bienvenidos** lessons. If there is no number following an entry, this means that the word or expression is included for receptive purposes only.*

a at
    ¿A cuánto está(n)... ? How much is (are) . . . ?, **5.2**
    a la una (las dos...) at one o'clock (two o'clock . . .), **BV**
    a pie on foot, **5.2**
    ¿a qué hora? at what time?, **BV**
    a veces at times, sometimes, **3.1**
el **abarrote** grocery
    la tienda de abarrotes grocery store
abril April, **BV**
abrir to open
la **abuela** grandmother, **2.1**
el **abuelo** grandfather, **2.1**
los **abuelos** grandparents, **2.1**
aburrido(a) bored
aburrir to bore, **6.2**
la **academia** academy, school
acariciar to caress
aceptar to accept
acompañado(a) accompanied
la **actividad** activity
además (de) besides
adiós good-bye, **BV**
adivinar to guess
¿adónde? where?, **3.2**
adorable adorable
adverso(a) opposing, opposite
el/la **aficionado(a)** fan
agosto August, **BV**
agradable pleasant
el **agua** water, **5.2**
    el agua mineral mineral water, **5.2**
el **agujero** hole
ahora now
ahorrar to save
el **ahorro** saving
    la cuenta de ahorros savings account
el **aire** air
el **álbum** album

alegre happy
la **alfombrilla** (mouse) pad
algo something
    algo más something (anything) else, **5.2**
algunos(as) some
el **alimento** food
allí there
el **almuerzo** lunch, **3.2**
    tomar el almuerzo to have lunch
alrededor de around
alto(a) tall, **1.1**; high, **4.2**
el/la **alumno(a)** student, **1.2**
amarillo(a) yellow, **4.2**
la **América del Sur** South America
americano(a) American, **1.1**
el/la **amigo(a)** friend, **1.1**
la **anatomía** anatomy
andar to walk
andino(a) Andean
antes (de) before
el **año** year
    ¿Cuántos años tiene? How old is he (she)?
el **aparato** system
    el aparato respiratorio respiratory system
el **apartamento** apartment, **2.2**
el **apodo** nickname
aprender to learn, **5.1**
el **apunte** note
    tomar apuntes to take notes, **3.2**
aquí here
el **árbol** tree
    el árbol genealógico family tree
argentino(a) Argentine, **1.1**
la **aritmética** arithmetic
el **arroz** rice, **5.2**
el **arte** art, **1.2**
la **artería** artery
el/la **artista** artist
la **ascendencia** background
así so
la **atención** attention
    prestar atención to pay attention, **3.2**
atrapar to catch, **6.2**

Spanish-English Dictionary

el **atún** tuna, **5.2**
el/la **autor(a)** author
la **avenida** avenue
    ayudar to help
    azul blue, **4.2**

    bailar to dance, **3.1**
    bajar to lower
    bajo under, below
    bajo(a) short, **1.1**; low, **4.2**
        la planta baja ground floor, **2.2**
el **balcón** balcony, **2.2**
el **balón** ball, **6.1**
el **baloncesto** basketball, **6.2**
el **banco** bank
el **baño** bath, **2.2**
        el cuarto de baño bathroom, **2.2**
    barato(a) cheap, inexpensive, **4.2**
el **barrio** district, area, region
    basado(a) based
la **base** base, **6.2**
el **básquetbol** basketball, **6.2**
        la cancha de básquetbol basketball
            court, **6.2**
    bastante enough, rather, quite, **1.2**
el **bate** bat, **6.2**
el/la **bateador(a)** batter, **6.2**
    batear to bat, **6.2**
el/la **bebé** baby
    beber to drink, **5.1**
el **béisbol** baseball, **6.2**
        el campo de béisbol baseball field, **6.2**
        el/la jugador(a) de béisbol baseball
            player, **6.2**
la **bicicleta** bicycle
    bien well, fine
        muy bien very well, **BV**
el **biftec** steak
la **biología** biology
    blanco(a) white, **4.2**
    blando(a) short
el **bloc** notebook, writing pad, **4.1**
    bloquear to block, **6.1**
el **blue jean** jeans, **4.2**
los **blue jeans** jeans, **4.2**
la **blusa** blouse, **4.2**
la **boca** mouth
el **bocadillo** sandwich, **5.1**

la **bodega** grocery store
el **bolígrafo** pen, **4.1**
el **bolívar** currency of Venezuela
la **bolsa** bag, **5.2**
el **bolsillo** pocket
    bonito(a) pretty, **1.1**
el **borrador** eraser, **4.1**
    borrar to erase
        la goma (de borrar) eraser, **4.1**
el **bote** can, **5.2**
la **botella** bottle, **5.2**
    brasileño(a) Brazilian
el **brazo** arm, **6.1**
    brillante bright
el **bronquio** bronchial tube
    bueno(a) good, **1.1**
        Buenos días. Good morning., **BV**
        Buenas noches. Good evening., **BV**
        Buenas tardes. Good afternoon., **BV**
        Hace buen tiempo. The weather is nice.
el **bus** bus, **3.2**
        el bus escolar school bus, **3.2**
    buscar to look for, **4.1**

el **caballete** easel
la **cabeza** head, **6.1**
    cada each
el **café** café, coffee, **5.1**
la **cafetería** cafeteria, **3.1**
la **caja** cash register, **4.1**
el **calcetín** sock, **4.2**
los **calcetines** socks, **4.2**
la **calculadora** calculator, **4.1**
la **calle** street
el **calor** heat
        Hace calor. It's hot (weather).
    calzar to take, to wear (shoe size)
la **cámara** camera
la **camarera** waitress, **5.1**
el **camarero** waiter, **5.1**
    cambiar to change
la **camisa** shirt, **4.2**
la **camiseta** T-shirt, undershirt, **4.2**
el/la **campeón(ona)** champion, **6.2**
el **campo** field, **6.1**; country
        el campo de béisbol baseball field, **6.2**
        el campo de fútbol soccer field, **6.1**
la **canasta** basket, **6.2**

Spanish-English Dictionary

el **canasto** basket
la **cancha** court, field, **6.2**
    la cancha de básquetbol basketball
        court, **6.2**
la **canción** song
el/la **cantante** singer
    cantar to sing, **3.1**
la **cantina** cafeteria
la **capital** capital
el **carbono** carbon
    el dióxido de carbono carbon dioxide
    cargado(a) full
    caribe Caribbean
    el mar Caribe Caribbean Sea
la **carne** meat, **5.2**
    caro(a) expensive, **4.2**
la **carpeta** folder, **4.1**
el **carro** car, **2.2**
    en carro by car, **3.2**
el **cartel** poster
la **casa** house, **2.2**
    en casa at home
el **caso** case
el **catálogo** catalogue
el/la **cátcher** catcher, **6.2**
    catorce fourteen, **1.1**
el **CD** compact disc (CD), **3.2**
la **cebolla** onion
la **celebración** celebration
    celebrar to celebrate, **3.1**
la **cena** dinner, **3.1**
    cenar to have dinner, **3.1**
el **centro** center
el **cereal** cereal
    cero zero
    cerrado(a) closed, shut
el **cesto** basket, **6.2**
el **chaleco** vest
    ¡Chao! Good-bye!, **BV**
la **chaqueta** jacket, **4.2**
    chileno(a) Chilean, **1.1**
el **chocolate** chocolate, **5.1**
    el helado de chocolate chocolate ice
        cream, **5.1**
el **churro** (type of) doughnut
la **ciencia** science, **1.2**
    cien(to) one hundred, **2.1**
    cinco five, **1.1**
    cincuenta fifty, **2.1**
el **cine** movie theater

la **circulación** circulation
la **ciudad** city
    claro(a) clear
    claro que of course
la **clase** class, **1.2**
    la sala de clase classroom
el/la **cliente** customer, client, **5.1**
el **club** club
    el Club de español Spanish club
la **cocina** kitchen, **2.2**
la **coincidencia** coincidence
la **cola** cola, **5.1**
la **colección** collection
el **colegio** school, **1.3**
    colgado(a) hung
    colgar (ue) to hang
    colombiano(a) Colombian, **1.1**
el **color** color, **4.2**
    ¿de qué color? what color?, **4.2**
el **comedor** dining room, **2.2**
    comenzar (ie) to begin
    comer to eat, **5.1**
    comercial commercial
el **comestible** food
    cómico(a) funny, comical, **1.1**
la **comida** meal, food, **3.1**
    como like, as
    ¿cómo? how?, **1.1**
    compacto(a) compact
    el disco compacto compact disc (CD)
el/la **compañero(a)** friend
la **competencia** competetion
la **compra** purchase
    ir de compras to go shopping, to shop, **5.2**
    comprar to buy, **4.1**
    comprender to understand, **5.1**
la **computadora** computer
    con with
el **concierto** concert
    conectado(a) connected
    conectar to connect
la **conexión** connection
    congelado(a) frozen
    los productos congelados frozen
        foods, **5.2**
    consecutivo(a) consecutive
la **consonante** consonant
el **contacto** contact
    contar (ue) to count
    contar (ue) con to rely on

Spanish-English Dictionary

contener (ie) to contain
contento(a) happy
contestar to answer
    contestar (a) la pregunta to answer the question, **3.2**
el **continente** continent
continuar to continue, **6.2**
contra against, **6.1**
la **conversación** conversation
la **Copa mundial** World Cup
el **corazón** heart
la **corbata** tie, **4.2**
el **correo** mail
    el correo electrónico e-mail
correr to run, **6.2**
la **cortesía** courtesy
corto(a) short
    la manga corta short sleeve, **4.2**
    el pantalón corto shorts, **4.2**
la **cosa** thing
coser to sew
la **costa** coast
costar (ue) to cost
la **costura** sewing
el **cuaderno** notebook, **4.1**
el **cuadro** painting
¿cuál? which?, what?
    ¿Cuál es la fecha de hoy? What is today's date?
cualquier(a) any
    cualquier otro any other
cuando when
¿cuándo? when?, **3.1**
¿cuánto? how much?
    ¿A cuánto está(n)... ? How much is (are) . . . ?, **5.2**
    ¿Cuánto es? How much does it cost?, **4.1**
¿cuántos(as)? how much?, how many?, **2.1**
    ¿Cuántos años tiene? How old is he (she)?, **2.1**
cuarenta forty, **2.1**
el **cuarto** room, **2.2**; quarter
    el cuarto de baño bathroom, **2.2**
    el cuarto de dormir bedroom, **2.2**
cuatro four, **1.1**
cuatrocientos(as) four hundred, **3.1**
cubano(a) Cuban, **1.1**
cubanoamericano(a) Cuban American
la **cuenta** bill, check, **5.1**; account
    la cuenta de ahorros savings account

el/la **cuentista** short-story writer
el **cuento** story
el **cuerpo** body
    el cuerpo humano human body
la **cultura** culture
el **cumpleaños** birthday, **2.2**
el **curso** course, **1.2**

la **dama** lady-in-waiting
dar to give, **3.1**
los **datos** data
de of, from
    ¿de dónde? from where?, **1.1**
    de habla española Spanish-speaking
    de moda in style
    De nada. You're welcome., **BV**
    ¿de qué color? what color?, **4.2**
    ¿de qué nacionalidad? what nationality?, **1.1**
    ¿de quién? whose?
    No hay de qué. You're welcome., **BV**
debajo (de) under
deber to owe
débil weak
decidir to decide
decimal decimal
el **dedo** finger
delante de in front of
delicioso(a) delicious
demás rest
el **departamento** apartment
el/la **dependiente(a)** employee, **4.1**
el **deporte** sport, **6.1**
    el deporte de equipo team sport
    el deporte individual individual sport
deportivo(a) (related to) sports
    la emisión deportiva sports program
depositar to deposit
derecho(a) right, **6.1**
el **desayuno** breakfast, **3.1**
    tomar el desayuno to have breakfast, **3.1**
la **descripción** description
desde since
desear to wish, to want
después de after, **3.1**
determinado(a) determined, definite
devolver (ue) to return (something), **6.1**

Spanish-English Dictionary

el **día** day

Buenos días. Good morning., **BV**

el Día de los Muertos All Souls' Day, Day of the Dead

¿Qué día es (hoy)? What day is it (today)?

el **dibujo** drawing, **1.2**

diciembre December, **BV**

diecinueve nineteen, **1.1**

dieciocho eighteen, **1.1**

dieciséis sixteen, **1.1**

diecisiete seventeen, **1.1**

diez ten, **1.1**

de diez en diez by tens

la **diferencia** difference

diferente different

difícil hard, difficult, **1.2**

el **dinero** money

directamente directly

el **disco** record, disc

el disco compacto compact disc (CD)

distinto(a) different

la **diversión** amusement, pastime

divertido(a) fun, amusing

divino(a) divine

doce twelve, **1.1**

el **domingo** Sunday, **BV**

dominicano(a) Dominican

La República Dominicana Dominican Republic

¿dónde? where?, **1.1**

¿de dónde? from where?, **1.1**

dormido(a) asleep

dormir (ue) to sleep, **6.1**

el cuarto de dormir bedroom, **2.2**

el **dormitorio** bedroom, **2.2**

dos two, **1.1**

doscientos(as) two hundred, **3.1**

el/la **dramaturgo(a)** playwright

driblar to dribble, **6.2**

la **duda** doubt

durante during, **3.1**

duro(a) hard, difficult, **1.2**

el **DVD** digital video disc (DVD), **3.2**

ecuatoriano(a) Ecuadorean

el **edificio** building, **2.2**

la **educación** education

la educación física physical education, **1.2**

el **ejemplo** example

por ejemplo for example

el **ejote** string bean, **5.2**

el the

él he

electrónico(a) electronic

el correo electrónico e-mail

elegante elegant

ella she

ellos(as) they

la **emisión** program, **3.1**

la emisión deportiva sports program

empatado(a) tied (score), **6.1**

empezar (ie) to begin, **6.1**

el/la **empleado(a)** employee, **4.1**

en in, on

en carro by car, **3.2**

en casa at home

en cuanto a as for

encender (ie) to light

el **encestado** basket

encestar to make a basket, **6.2**

la **enchilada** enchilada

enero January, **BV**

enrollado(a) rolled up

la **ensalada** salad, **5.1**

enseñar to teach

la **entrada** inning, **6.2**

entrar to enter, **3.2**

entre between, among

entregar to deliver

el/la **entrenador(a)** trainer, coach

la **entrevista** interview

el **envase** container, **5.2**

el **equipo** team, **6.1**; equipment

el deporte de equipo team sport

equivaler to be equivalent

escamotear to secretly take out

escoger to choose

escolar (related to) school

el bus escolar school bus, **3.2**

los materiales escolares school supplies, **4.1**

esconder to hide

escribir to write, **5.1**

escuchar to listen (to), **3.2**

la **escuela** school, **1.2**

la escuela intermedia middle school

la escuela primaria elementary school

la escuela superior high school

Spanish-English Dictionary

el/la **escultor(a)** sculptor
la **escultura** sculpture
la **espalda** back
España Spain
el **español** Spanish, **1.2**
    el Club de español Spanish club
    de habla española Spanish-speaking
especialmente especially
el/la **espectador(a)** spectator, **6.1**
el **espejo** mirror
esperar to wait for, **5.1**
esquelético(a) skeletal
el **esqueleto** skeleton
establecer to establish
la **estación** season
el **estadio** stadium, **6.1**
el **estado** state
Estados Unidos United States
estar to be, **3.1**
    ¿A cuánto está(n)? How much is it
      (are they)?
    estar en clase to be in class, **3.2**
la **estatua** statue
el **estilo** style
la **estrella** star
estudiar to study, **3.1**
el **estudio** study
    los estudios sociales social studies, **1.2**
estupendo(a) stupendous
el **euro** euro (currency of all countries of the
    European Common Market)
el **examen** test, exam
examinar to examine
excelente excellent
explicar to explain
la **expresión** expression
extraordinario(a) extraordinary

fácil easy, **1.2**
la **falda** skirt, **4.2**
falso(a) false
la **familia** family, **2.1**
familiar (related to) family
famoso(a) famous
fantástico(a) fantastic
el **favor** favor
    por favor please, **BV**
favorito(a) favorite
febrero February, **BV**

la **fecha** date
    ¿Cuál es la fecha de hoy? What is today's
      date?, **BV**
feo(a) ugly, **1.1**
la **fiesta** party, **2.2**; holiday
físico(a) physical
    la educación física physical
      education, **1.2**
la **flor** flower
formal formal
formar to form
la **foto** photo
la **fotografía** photograph
el **francés** French
frecuentemente frequently
fresco(a) fresh (food), **5.2**; cool
    Hace fresco. It's cool (weather).
el **frijol** bean, **5.2**
el **frío** cold
    Hace frío. It's cold (weather).
frito fried
    las papas (patatas) fritas French fries, **5.1**
la **fruta** fruit, **5.2**
fuerte strong
funcionar to operate
la **fundación** foundation
fundar to found, to establish
el **fútbol** soccer, **6.1**
    el campo de fútbol soccer field, **6.1**

el **galón** gallon
ganar to win, **6.1**; to earn
el **garaje** garage, **2.2**
la **gaseosa** carbonated drink, **5.1**
gastar to spend
el **gasto** expense
el/la **gato(a)** cat, **2.1**
genealógico(a) genealogical
    el árbol genealógico family tree
general general
    en general generally
la **gente** people
la **geografía** geography
el/la **gobernador(a)** governor
el **gol** goal, **6.1**
    meter un gol to score a goal, **6.1**
el **golf** golf, **6.2**
golpear to hit
la **goma (de borrar)** eraser, **4.1**

Spanish-English Dictionary

la **gorra** cap, **4.2**
gozar (de) to enjoy
Gracias. Thank you., **BV**
gracioso(a) funny, **1.1**
el **gramo** gram
gran, grande big, large, great, **1.2**
las **Grandes Ligas** Major Leagues
gris gray, **4.2**
el **grupo** group
el **guante** glove, **6.2**
guapo(a) handsome, good-looking, **1.1**
guardar to guard, **6.1**; to keep
el **guisante** pea, **5.2**
gustar to please; to like, **6.2**
el **gusto** pleasure; like; taste
Mucho gusto. Nice to meet you.

la **habichuela** bean, **5.2**
el **habla** speech, language
de **habla española** Spanish-speaking
hablar to talk, to speak, **3.1**
hablar por teléfono to speak on the phone, **3.1**
hacer to do, to make
Hace buen tiempo. The weather is nice.
Hace calor. It's hot (weather).
Hace fresco. It's cool (weather).
Hace frío. It's cold (weather).
Hace mal tiempo. The weather is bad.
Hace (Hay) sol. It's sunny.
Hace viento. It's windy.
¿Qué tiempo hace? What is the weather (like)?
hallar to find
el **hambre** hunger
tener hambre to be hungry, **5.1**
la **hamburguesa** hamburger, **5.1**
el **hardware** hardware
la **harina** flour
hasta until
¡Hasta luego! See you later!, **BV**
¡Hasta mañana! See you tomorrow!, **BV**
¡Hasta pronto! See you soon!, **BV**
hay there is, there are, **2.2**
Hay sol. It's sunny.
No hay de qué. You're welcome., **BV**
¿Qué hay? What's new (up)?

helado(a) frozen, iced
el **té helado** iced tea, **5.1**
el **helado** ice cream, **5.1**
el **helado de chocolate** chocolate ice cream, **5.1**
el **helado de vainilla** vanilla ice cream, **5.1**
la **hermana** sister, **2.1**
la **hermanastra** stepsister, **2.1**
el **hermanastro** stepbrother, **2.1**
el **hermano** brother, **2.1**
el **héroe** hero
la **heroína** heroine
la **hija** daughter, **2.1**
el **hijo** son, **2.1**
el **hipermercado** (wholesale) supermarket
hispano(a) Hispanic
la **historia** history, **1.2**
la **historieta** short story
la **hoja** leaf, sheet
la **hoja de papel** sheet of paper, **4.1**
¡Hola! Hello!, **BV**
el **honor** honor
la **hora** hour, time
¿A qué hora? At what time?, **BV**
¿Qué hora es? What time is it?, **BV**
el **horario** schedule
hoy today, **BV**
¿Cuál es la fecha de hoy? What is today's date?
¿Qué día es (hoy)? What day is it (today)?
el **hueso** bone
el **huevo** egg, **5.2**
humano(a) human
el **cuerpo humano** human body
humilde humble

la **idea** idea
la **igualdad** equality
importante important
imposible impossible
la **impresora** printer
increíble incredible
la **independencia** independence
el **indicador** indicator
el **tablero indicador** scoreboard, **6.1**
indicar to indicate, **6.1**
indígena native, indigenous
el/la **indígena** native person

indio(a) Indian
individual individual
   el deporte individual individual sport
el inglés English, **1.2**
el instituto high school, secondary school,
   institute
la instrucción instruction
inteligente intelligent, **1.2**
el interés interest
interesante interesting, **1.2**
interesar to interest, **6.2**
intermedio(a) intermediate, **1.2**
   la escuela intermedia middle school
el/la Internet Internet
interno(a) internal
la introducción introduction
el/la intruso(a) intruder
la invención invention
la investigación research, investigation
el invierno winter, **BV**
invitar to invite, **3.1**
ir to go, **3.1**
   ir a pie to walk, **3.2**
   ir de compras to go shopping, **5.2**
   irse por to go (fall) through
la isla island
italiano(a) Italian
izquierdo(a) left, **6.1**

el jamón ham, **5.1**
   el sándwich de jamón y queso ham and
   cheese sandwich, **5.1**
el jardín garden, **2.2**
el/la jardinero(a) outfielder, **6.2**
el jean jeans, **4.2**
el jonrón home run, **6.2**
joven young
el/la joven young person
la judía bean
   la judía verde green bean, **5.2**
el juego game
el jueves Thursday, **BV**
el/la jugador(a) player, **6.1**
   el/la jugador(a) de béisbol baseball
   player, **6.2**
jugar (ue) to play, **6.1**
el juguete toy
julio July, **BV**

la jungla jungle
junio June, **BV**
junto(a) together

el kilo kilo, **5.2**
el kilogramo kilogram

la the
el laboratorio laboratory
lacustre (related to) lake
el lado side
ladrar to bark
la lana wool
el/la lanzador(a) pitcher, **6.2**
lanzar to throw, to kick, **6.1**
el lápiz pencil, **4.1**
largo(a) long
   la manga larga long sleeve, **4.2**
   el pantalón largo long pants, **4.2**
la lata can, **5.2**
el latín Latin (language)
latino(a) Latin
latinoamericano(a) Latin American
la lección lesson, **3.1**
la leche milk, **5.2**
la lechuga lettuce, **5.2**
la lectura reading
leer to read, **5.1**
la legumbre vegetable, **5.2**
la lengua language, tongue
levantar to raise, to lift
   levantar la mano to raise your hand, **3.2**
el/la libertador(a) liberator
la libra pound
libre free, unoccupied, **5.1**
el libro book, **4.1**
el liceo high school
la liga league
   las Grandes Ligas Major Leagues
la limonada lemonade
la liquidación sale, **4.2**
el líquido liquid
la lista list
listo(a) ready
la literatura literature
el litro liter

Spanish-English Dictionary

llegar to arrive, **5.1**
lleno(a) full
llevar to wear, **3.2**; to carry, **4.1**
llover (ue) to rain, it's raining
lógico(a) logical
luchar to fight
luego later; then
    ¡Hasta luego! See you later!, **BV**
la **luna** moon
el **lunes** Monday, **BV**
la **luz** light

M

la **madrastra** stepmother, **2.1**
la **madre** mother, **2.1**
madrileño(a) native of Madrid
el/la **maestro(a)** teacher
el **maíz** corn, **5.2**
mal bad
    Hace mal tiempo. The weather is bad., **BV**
malagueño(a) native of Malaga, Spain
malhumorado(a) bad-tempered
malo(a) bad, **1.2**
la **mamá** mom
la **manga** sleeve
    la manga corta short sleeve, **4.2**
    la manga larga long sleeve, **4.2**
la **mano** hand, **6.1**
    ¡Manos a la obra! Let's get to work!
el **mantel** tablecloth
la **manzana** apple, **5.2**
mañana tomorrow, **BV**
    ¡Hasta mañana! See you tomorrow!, **BV**
la **mañana** morning
    por la mañana in the morning, **5.2**
el **mapa** map
la **máquina** machine
el **mar** sea
    el mar Caribe Caribbean Sea
el **marcador** marker, **4.1**
marcar to score
    marcar un tanto to score a point, **6.1**
los **mariscos** shellfish, **5.2**
    marrón brown, **4.2**
martes Tuesday, **BV**
marzo March, **BV**
más more
    más que more than
    ¡Qué... más... ! What a . . . !

las **matemáticas** mathematics, **1.2**
el **material** material
    los materiales escolares school supplies, **4.1**
mayo May, **BV**
mayor older, **2.1**
el/la **mayor** oldest, **2.1**
la **medalla** medal
médico(a) medical
la **medida** measure
medio(a) half
el **medio** means
    por medio de by means of
el/la **mejor** best
melancólico(a) sad, melancholic
el/la **menino(a)** young page of a royal family
menor younger, **2.1**
el/la **menor** youngest, **2.1**
menos less; minus
el **menú** menu, **5.1**
el **mercado** market, **5.2**
la **mermelada** marmalade
el **mes** month
la **mesa** table, **5.1**
la **mesera** waitress, **5.1**
el **mesero** waiter, **5.1**
meter to put, to place
    meter un gol to score a goal, **6.1**
métrico(a) metric
mexicano(a) Mexican, **1.1**
mi my
mí me
el **miedo** fear
    tener miedo to be afraid
el **miembro** member
el **miércoles** Wednesday, **BV**
mil one thousand, **3.1**
el **millón** million, **4.1**
mineral mineral
    el agua mineral mineral water, **5.2**
mirar to watch, to look at, **3.1**
mismo(a) same, **1.2**; himself, herself
la **mochila** knapsack, backpack, **4.1**
la **moda** style
    de moda in style
el/la **modelo** model
moderno(a) modern
la **moneda** coin
    la moneda de oro gold coin
el **monitor** monitor

Spanish-English Dictionary

la **montaña** mountain
el **monto** sum, total
morder (ue) to bite
moreno(a) dark, brunette, **1.1**
la **mosca** fly
la **muchacha** girl, **1.1**
el **muchacho** boy, **1.1**
mucho(a) a lot, many, much, **2.1**
Mucho gusto. Nice to meet you.
el/la **muerto(a)** dead (person)
el Día de los Muertos All Souls' Day,
Day of the Dead
la **mujer** wife
mundial (related to) world
la Copa mundial World Cup
la Serie mundial World Series
el **mundo** world
municipal municipal
muscular muscular
el **músculo** muscle
la **música** music, **1.2**
muy very, **1.2**
muy bien very well, **BV**

nacer to be born
nacional national
la **nacionalidad** nationality
¿de qué nacionalidad? what nationality?,
1.1
nada nothing
De nada. You're welcome., **BV**
Por nada. You're welcome., **BV**
nada más nothing else, **5.2**
nadie no one
naranja orange (color), **4.2**
la **naranja** orange (fruit), **5.2**
natal native
navegar to navigate
navegar la red to surf the Net
la **Navidad** Christmas
necesitado(a) needy
necesitar to need, **4.1**
negro(a) black, **4.2**
nevar (ie) to snow, it's snowing
la **nieta** granddaughter, **2.1**
el **nieto** grandson, **2.1**
el/la **niño(a)** child

no no, not
No hay de qué. You're welcome., **BV**
la **noche** night, evening
Buenas noches. Good evening., **BV**
por la noche at night
la **Nochebuena** Christmas Eve
nombrar to name
el **norte** north
nosotros(as) we
la **nota** grade, mark
sacar notas (buenas/malas) to get
(good/bad) grades, **3.2**
notar to note, to notice
novecientos(as) nine hundred, **3.1**
el/la **novelista** novelist
noveno(a) ninth
noventa ninety, **2.1**
noviembre November, **BV**
nuestro(a) our
nueve nine, **1.1**
nuevo(a) new, **1.2**
el **número** number, size, **4.2**

o or
objetivo objective
obligatorio(a) required, obligatory
ochenta eighty, **2.1**
ocho eight, **1.1**
ochocientos(as) eight hundred, **3.1**
octubre October, **BV**
ocupado(a) occupied, **5.1**
oír to hear
el **ojo** eye
once eleven, **1.1**
la **onza** ounce
opcional optional
la **oración** sentence
el **orden** order (sequential)
la **orden** order (restaurant), **5.1**
el **ordenador** computer
el **órgano** organ
el **oro** gold
la moneda de oro gold coin
oscuro(a) dark
el **otoño** fall, **BV**
otro(a) other
cualquier otro any other
¡Oye! Listen!

Spanish-English Dictionary

P

el **padrastro** stepfather, **2.1**

el **padre** father, **2.1**

los **padres** parents, **2.1**

  pagar to pay, **4.1**

la **página** page

    la página Web Web page

el **país** country

    los países de habla española Spanish-speaking countries

la **paja** straw

la **palabra** word

el **palo** pole

el **pan** bread, **5.1**

    el pan tostado toast, **5.1**

el **panqueque** pancake

la **pantalla** screen (movie theater)

el **pantalón** pants, **4.2**

    el pantalón largo long pants, **4.2**

    el pantalón corto shorts, **4.2**

la **papa** potato, **5.2**

    las papas fritas French fries, **5.1**

el **papá** dad

el **papel** paper, **4.1**

    la hoja de papel sheet of paper, **4.1**

la **papelería** stationery store, **4.1**

el **paquete** package, **5.2**

el **par** pair

    el par de tenis pair of tennis shoes (sneakers), **4.2**

  para for

  parar to stop, **6.1**

  parecido(a) similar

el/la **pariente(a)** relative, **2.1**

  el **parque** park

  la **parte** part

  participar to participate

el **partido** game, **6.1**

  pasar to pass, **6.2**; to spend (time)

    pasar por to pass (walk) through

el **paso** step

el **pastel** cake, **2.2**

la **patata** potato, **5.2**

    las patatas fritas French fries, **5.1**

el **pecho** chest

  pelirrojo(a) redheaded, **1.1**

la **pelota** ball, **6.2**

la **pena** pain

    ¡Qué pena! What a shame!

  pequeño(a) small, **1.2**

  perder (ie) to lose, **6.1**

  ¡Perdón! Excuse me!

  perfecto(a) perfect

  pero but

el **perrito** puppy, **2.1**

el/la **perro(a)** dog, **2.1**

la **persona** person

el **personaje** character

  peruano(a) Peruvian, **1.1**

  pesar to weigh

el **pescado** fish, **5.2**

el **peso** peso; weight

  picado(a) chopped, ground

el **pícher** pitcher, **6.2**

el **pie** foot, **6.1**

    a pie on foot, **3.2**

    ir a pie to walk, **3.2**

la **piedra** stone

la **pierna** leg, **6.1**

la **pieza** room

la **pinta** pint

el/la **pintor(a)** painter

la **pintura** painting

el **piso** floor, **2.2**

la **pizza** pizza

el **plan** plan

la **planta** floor

    la planta baja ground floor, **2.2**

el **plátano** banana, **5.2**

el **platillo** home plate, **6.2**

el **plato** plate, dish

la **pluma** pen, **4.1**

la **población** population

  pobre poor

  poco(a) a little, few, **2.1**

  poder (ue) to be able, **6.1**

el/la **poeta** poet

  el **pollo** chicken, **5.2**

  poner to put, to place

  ponerse to put on

la **popularidad** popularity

  por for, by

    irse por to go (fall) through

    por ejemplo for example

    por favor please, **BV**

    por la mañana in the morning, **5.2**

por la noche at night
por medio de by means of
Por nada. You're welcome., **BV**
¿por qué? Why?
porque because
la **portería** goal, **6.1**
el/la **portero(a)** goalie, **6.1**
posible possible
el **postre** dessert, **5.1**
practicar to practice
el **precio** price, **4.2**
preferir (ie) to prefer, **6.1**
la **pregunta** question, **3.2**
   contestar (a) la pregunta to answer the
   question, **3.2**
preguntar to ask
preparar to prepare, **3.1**
presentar to present
el/la **presidente(a)** president
prestar to lend
   prestar atención to pay attention, **3.2**
el **presupuesto** budget
primario(a) primary, elementary
   la escuela primaria elementary school
la **primavera** spring, **BV**
primero(a) first
el/la **primo(a)** cousin, **2.1**
la **princesa** princess
principal main, principal
privado(a) private, **2.2**
el **problema** problem
procesar to process
producir to produce
el **producto** product
   los productos congelados frozen foods,
   5.2
la **profesión** occupation, profession
profesional professional
el/la **profesor(a)** teacher, **1.2**
el **programa** program
pronto soon
   ¡Hasta pronto! See you soon!, **BV**
publicar to publish
el **pueblo** town
la **puerta** door
el **puerto** port
puertorriqueño(a) Puerto Rican, **1.1**
pues well
el **pulmón** lung

el **punto** point
purificado(a) purified

que that
¿qué? what? how? **3.1**
   ¿A qué hora? At what time?, **BV**
   ¿de qué color? what color?, **4.2**
   ¿de qué nacionalidad? what nationality?,
   1.1
   No hay de qué. You're welcome., **BV**
   ¿Qué desea Ud.? May I help you? (in a
   store), **4.2**
   ¿Qué día es (hoy)? What day is it (today)?
   ¿Qué hay? What's new (up)?
   ¿Qué hora es? What time is it?, **BV**
   ¡Qué... más... ! What a . . . !
   ¿Qué número usa Ud.? What size do you
   wear?, **4.2**
   ¡Qué pena! What a shame!
   ¿Qué tal? How are you?, **BV**
   ¿Qué talla usa Ud.? What size do you
   wear?, **4.2**
   ¿Qué tiempo hace? What is the weather
   (like)?
quedar to remain, **6.1**
querer (ie) to want, to wish
querido(a) dear
el **queso** cheese, **5.1**
   el sándwich de jamón y queso ham and
   cheese sandwich, **5.1**
el **quetzal** currency of Guatemala
¿quién? who?, **1.1**
   ¿de quién? whose?
¿quiénes? who?, **1.1**
quince fifteen, **1.1**
la **quinceañera** fifteen-year-old (girl), **2.2**
quinientos(as) five hundred, **3.1**
quitarse to take off

rápido(a) fast, quickly
el **rato** while
el **ratón** mouse
real royal
realmente really
la **recámara** bedroom, **2.2**

Spanish-English Dictionary

el/la **receptor(a)** catcher, **6.2**
recibir to receive, **5.1**
recoger to pick up
la **red** network
navegar la red to surf the Net
reducido(a) reduced
reflejar to reflect
el **reflejo** reflection
reflexionar to reflect
el **refresco** refreshment, drink, **5.1**
el **regalo** gift, **2.2**
la **región** region
la **reina** queen
relleno(a) full, stuffed
relleno de stuffed with
el **repaso** review
la **república** republic
la **República Dominicana** Dominican
Republic
respiratorio(a) respiratory
el aparato respiratorio respiratory system
el **restaurante** restaurant
el **resto** rest, remainder
el **retintín** jingle
el **retrato** portrait
el **rey** king
rico(a) rich
el **río** river
la **rodilla** knee, **6.1**
rojo(a) red, **4.2**
el **rompecabezas** puzzle
la **ropa** clothing, **4.2**
la tienda de ropa clothing store, **4.2**
rosado(a) pink, **4.2**
rubio(a) blond(e), **1.1**
la **rutina** routine

S

el **sábado** Saturday, **BV**
sacar to get, **3.2**
sacar notas (buenas/malas) to get
(good/bad) grades, **3.2**
el **saco** jacket
la **sala** room, living room, **2.2**
la sala de clase classroom
salir to leave
saltar to jump

el **sándwich** sandwich, **5.1**
el sándwich de jamón y queso ham and
cheese sandwich, **5.1**
la **sangre** blood
secundario(a) secondary
la **sed** thirst
tener sed to be thirsty, **5.1**
segundo(a) second
el segundo tiempo second half (soccer),
6.1
seis six, **1.1**
seiscientos(as) six hundred, **3.1**
la **semana** week, **BV**
sencillo(a) simple
el **señor** sir, Mr., gentleman, **BV**
la **señora** Ms., Mrs., madam, **BV**
la **señorita** Miss, Ms., **BV**
septiembre September, **BV**
ser to be, **1.1**
¿Cuánto es? How much does it cost (is it)?
la **serie** series
la Serie mundial World Series
serio(a) serious, **1.1**
sesenta sixty, **2.1**
setecientos(as) seven hundred, **3.1**
setenta seventy, **2.1**
si if
sí yes
siete seven, **1.1**
el **siglo** century
la **silla** chair, **5.1**
similar similar
simpático(a) nice, **1.1**
sincero(a) sincere, **1.1**
el **sistema** system
situado(a) situated
sobre on, on top of, about
sobre todo especially, above all
sobresaltar to jump up
la **sobrina** niece, **2.1**
el **sobrino** nephew, **2.1**
social social
los estudios sociales social studies, **1.2**
el **software** software
el **sol** sun
Hace (Hay) sol. It's sunny.
sólo only
el **sombrero** hat
la **sopa** soup, **5.1**

Spanish-English Dictionary

su his, her, their, your
el **suburbio** suburb
sudamericano(a) South American
el **suelo** ground
el **sueño** dream
la **suerte** luck
   tener (ie) suerte to be lucky
superior superior, high
   la escuela superior high school
el **supermercado** supermarket, **5.2**
el **sur** south
   la América del Sur South America
sus their, your *(pl.)*
suspirar to sigh

T

el **T-shirt** T-shirt, **4.2**
el **tablero** board
   el tablero indicador scoreboard, **6.1**
el **taco** taco
tal such (a thing)
   ¿Qué tal? How are things?, How are you?, **BV**
la **talla** size, **4.2**
también also, too, **1.1**
tanto(a) so much
el **tanto** point, score, **6.1**
   marcar un tanto to score a point, **6.1**
la **tarde** afternoon
   Buenas tardes. Good afternoon., **BV**
el **té** tea
   el té helado iced tea, **5.1**
el **techo** roof
el **teclado** keyboard
la **tecnología** technology
la **tele** TV, television
el **teléfono** telephone, **3.1**
   hablar por teléfono to speak on the phone, **3.1**
la **televisión** television, **3.1**
temprano early
el **tendón** tendon
tener to have, **2.1**
   tener... años to be . . . years old, **2.1**
   tener hambre to be hungry, **5.1**
   tener miedo to be afraid
   tener que to have to, **4.1**
   tener sed to be thirsty, **5.1**
   tener suerte to be lucky

el **tenis** tennis
   el par de tenis pair of tennis shoes (sneakers), **4.2**
   los tenis tennis shoes, sneakers, **4.2**
la **terminal** terminal
la **terraza** terrace, **2.2**
el **terror** fear, terror
el **tesoro** treasure
ti you
la **tía** aunt, **2.1**
el **tiempo** half (soccer), **6.1**; time; weather
   Hace buen tiempo. The weather is nice.
   Hace mal tiempo. The weather is bad.
   ¿Qué tiempo hace? What is the weather (like)?
   el segundo tiempo second half (soccer), **6.1**
la **tienda** store, **4.2**
   la tienda de abarrotes grocery store
   la tienda de ropa clothing store, **4.2**
tierno(a) tender
las **tijeras** scissors, **4.1**
tímido(a) timid, shy, **1.1**
el **tío** uncle, **2.1**
típico(a) typical
el **tipo** type
   tirar to throw, **6.2**
   tocar to touch
      ¡Te toca a ti! It's your turn!
   todo(a) all, everything, **2.1**
      sobre todo above all, especially
   todos(as) everyone, everything, all
   tomar to take, **3.1**
      tomar apuntes to take notes, **3.2**
      tomar el almuerzo to have lunch, **3.2**
      tomar el desayuno to have breakfast, **3.1**
el **tomate** tomato, **5.2**
la **tonelada** ton
la **torta** cake, **2.2**
la **tortilla** tortilla
la **tostada** toast
   tostado(a) toasted
      el pan tostado toast, **5.1**
el **total** total
   trabajar to work, **4.2**
el **trabajo** work
el **trabalenguas** tongue twister
   tradicional traditional
el **traje** suit, **4.2**
   trece thirteen, **1.1**

Spanish-English Dictionary

treinta thirty, **1.1**
treinta y cinco thirty-five, **2.1**
treinta y cuatro thirty-four, **2.1**
treinta y dos thirty-two, **2.1**
treinta y nueve thirty-nine, **2.1**
treinta y ocho thirty-eight, **2.1**
treinta y seis thirty-six, **2.1**
treinta y siete thirty-seven, **2.1**
treinta y tres thiry-three, **2.1**
treinta y uno thirty-one, **1.1**
la **trenza** braid
tres three, **1.1**
trescientos(as) three hundred, **3.1**
triste sad
el **trofeo** trophy, **6.2**
tropical tropical
tu your
tú you

Ud., usted you *(sing.)*
Uds., ustedes you *(pl.)*
un a, an
el **uniforme** uniform, **3.2**
la **universidad** university
uno(a) one, a, **1.1**
usar to use, **4.2**

la **vainilla** vanilla
    el **helado de vainilla** vanilla ice cream, **5.1**
valer to be worth
variar to change
vario(a) various
el **vegetal** vegetable
veinte twenty, **1.1**
veinticinco twenty-five, **1.1**
veinticuatro twenty-four, **1.1**
veintidós twenty-two, **1.1**
veintinueve twenty-nine, **1.1**
veintiocho twenty-eight, **1.1**
veintiséis twenty-six, **1.1**

veintisiete twenty-seven, **1.1**
veintitrés twenty-three, **1.1**
veintiuno twenty-one, **1.1**
la **vela** candle, **2.2**
la **vena** vein
vender to sell, **5.2**
venezolano(a) Venezuelan, **1.1**
ver to see, **5.1**
el **verano** summer, **BV**
la **verdad** truth
    ¡verdad! that's right (true)!
    verde green, **4.2**
        la **judía verde** green bean, **5.2**
        verde olivo olive green, **4.2**
la **vez** time
    a veces at times, sometimes, **3.1**
el **video** video, **3.2**
    viejo(a) old, **2.2**
el **viento** wind
        Hace viento. It's windy.
el **viernes** Friday, **BV**
    violeta violet, purple, **4.2**
la **vista** view
    vital vital
    vivir to live, **5.2**
la **vocal** vowel
el **voleibol** volleyball
    volver (ue) to return, **6.1**
    vosotros(as) you
la **voz** voice
el **vuelo** flight

y and
ya already
yo I

la **zanahoria** carrot, **5.2**
el **zapato** shoe, **4.2**
la **zona** zone
el **zumo** juice

English-Spanish Dictionary

This English-Spanish Dictionary contains all productive and receptive vocabulary from the text. The numbers following each productive entry indicate the unit and vocabulary section in which the word is introduced. For example, **3.2** means that the word was taught in **Unidad 3, Paso 2**. **BV** refers to the preliminary **Bienvenidos** lessons. If there is no number following an entry, this means that the word or expression is included for receptive purposes only.

a un(a)
able: to be able poder (ue), **6.1**
above sobre
   above all sobre todo
academy la academia
to **accept** aceptar
accompanied acompañado(a)
account la cuenta
   savings account la cuenta de ahorros
activity la actividad
adorable adorable
afraid: to be afraid tener miedo
after después de, **3.1**
afternoon la tarde
   Good afternoon. Buenas tardes., **BV**
against contra, **6.1**
air el aire
album el álbum
all todo(a), **2.1;** todos(as)
   above all sobre todo
All Souls' Day el Día de los Muertos
already ya
also también, **1.1**
American americano(a), **1.1**
among entre
amusement la diversión
amusing divertido(a)
anatomy la anatomía
and y
Andean andino(a)
to **answer** contestar
   to answer the question contestar (a) la pregunta, **3.2**
any other cualquier otro
apartment el apartamento, **2.2;** el departamento

apple la manzana, **5.2**
April abril, **BV**
Argentine argentino(a), **1.1**
arithmetic la aritmética
arm el brazo, **6.1**
around alrededor de
to **arrive** llegar, **5.1**
art el arte, **1.2**
artery la artería
artist el/la artista
as como
to **ask (a question)** preguntar
asleep dormido(a)
at a
   at home en casa
   at night por la noche
   at one o'clock (two o'clock . . .) a la una (las dos...), **BV**
   at times a veces, **3.1**
   At what time? ¿A qué hora?, **BV**
attention la atención
   to pay attention prestar atención, **3.2**
August agosto, **BV**
aunt la tía, **2.1**
author el/la autor(a)
avenue la avenida

baby el/la bebé
back la espalda
background la ascendencia
bad malo(a), **1.2;** mal
   The weather is bad. Hace mal tiempo.
bad-tempered malhumorado(a)
bag la bolsa, **5.2**
balcony el balcón, **2.2**
ball el balón, **6.1;** la pelota, **6.2**
banana el plátano, **5.2**

English-Spanish Dictionary

bank el banco

to **bark** ladrar

base la base, **6.2**

baseball el béisbol, **6.2**

  baseball field el campo de béisbol, **6.2**

  baseball player el/la jugador(a) de béisbol, **6.2**

based basado(a)

basket el cesto, la canasta, **6.2;** el canasto, el encestado

basketball el baloncesto, el básquetbol, **6.2**

  basketball court la cancha de básquetbol, **6.2**

bat el bate, **6.2**

to **bat** batear, **6.2**

bath el baño, **2.2**

bathroom el cuarto de baño, **2.2**

batter el/la bateador(a), **6.2**

to **be** ser, **1.1;** estar, **3.1**

  to be able poder (ue), **6.1**

  to be afraid tener miedo

  to be born nacer

  to be equivalent equivaler

  to be hungry tener hambre, **5.1**

  to be in class estar en clase, **3.2**

  to be lucky tener suerte

  to be thirsty tener sed, **5.1**

  to be worth valer

  to be . . . years old tener... años, **2.1**

bean la habichuela, el frijol, **5.2;** la judía

  green bean la judía verde, **5.2**

  string bean ejote, **5.2**

because porque

bedroom el cuarto de dormir, el dormitorio, la recámara, **2.2**

before antes (de)

to **begin** empezar (ie), **6.1;** comenzar (ie)

below bajo

besides además (de)

best el/la mejor

between entre

bicycle la bicicleta

big gran, grande, **1.2**

bill la cuenta, **5.1**

biology la biología

birthday el cumpleaños, **2.2**

to **bite** morder (ue)

black negro(a), **4.2**

block bloquear, **6.1**

blond(e) rubio(a), **1.1**

blood la sangre

blouse la blusa, **4.2**

blue azul, **4.2**

board el tablero, **6.1**

  scoreboard el tablero indicador, **6.1**

body el cuerpo

  human body el cuerpo humano

bone el hueso

book el libro, **4.1**

to **bore** aburrir, **6.2**

bored aburrido(a)

born: to be born nacer

bottle la botella, **5.2**

boy el muchacho, **1.1**

braid la trenza

Brazilian brasileño(a)

bread el pan, **5.1**

breakfast el desayuno, **3.1**

  to have breakfast tomar el desayuno, **3.1**

bright brillante

bronchial tube el bronquio

brother el hermano, **2.1**

brown marrón, **4.2**

brunette moreno(a), **1.1**

budget el presupuesto

building el edificio, **2.2**

bus el bus, **3.2**

  school bus el bus escolar, **3.2**

but pero

to **buy** comprar, **4.1**

  by por

  by car en carro, **3.2**

  by means of por medio de

  by tens de diez en diez

café el café, **5.1**

cafeteria la cafetería, **3.1;** la cantina

cake la torta, el pastel, **2.2**

English-Spanish Dictionary

calculator la calculadora, **4.1**

camera la cámara

can la lata, el bote, **5.2**

candle la vela, **2.2**

cap la gorra, **4.2**

capital la capital

car el carro, **2.2**

    by car en carro, **3.2**

carbonated drink la gaseosa, **5.1**

carbon dioxide el dióxido de carbono

to **caress** acariciar

Caribbean caribe

    Caribbean Sea el mar Caribe

carrot la zanahoria, **5.2**

to **carry** llevar, **4.1**

case el caso

cash register la caja, **4.1**

cat el/la gato(a), **2.1**

catalogue el catálogo

to **catch** atrapar, **6.2**

    catcher el/la cátcher, el/la receptor(a), **6.2**

CD (compact disc) el CD, **3.2**

to **celebrate** celebrar, **3.1**

    celebration la celebración

center el centro

century el siglo

cereal el cereal

chair la silla, **5.1**

champion el/la campeón(ona), **6.2**

to **change** cambiar, variar

character el personaje

cheap barato(a), **4.2**

check la cuenta, **5.1**

cheese el queso, **5.1**

    ham and cheese sandwich el sándwich de jamón y queso, **5.1**

chest el pecho

chicken el pollo, **5.2**

child el/la niño(a)

Chilean chileno(a), **1.1**

chocolate el chocolate, **5.1**

    chocolate ice cream el helado de chocolate, **5.1**

to **choose** escoger

chopped picado(a)

Christmas la Navidad

Christmas Eve la Nochebuena

circulation la circulación

city la ciudad

class la clase, **1.2**

classroom la sala de clase

clear claro(a)

client el/la cliente, **5.1**

closed cerrado(a)

clothing la ropa, **4.2**

    clothing store la tienda de ropa, **4.2**

club el club

    Spanish club el Club de español

coach el/la entrenador(a)

coast la costa

coffee café, **5.1**

coin la moneda

    gold coin la moneda de oro

coincidence la coincidencia

cola la cola

cold el frío

    It's cold (weather). Hace frío.

collection la colección

Colombian colombiano(a), **1.1**

color el color, **4.2**

    what color? ¿de qué color?, **4.2**

comical cómico(a), **1.1**

commercial comercial

compact compacto(a)

    compact disc (CD) el CD, **3.2**; el disco compacto

competition la competencia

computer la computadora, el ordenador

concert el concierto

to **connect** conectar

connected conectado(a)

connection la conexión

consecutive consecutivo(a)

consonant la consonante

contact el contacto

to **contain** contener (ie)

container el envase, **5.2**

continent el continente

English-Spanish Dictionary

to **continue** continuar, **6.2**

  conversation la conversación

  cool fresco

    It's cool (weather). Hace fresco.

  corn el maíz, **5.2**

to **cost** costar (ue)

to **count** contar (ue)

  country el país; el campo

    Spanish-speaking countries los países de habla española

  course el curso, **1.2**

    of course! ¡claro!

  court la cancha, **6.2**

    basketball court la cancha de básquetbol, **6.2**

  courtesy la cortesía

  cousin el/la primo(a), **2.1**

  Cuban cubano(a), **1.1**

  Cuban American cubanoamericano(a)

  culture la cultura

  customer el/la cliente, **5.1**

  dad el papá, **3.1**

to **dance** bailar, **3.1**

  dark moreno(a), **1.1;** oscuro(a)

  data los datos

  date la fecha

    What is today's date? ¿Cuál es la fecha de hoy?

  daughter la hija, **2.1**

  day el día

    All Souls' Day el Día de los Muertos

    What day is it (today)? ¿Qué día es (hoy)?

  dead (person) el/la muerto(a)

  dear querido(a)

  December diciembre, **BV**

to **decide** decidir

  decimal decimal

  definite determinado(a)

  delicious delicioso(a)

to **deliver** entregar

to **deposit** depositar

  description la descripción

  dessert el postre, **5.1**

  determined determinado(a)

  difference la diferencia

  different diferente, distinto(a)

  difficult difícil, duro(a), **1.2**

  dining room el comedor, **2.2**

  dinner la cena, **3.1**

    to have dinner cenar, **3.1**

  directly directamente

  disc el disco

    compact disc (CD) el CD, **3.2;** el disco compacto

  dish el plato

  district el barrio

  divine divino(a)

to **do** hacer

  dog el/la perro(a), **2.1**

  Dominican dominicano(a)

    Dominican Republic la República Dominicana

  door la puerta

  doubt la duda

  doughnut (type of) el churro

  drawing el dibujo, **1.2**

  dream el sueño

to **dribble** driblar, **6.2**

  drink el refresco, **5.1**

to **drink** beber, **5.1**

  during durante, **3.1**

  DVD el DVD, **3.2**

  each cada, **2.2**

  early temprano

to **earn** ganar

  easel el caballete

  easy fácil, **1.2**

to **eat** comer, **5.1**

  Ecuadorean ecuatoriano(a)

  education la educación

    physical education la educación física, **1.2**

  egg el huevo, **5.2**

eight ocho, **1.1**
eight hundred ochocientos(as), **3.1**
eighteen dieciocho, **1.1**
eighty ochenta, **2.1**
electronic electrónico(a)
elegant elegante
elementary primario(a)
    elementary school la escuela primaria
eleven once, **1.1**
e-mail el correo electrónico
employee el/la empleado(a), el/la
    dependiente(a), **4.1**
enchilada la enchilada
English el inglés
to enjoy gozar (de)
enough bastante, **1.2**
to enter entrar, **3.2**
equality la igualdad
equipment el equipo
equivalent: to be equivalent equivaler
to erase borrar
eraser la goma (de borrar), el borrador, **4.1**
especially sobre todo, especialmente
to establish establecer, fundar
evening la noche
    Good evening. Buenas noches., **BV**
everyone todos
everything todo(a), **2.1**; todos(as)
exam el examen
to examine examinar
example el ejemplo
    for example por ejemplo
excellent excelente
Excuse (me)! ¡Perdón!
expense el gasto
expensive caro(a), **4.2**
to explain explicar
expression la expresión
extraordinary extraordinario(a)
eye el ojo

fall el otoño, **BV**
false falso(a)

family la familia, **2.1**
family (related to) familiar
    family tree el árbol genealógico
famous famoso(a)
fan el/la aficionado(a)
fantastic fantástico(a)
fast rápido(a)
father el padre, **2.1**
favor el favor
favorite favorito(a)
fear el miedo, el terror
February febrero, **BV**
few poco(a), **2.1**; pocos(as)
field el campo, **6.1**
    baseball field el campo de béisbol, **6.2**
    soccer field el campo de fútbol, **6.1**
fifteen quince, **1.1**
fifteen-year-old (girl) la quinceañera, **2.2**
fifty cincuenta, **2.1**
to fight luchar
to find hallar
fine bien
finger el dedo
first primero(a)
fish el pescado, **5.2**
five cinco, **1.1**
five hundred quinientos(as), **3.1**
flight el vuelo
floor el piso, **2.2**; la planta
    ground floor la planta baja, **2.2**
flour la harina
flower la flor
fly la mosca
folder la carpeta, **4.1**
food la comida, **3.1**; el alimento; el comestible
    frozen foods los productos congelados, **5.2**
foot el pie, **6.1**
    on foot a pie, **3.2**
for por; para
    for example por ejemplo
to form formar
formal formal
forty cuarenta, **2.1**
to found fundar

English-Spanish Dictionary

foundation la fundación

four cuatro, **1.1**

four hundred cuatrocientos(as), **3.1**

fourteen catorce, **1.1**

free libre, **5.1**

French el francés

frequently frecuentemente

fresh (food) fresco, **5.2**

Friday el viernes, **BV**

fried frito(a)

    fried potatoes las papas (patatas) fritas, **5.1**

friend el/la amigo(a), **1.1;** el/la compañero(a)

from de

    from where? ¿de dónde?, **1.1**

front: in front of delante de

frozen helado(a), congelado(a)

    frozen foods los productos congelados, **5.2**

fruit la fruta, **5.2**

full lleno(a); cargado(a); relleno(a)

fun divertido(a)

funny gracioso(a), **1.1;** cómico(a), **1.1**

gallon el galón

game el partido, **6.1;** el juego

garage el garaje, **2.2**

garden el jardín, **2.2**

genealogical genealógico(a)

general general

generally en general

gentleman el señor, **BV**

geography la geografía

to **get** sacar, **3.2**

    to get a good (bad) grade sacar una nota buena (mala), **3.2**

gift el regalo, **2.2**

girl la muchacha, **1.1**

to **give** dar, **3.1**

    glove el guante, **6.2**

to **go** ir, **3.1**

    to go (fall) through irse por

    to go shopping ir de compras, **5.2**

goal el gol, **6.1**

    goal (box) la portería, **6.1**

    to score a goal meter un gol, **6.1**

goalie el/la portero(a), **6.1**

gold el oro

    gold coin la moneda de oro

golf el golf, **6.2**

good bueno(a), **1.1**

    Good afternoon. Buenas tardes., **BV**

    Good evening. Buenas noches., **BV**

    Good morning. Buenos días., **BV**

good-bye adiós, ¡chao!, **BV**

governor el/la gobernador(a)

grade la nota

    to get a good (bad) grade sacar una nota buena (mala), **3.2**

gram el gramo

granddaughter la nieta, **2.1**

grandfather el abuelo, **2.1**

grandmother la abuela, **2.1**

grandparents los abuelos, **2.1**

grandson el nieto, **2.1**

gray gris, **4.2**

great gran, grande, **1.2**

green verde, **4.2**

    green bean la judía verde, **5.2**

    olive green verde olivo, **4.2**

grocery el abarrote

    grocery store la tienda de abarrotes, la bodega

ground el suelo

group el grupo

to **guard** guardar, **6.1**

to **guess** adivinar

half medio(a)

    half (soccer) el tiempo, **6.1**

    second half (soccer) el segundo tiempo, **6.1**

ham el jamón, **5.1**

    ham and cheese sandwich el sándwich de jamón y queso, **5.1**

hamburger la hamburguesa, **5.1**

English-Spanish Dictionary

hand la mano, **6.1**

handsome guapo(a), **1.1**

to **hang** colgar (ue)

happy contento(a), alegre

hard duro(a), difícil, **1.2**

hardware el hardware

hat el sombrero

to **have** tener, **2.1**

    to have breakfast tomar el desayuno, **3.1**

    to have dinner cenar, **3.1**

    to have (give) a party dar una fiesta

    to have lunch tomar el almuerzo, **3.2**

    to have to tener que, **4.1**

he él

head la cabeza, **6.1**

to **hear** oír

heart el corazón

heat el calor

Hello! ¡Hola!, **BV**

to **help** ayudar

her su(s)

here aquí

hero el héroe

heroine la heroína

to **hide** esconder

high alto(a), **4.2**; superior

    high school el colegio, la escuela superior, la escuela secundaria

his su(s)

Hispanic hispano(a)

history la historia

to **hit** golpear

hole el agujero

holiday la fiesta

home la casa, **2.2**

    at home en casa

home plate el platillo, **6.2**

home run el jonrón, **6.2**

honor el honor

hot: It's hot. Hace calor.

hour la hora

house la casa, **2.2**

how? ¿cómo?, **1.1**; ¿qué?

    How are you? ¿Qué tal?, **BV**

    How much? ¿Cuánto?

    How much does it cost? ¿Cuánto es?, **4.1**

    How much is (are) . . . ? ¿A cuánto está(n)... ?, **5.2**

human humano(a)

    human body el cuerpo humano

humble humilde

hunger hambre

hungry: to be hungry tener hambre, **5.1**

I yo

ice cream el helado, **5.1**

    chocolate ice cream el helado de chocolate, **5.1**

    vanilla ice cream el helado de vainilla, **5.1**

idea la idea

if si

important importante

impossible imposible

in en

    in front of delante de

    in style de moda

incredible increíble

independence la independencia

Indian indio(a)

to **indicate** indicar, **6.1**

indicator el indicador

indigenous indígena

individual individual

    individual sport el deporte individual

inexpensive barato(a), **4.2**

inning la entrada, **6.2**

institute el instituto

instruction la instrucción

intelligent inteligente, **1.2**

interest el interés

to **interest** interesar, **6.2**

interesting interesante, **1.2**

internal interno(a)

English-Spanish Dictionary

Internet el/la Internet
interview la entrevista
introduction la introducción
invention la invención
investigation la investigación
to **invite** invitar, **3.1**
island la isla
Italian italiano(a)

jacket la chaqueta, **4.2**; el saco
January enero, **BV**
jeans el jean, el blue jean, los blue jeans, **4.2**
jingle el retintín
juice el zumo
July julio, **BV**
to **jump** saltar
    to jump up sobresaltar
June junio, **BV**
jungle la jungla

to **keep** guardar
keyboard el teclado
to **kick** lanzar, **6.1**
kilo el kilo, **5.2**
kilogram el kilogramo
king el rey
kitchen la cocina, **2.2**
knapsack la mochila, **4.1**
knee la rodilla, **6.1**

laboratory el laboratorio
lady-in-waiting la dama
lake (related to) lacustre
language la lengua, el habla
large gran, grande, **1.2**
later luego
    See you later! ¡Hasta luego!, **BV**
Latin el latín
Latin latino(a)
Latin American latinoamericano(a)
leaf la hoja

league la liga
    Major Leagues las Grandes Ligas
to **learn** aprender, **5.1**
to **leave** salir
  left izquierdo(a), **6.1**
  leg la pierna, **6.1**
  lemonade la limonada
to **lend** prestar
  less menos
  lesson la lección
  lettuce la lechuga, **5.2**
  liberator el/la libertador(a)
to **lift** levantar
  light la luz
to **light** encender (ie)
  like el gusto
to **like** gustar, **6.2**
  liquid el líquido
  list la lista
to **listen (to)** escuchar, **3.2**
    Listen! ¡Oye!
  liter el litro
  literature la literatura
  little: a little poco(a)
to **live** vivir, **5.2**
  living room la sala, **2.2**
  logical lógico(a)
  long largo(a)
    long pants el pantalón largo, **4.2**
    long sleeve la manga larga, **4.2**
to **look at** mirar, **3.1**
to **look for** buscar, **4.1**
to **lose** perder (ie), **6.1**
  lot: a lot mucho(a), **2.1**
  low bajo(a), **4.2**
to **lower** bajar
  lucky: to be lucky tener suerte
  lunch el almuerzo, **3.2**
    to have lunch tomar el almuerzo
  lung el pulmón

machine la máquina
madam la señora, **BV**

English-Spanish Dictionary

mail el correo
    e-mail el correo electrónico
main principal
Major Leagues las Grandes Ligas
to **make** hacer
    to make a basket encestar, **6.2**
many muchos(as)
map el mapa
March marzo, **BV**
mark la nota, **3.2**
marker el marcador, **4.1**
market el mercado, **5.2**
marmalade la mermelada
material el material
mathematics las matemáticas
May mayo, **BV**
me mí
meal la comida, **3.1**
means el medio
    by means of por medio de
measure la medida
meat la carne, **5.2**
medal la medalla
medical médico(a)
melancholic melancólico(a)
member el miembro
menu el menú, **5.1**
metric métrico(a)
Mexican mexicano(a)
middle: middle school la escuela intermedia
milk la leche, **5.2**
million el millón, **4.1**
mineral mineral
    mineral water el agua mineral, **5.2**
minus menos
mirror el espejo
Miss la señorita, **BV**
model el/la modelo
modern moderno(a)
Monday el lunes, **BV**
money el dinero
monitor el monitor
month el mes

moon la luna
more más
morning la mañana
    Good morning. Buenos días., **BV**
    in the morning por la mañana, **5.2**
mother la madre, **2.1**
mountain la montaña
mouse el ratón
    (mouse) pad la alfombrilla
mouth la boca
movie theater el cine
Mr. el señor, **BV**
Mrs. la señora, **BV**
Ms. la señorita, la señora, **BV**
much mucho(a), **2.1**
    How much? ¿Cuánto?
    How much does it cost? ¿Cuánto es?, **4.1**
    How much is (are) . . . ? ¿A cuánto está(n)... ?, **5.2**
municipal municipal
muscle el músculo
muscular muscular
music la música, **1.2**
my mi

to **name** nombrar
national nacional
nationality la nacionalidad
    what nationality? ¿de qué nacionalidad?, **1.1**
native indígena
    native person el/la indígena
to **navigate** navegar
to **need** necesitar, **4.1**
needy necesitado(a)
nephew el sobrino, **2.1**
Net la red
    to surf the Net navegar la red
new nuevo(a), **1.2**
nice simpático(a), **1.1**
nickname el apodo
niece la sobrina, **2.1**

English-Spanish Dictionary

night la noche
   at night por la noche
nine nueve, **1.1**
nine hundred novecientos(as), **3.1**
nineteen diecinueve, **1.1**
ninety noventa, **2.1**
ninth noveno(a)
no no
   no one nadie
north el norte
not no, **1.1**
note el apunte
   to take notes tomar apuntes, **3.2**
to **note** notar
notebook el bloc, el cuaderno, **4.1**
nothing nada
   nothing else nada más, **5.2**
to **notice** notar
novelist el/la novelista
November noviembre, **BV**
now ahora
number el número

objective el objetivo
obligatory obligatorio(a)
occupation la profesión
occupied ocupado(a), **5.1**
October octubre, **BV**
of de
   of course! ¡claro!
old viejo(a), **2.2**
   How old is he (she)? ¿Cuántos años
     tiene?, **2.1**
older mayor, **2.1**
oldest el/la mayor, **2.1**
olive green verde olivo, **4.2**
on en, sobre
   on foot a pie, 3.2
   on top of sobre
one uno(a), **1.1**
one hundred cien(to), **2.1**
one thousand mil, **3.1**
onion la cebolla

only sólo
to **open** abrir
to **operate** funcionar
opposing adverso(a)
opposite adverso(a)
optional opcional
or o
orange (color) naranja, **4.2**
orange (fruit) la naranja, **5.2**
order (restaurant) la orden, **5.1;** (sequential)
   el orden
organ el órgano
other otro(a)
   any other cualquier otro
ounce la onza
our nuestro(a)
outfielder el/la jardinero(a), **6.2**
to **owe** deber

package el paquete, **5.2**
pad (writing) el bloc, **4.1**
   (mouse) pad la alfombrilla
page la página
   Web page la página Web
pain la pena
painter el/la pintor(a)
painting la pintura, el cuadro
pair el par
   pair of tennis shoes (sneakers) el par de
     tenis, **4.2**
pancake el panqueque
pants el pantalón, **4.2**
   long pants el pantalón largo, **4.2**
   shorts el pantalón corto, **4.2**
paper el papel, **4.1**
   sheet of paper la hoja de papel, **4.1**
parents los padres, **2.1**
park el parque
part la parte
to **participate** participar
party la fiesta, **2.2**
   to have (give) a party dar una fiesta
to **pass** pasar, **6.2**
   to pass (walk) through pasar por

English-Spanish Dictionary

pastime la diversión
to **pay** pagar, **4.1**
    to pay attention prestar atención, **3.2**
pea el guisante, **5.2**
pen el bolígrafo, la pluma, **4.1**
pencil el lápiz, **4.1**
people la gente
perfect perfecto(a)
person la persona
    young person el/la joven
Peruvian peruano(a), **1.1**
peso el peso
photo la foto
photograph la fotografía
physical físico(a)
    physical education la educación física, **1.2**
to **pick up** recoger
pink rosado(a), **4.2**
pint la pinta
pitcher el/la lanzador(a), el/la pícher, **6.2**
pizza la pizza
to **place** meter, poner
plan el plan
plate el plato
to **play** jugar (ue), **6.1**
    player el/la jugador(a), **6.1**
        baseball player el/la jugador(a) de béisbol, **6.2**
    playwright el/la dramaturgo(a)
pleasant agradable
please por favor, **BV**
to **please** gustar, **6.2**
    pleasure el gusto
        It's a pleasure to meet you. (Nice to meet you.) Mucho gusto.
pocket el bolsillo
poet el/la poeta
point el tanto, **6.1**; el punto
    to score a point marcar un tanto, **6.1**
pole el palo
poncho el poncho
poor pobre
popular popular
popularity la popularidad
population la población

port el puerto
portrait el retrato
possible posible
poster el cartel
potato la papa, la patata, **5.2**
    fried potatoes las papas (patatas) fritas, **5.1**
pound la libra
to **practice** practicar
to **prefer** preferir (ie), **6.1**
to **prepare** preparar, **3.1**
to **present** presentar
    president el/la presidente(a)
    pretty bonito(a), **1.1**
    price el precio, **4.2**
    primary primario(a)
    princess la princesa
    principal principal
    printer la impresora
    private privado(a), **2.2**
    problem el problema
to **process** procesar
to **produce** producir
    product el producto
        frozen products (foods) los productos congelados, **5.2**
    profession la profesión
    professional profesional
    program la emisión, **3.1**; el programa
        sports program la emisión deportiva
to **publish** publicar
Puerto Rican puertorriqueño(a), **1.1**
pulmonary pulmonar
puppy el perrito, **2.1**
purchase la compra
purified purificado(a)
purple violeta, **4.2**
to **put** poner; meter
    to put on ponerse
puzzle el rompecabezas

Q

quarter el cuarto
queen la reina
question la pregunta, **3.2**

English-Spanish Dictionary

quickly rápido
quite bastante, **1.2**

racial racial
to **rain** llover (ue)
to **raise** levantar
    to raise your hand levantar la mano, **3.2**
  rather bastante, **1.2**
to **read** leer, **5.1**
  reading la lectura
  ready listo(a)
  really realmente
to **receive** recibir, **5.1**
  record el disco
  red rojo(a), **4.2**
  redheaded pelirrojo(a), **1.1**
  reduced reducido(a)
to **reflect** reflexionar, reflejar
  reflection el reflejo
  refreshment el refresco, **5.1**
  region el barrio, la región
  relative el/la pariente(a), **2.1**
to **rely on** contar (ue) con
to **remain** quedar, **6.1**
  remainder el resto
  republic la república
    Dominican Republic la República Dominicana
  required obligatorio(a)
  research la investigación
  respiratory respiratorio(a)
    respiratory system el aparato respiratorio
  rest lo demás; el resto
  restaurant el restaurante
to **return** volver (ue), **6.1**
    to return something devolver (ue), **6.1**
  review el repaso
  rice el arroz, **5.2**
  rich rico(a)
  right derecho(a), **6.1**
  river el río
  rolled up enrollado(a)
  roof el techo

room el cuarto, **2.2;** la sala; la pieza
  classroom la sala de clase
  dining room el comedor, **2.2**
  living room la sala, **2.2**
 routine la rutina
 royal real
to **run** correr, **6.2**

 sad triste, melancólico(a)
 salad la ensalada, **5.1**
 sale la liquidación, **4.2**
 same mismo(a), **1.2**
 sandwich el sándwich, **5.1;** el bocadillo, **5.1**
  ham and cheese sandwich el sándwich de jamón y queso, **5.1**
 Saturday el sábado, **BV**
to **save** ahorrar
 saving el ahorro
  savings account la cuenta de ahorros
 schedule el horario
 school la escuela, **1.2;** la academia, el colegio, **1.3**
  elementary school la escuela primaria
  high school el colegio, la escuela superior, la escuela secundaria,
  middle school la escuela intermedia
 school (related to) escolar
  school bus el bus escolar, **3.2**
  school supplies los materiales escolares, **4.1**
 science la ciencia, **1.2**
 scissors las tijeras, **4.1**
 score el tanto, **6.1**
to **score** marcar
  to score a goal meter un gol, **6.1**
  to score a point marcar un tanto, **6.1**
 scoreboard el tablero indicador, **6.1**
 screen la pantalla
 sculptor el/la escultor(a)
 sculpture la escultura
 sea el mar
  Caribbean Sea el mar Caribe
 season la estación

English-Spanish Dictionary

second segundo(a)

  second half (soccer) el segundo tiempo, **6.1**

secondary secundario(a)

to **see** ver, **5.1**

  See you later! ¡Hasta luego!, **BV**

  See you soon! ¡Hasta pronto!, **BV**

  See you tomorrow! ¡Hasta mañana!, **BV**

to **sell** vender, **5.2**

sentence la oración

September septiembre, **BV**

series la serie

  World Series la Serie mundial

serious serio(a), **1.1**

seven siete, **1.1**

seven hundred setecientos(as), **3.1**

seventeen diecisiete, **1.1**

seventy setenta, **2.1**

to **sew** coser

she ella

sheet la hoja

  sheet of paper la hoja de papel, **4.1**

shellfish los mariscos, **5.2**

shirt la camisa, **4.2**

shoe el zapato, **4.2**

  pair of tennis shoes (sneakers) el par de tenis, **4.2**

  tennis shoes (sneakers) los tenis, **4.2**

to **shop** ir de compras, **5.2**

short bajo(a), **1.1;** corto(a)

  short sleeve la manga corta, **4.2**

shorts el pantalón corto, **4.2**

short-story writer el/la cuentista

shut cerrado(a)

shy tímido(a), **1.1**

side el lado

to **sigh** suspirar

similar parecido(a), similar

simple sencillo(a)

since desde

sincere sincero(a), **1.1**

to **sing** cantar, **3.1**

  singer el/la cantante

sir el señor, **BV**

sister la hermana, **2.1**

situated situado(a)

six seis, **1.1**

six hundred seiscientos(as), **3.1**

sixteen dieciséis, **1.1**

sixty sesenta, **2.1**

size la talla, **4.2**

skeletal esquelético(a)

skeleton el esqueleto

skirt la falda, **4.2**

to **sleep** dormir (ue), **6.1**

sleeve la manga

  long sleeve la manga larga, **4.2**

  short sleeve la manga corta, **4.2**

small pequeño(a), **1.2**

to **snow** nevar (ie)

so así

  so much tanto(a)

soccer el fútbol, **6.1**

  soccer field el campo de fútbol, **6.1**

social social

  social studies los estudios sociales, **1.2**

sock el calcetín, **4.2**

socks los calcetines, **4.2**

soda la soda

soft blando(a)

software el software

some algunos(as)

something algo

sometimes a veces, **3.1**

son el hijo, **2.1**

song la canción

soon pronto

  See you soon! ¡Hasta pronto!, **BV**

soup la sopa, **5.1**

south el sur

South America la América del Sur

South American sudamericano(a)

Spain España

Spanish español

  Spanish club el Club de español

Spanish-speaking de habla española

English-Spanish Dictionary

to **speak** hablar, **3.1**

    to speak on the phone hablar por teléfono, **3.1**

spectator el/la espectador(a), **6.1**

speech el habla

to **spend** gastar

    to spend time pasar

sport el deporte, **6.1**

    individual sport el deporte individual

    team sport el deporte de equipo

sports (related to) deportivo(a)

    sports program la emisión deportiva

spring la primavera, **BV**

stadium el estadio, **6.1**

star la estrella

state el estado

stationery: stationery store la papelería, **4.1**

statue la estatua

steak el biftec

step el paso

stepbrother el hermanastro, **2.1**

stepfather el padrastro, **2.1**

stepmother la madrastra, **2.1**

stepsister la hermanastra, **2.1**

stone la piedra

to **stop** parar, **6.1**

store la tienda, **4.2**

    clothing store la tienda de ropa, **4.2**

    grocery store la tienda de abarrotes, la bodega

    stationery store la papelería, **4.1**

story el cuento

    short story la historieta

    short-story writer el/la cuentista

straw la paja

street la calle

string bean el ejote, **5.2**

strong fuerte

student el/la alumno(a), **1.2**

study el estudio

    social studies los estudios sociales, **1.2**

to **study** estudiar, **3.1**

stuffed relleno(a)

    stuffed with relleno de

stupendous estupendo(a)

style la moda, el estilo

    in style de moda

suburb el suburbio

such tal

suit el traje, **4.2**

sum el monto

summer el verano, **BV**

sun el sol

Sunday el domingo, **BV**

sunny: It's sunny. Hace (Hay) sol.

superior superior

supermarket el supermercado, **5.2**

    (wholesale) supermarket el hipermercado

supplies: school supplies los materiales escolares, **4.1**

to **surf the Net** navegar la red

system el aparato; el sistema

    respiratory system el aparato respiratorio

T-shirt el T-shirt, la camiseta, **4.2**

table la mesa, **5.1**

tablecloth el mantel

to **take** tomar, **3.1**

    to take (clothing size) usar, **3.2**

    to take notes tomar apuntes, **3.2**

    to take off quitarse

    to take out (secretly) escamotear

    to take (shoe size) calzar

to **talk** hablar, **3.1**

tall alto(a), **1.1**

taste el gusto

tea el té

    iced tea el té helado, **5.1**

to **teach** enseñar

teacher el/la profesor(a), **1.2**; el/la maestro(a)

team el equipo, **6.1**

    team sport el deporte de equipo

technology la tecnología

telephone el teléfono, **3.1**

    to speak on the phone hablar por teléfono, **3.1**

television la televisión, **3.1**; la tele

English-Spanish Dictionary

ten diez, **BV**

    by tens de diez en diez

tender tierno(a)

tendon el tendón

tennis el tenis

    pair of tennis shoes (sneakers) el par de tenis, **4.2**

    tennis shoes (sneakers) los tenis, **4.2**

terminal la terminal

terrace la terraza, **2.2**

terror el terror

test el examen

Thank you. Gracias., **BV**

that's right (true)! ¡verdad!

the el, la

their su(s)

there allí

    there is, there are hay

they ellos(as)

thing la cosa

thirsty: to be thirsty tener sed, **5.1**

thirteen trece, **1.1**

thirty treinta, **1.1**

thirty-eight treinta y ocho, **2.1**

thirty-five treinta y cinco, **2.1**

thirty-four treinta y cuatro, **2.1**

thirty-nine treinta y nueve, **2.1**

thirty-one treinta y uno, **2.1**

thirty-seven treinta y siete, **2.1**

thirty-six treinta y seis, **2.1**

thirty-three treinta y tres, **2.1**

thirty-two treinta y dos, **2.1**

three tres, **1.1**

three hundred trescientos(as), **3.1**

to **throw** lanzar, **6.1;** tirar, **6.2**

Thursday el jueves, **BV**

tie la corbata, **4.2**

tied (score) empatado(a), **6.1**

time el tiempo; la vez; la hora

    at times (sometimes) a veces, **3.1**

    At what time? ¿A qué hora?, **BV**

    What time is it? ¿Qué hora es?, **BV**

timid tímido(a), **1.1**

toast el pan tostado, **5.1;** la tostada

toasted tostado(a)

today hoy

    What day is it (today)? ¿Qué día es (hoy)?

    What is today's date? ¿Cuál es la fecha de hoy?

together juntos(as)

tomato el tomate, **5.2**

tomorrow mañana

    See you tomorrow! ¡Hasta mañana!, **BV**

ton la tonelada

tongue twister el trabalenguas

too también, **1.1**

tortilla la tortilla

total el total, el monto

to **touch** tocar

town el pueblo

toy el juguete

traditional tradicional

trainer el/la entrenador(a)

treasure el tesoro

tree el árbol

    family tree el árbol genealógico

trophy el trofeo, **6.2**

tropical tropical

truth la verdad

Tuesday el martes, **BV**

tuna el atún, **5.2**

TV la tele

twelve doce, **1.1**

twenty veinte, **1.1**

twenty-eight veintiocho, **1.1**

twenty-five veinticinco, **1.1**

twenty-four veinticuatro, **1.1**

twenty-nine veintinueve, **1.1**

twenty-one veintiuno, **1.1**

twenty-seven veintisiete, **1.1**

twenty-six veintiséis, **1.1**

twenty-three veintitrés, **1.1**

twenty-two veintidós, **1.1**

two dos, **1.1**

two hundred doscientos(as), **3.1**

type el tipo

typical típico(a)

English-Spanish Dictionary

ugly feo(a), **1.1**
uncle el tío, **2.1**
under debajo (de); bajo
undershirt la camiseta, **4.2**
to understand comprender, **5.1**
uniform el uniforme, **3.2**
United States Estados Unidos
university la universidad
unoccupied, libre, **5.1**
until hasta
to use usar, **4.2**

vanilla vainilla
   vanilla ice cream el helado de vainilla, **5.1**
various vario(a)
vegetable la legumbre, el vegetal, **5.2**
vein la vena
Venezuelan venezolano(a), **1.1**
very muy, **1.2**
   very well muy bien, **BV**
vest el chaleco
video el video, **3.2**
view la vista
violet violeta, **4.2**
vital vital
voice la voz
volleyball el voleibol
vowel la vocal

to wait (for) esperar, **5.1**
   waiter el mesero, el camarero, **5.1**
   waitress la camarera, la mesera, **5.1**
to walk ir a pie, **3.2**; andar
to want desear, querer (ie)
to watch mirar, **3.1**
   water el agua, **5.2**
      mineral water el agua mineral, **5.2**

we nosotros(as)
weak débil
to wear llevar, **3.2**; (shoe size) calzar
   weather el tiempo
      It's cold (weather). Hace frío.
      It's cool (weather). Hace fresco.
      The weather is bad. Hace mal tiempo.
      The weather is nice. Hace buen tiempo.
      What is the weather (like)? ¿Qué tiempo hace?
   Web page la página Web
   Wednesday el miércoles, **BV**
   week la semana
to weigh pesar
   weight el peso
   welcome bienvenido(a)
      You're welcome. De nada., Por nada., No hay de qué., **BV**
   well bien; pues, **1.1**
      very well muy bien, **BV**
   what? ¿qué?, ¿cuál?, ¿cómo?
      At what time? ¿A qué hora?, **BV**
      What a . . . ! ¡Qué... más... !
      What a shame! ¡Qué pena!
      what color? ¿de qué color?, **4.2**
      What day is it (today)? ¿Qué día es (hoy)?
      What is he (she, it) like? ¿Cómo es?
      What is the weather (like)? ¿Qué tiempo hace?
      What is today's date? ¿Cuál es la fecha de hoy?
      what nationality? ¿de qué nacionalidad?, **1.1**
      What's new (up)? ¿Qué hay?
      What size do you wear? ¿Qué número usa Ud.?, ¿Qué talla usa Ud.?, **4.2**
      What time is it? ¿Qué hora es?, **BV**
   when cuando
   when? ¿cuándo?, **3.1**
   where? ¿dónde?, **1.1**; ¿adónde?, **3.2**
      from where? ¿de dónde?, **1.1**
   which? ¿cuál?
   while el rato
   white blanco(a), **4.2**

English-Spanish Dictionary

who? ¿quién?, ¿quiénes?, **1.1**

whose? ¿de quién?

wife la mujer

to **win** ganar, **6.1**

wind el viento

windy: It's windy. Hace viento.

winter el invierno, **BV**

to **wish** desear, querer (ie)

with con

wool la lana

word la palabra

work la obra, el trabajo

    Let's get to work! ¡Manos a la obra!

to **work** trabajar, **4.2**

world el mundo

world (related to) mundial

    World Cup la Copa mundial

    World Series la Serie mundial

worth: to be worth valer

to **write** escribir, **5.1**

writing pad el bloc, **4.1**

year el año

    to be . . . years old tener... años, **2.1**

yellow amarillo(a), **4.2**

yes sí

you tú, usted, ustedes, vosotros(as), ti, te

    You're welcome. De nada., Por nada., No hay de qué.

young joven

    young page (of a royal family) el/la menino(a)

    young person el/la joven

younger menor, **2.1**

youngest el/la menor, **2.1**

your tu(s), su(s)

    It's your turn! ¡Te toca a ti!

zero cero

zone la zona

Credits

Glencoe would like to acknowledge the artists and agencies who participated in illustrating this program: Joe Veno represented by Gwen Walters; Geo Parkin represented by American Artists Inc.; David Broad and Jane McCreary represented by Ann Remen-Willis; Susan Jaekel; Ortelius Design, Inc.; Lyle Miller; Andrew Shiff; Karen Maizel.

Cover CORBIS, Glow Images, (l)CORBIS, (b)Ed McDonald; **i** Glow Images; **iii** (l)(c)Pixtal/age Fotostock; **iv** Andrew Payti; **v** Larry Hamill; **vi** (t)Andrew Payti, (b)Larry Hamill; **vii** (l)Andrew Payti, (r)Anthony Azcona, (r)Anthony Azcona; **viii** (t)Curt Fischer, (bl)---, (br)Ann Summa; **ix** (t)Andrew Payti, (b)Andrew Payti; **x** (r)Larry Hamill; **xi** Digital Stock/CORBIS; (tr)Andrew Payti, (bl)Randy Faris/CORBIS, (br)PhotoDisc; **xxvi** (l)Curt Fischer, (c)Mark Smestad, (r)Timothy Fuller; **xxvii** (l)Timothy Fuller, (b)Ed McDonald; **0** Andrew Payti, Larry Hamill; **1** (l)EyeWire/Getty Images, (r)Ann Summa; **2** Ken Karp; **3** (tl)Ann Summa, (tc)Michelle Chaplow, (tr)Larry Hamill, (bl)Ann Summa, (br)Luis Delgado; **4** (l)Larry Hamill, (r)Ann Summa; **5** (l)Larry Hamill, (r)MAK 1; **6** Patrick Ward/CORBIS; **8** (cl)Philip Gould/CORBIS, (l)Ilene MacDonald/Alamy, (r)Susan See Photography; **10** (tl)Mark Burnett, (tc)Mark Burnett, (tr)Mark Burnett, (bl)Mark Burnett, (bc)Mark Burnett, (br)file photo; **12** (tl)Ann Summa, (tc)Ann Summa, (tr)Ann Summa, (b)Andrew Payti; **14** (tl)Larry Hamill, (tr)Larry Hamill, (bl)Larry Hamill; **15** (tl)Corbis, (tr)Digital Stock, (bl)Digital Stock, (br)Digital Stock; **17** Larry Hamill; **18** (b)Larry Hamill; **19** Andrew Payti, (l)Larry Hamill; **20** Luis Delgado; **21** (t)Larry Hamill, (bl)Larry Hamill, (br)Owen Franken/CORBIS; **22** (t)Image Source,(b)Getty Images; **25** (t)Randy Faris/CORBIS, (tl)Larry Hamill, (bl)McGraw-Hill Education/Digital Light Source, Richard Hutchings, (inset)Glow Images/Superstock; **26** Andrew Payti; **27** Ann Summa, Ann Summa, Ann Summa, Ann Summa, Ann Summa; **28** (t)Larry Hamill, (b)Andrew Payti; **30** (t)Larry Hamill, (b)Larry Hamill; **31** (t)Larry Hamill, (b)Keith Dannemiller/CORBIS SABA; **32** (l)Andrew Payti, (r)Andrew Payti; **34** Ann Summa; **37** (t)Larry Hamill, (b)Ken Karp; **38** (l)Larry Hamill, (r)Ed McDonald; **40** (tl)Larry Hamill, (tr)Larry Hamill, (bl)Luis Delgado; **41** PhotoDisc; **42** Andrew Payti; **43** Lori Shetler; **44** (l)Danny Lehman/CORBIS, (r)Andrew Payti; **47** Andrew Payti; **48** Courtesy Justo Lamas; **49** Lori Shetler; **52** (l)Reuters NewMedia Inc./CORBIS, (r)Chris Martinez/Getty Images; **55** Larry Hamill; **56** Larry Hamill; **57** (r)Ann Summa, (l)©Pixtal/age Fotostock; **58** (tl)Ann Summa, (tr)Ann Summa, (bl)Ann Summa, (br)Ann Summa; **59** (tl)Ann Summa, (tr)Ann Summa, (bl)Ann Summa, (bc)Andrew Payti, (br)Andrew Payti; **60** Andrew Payti; **62** Larry Hamill, (l)realia; **63** Andrew Payti; **65** (tl)Andrew Payti, (tr)Andrew Payti, (bl)Andrew Payti, (bc)Andrew Payti, (br)Luis Delgado; **66** (l)Andrew Payti, (r)Steve Torregrossa; **67** Andrew Payti; **68** (l)Andrew Payti, (r)Andrew Payti; **69** realia, Andrew Payti; **71** (l)Ann Summa, (r)Andrew Payti; **73** Andrew Payti; **75** Lori Shetler; **76** Larry Hamill; **78** Andrew Payti; **79** Inti St. Clair/Getty Images; **80** Jim Cummins/CORBIS; **81** (l)Andrew Payti, (r)Andrew Payti; **82** UpperCut Images/Alamy; **83** Realia; **85** Andrew Payti; **86** courtesy Justo Lamas; **88** Glow Images; **90** (t)Andrew Payti, (c)Jeremy Horner/CORBIS, (b)Alison Wright/CORBIS; **92** (br)Peter Willi/Superstock; **93** Passport Stock/AGE Fotostock; **95** Andrew Payti; **96** Larry Hamill; **97** (l)Andrew Payti, (r)Larry Hamill; **98** (l)Ann Summa, (r)Andrew Payti; **99** (t)Andrew Payti, (b)Ann Summa; **100** (t)Ann Summa; **102** Michelle Chaplow; **105** Andrew Payti, Michelle Chaplow; **106** (tl)Andrew Payti, (tr)Richard T. Nowitz/CORBIS, (b)Ann Summa, (inset)Michelle Chaplow, (inset)Michelle Chaplow, (inset)Michelle Chaplow; **107** Realia, Realia, (tr)Anthony Azcona, (cl)Ann Summa, (cr)Larry Hamill, (b)Michelle Chaplow; **108** (t)Andrew Payti, (b)Michelle Chaplow; **109** Andrew Payti; **110** Larry Hamill; **111** Andrew Payti; **112** (t)Andrew Payti, (b)Andrew Payti; **114** Ann Summa; **116** (l)Laura Sifferlin, (r)Andrew Payti, (inset)PhotoDisc; **117** Curt Fischer; **118** Pablo Corral V/CORBIS; **119** Pablo Corral Vega/Corbis; **120** Glow Images; **121** Andrew Payti; **122** Andrew Payti; **124** Courtesy Justo Lamas; **128** (tl)Anthony Azcona, (tr)PhotoDisc, (bl)©Buzzshotz/Alamy, (br)Sami Kilpelainen/Alamy; **129** (tl)Larry Hamill, (tc)Larry Hamill, (tr)©Hisham Ibrahim/Photov.com/Alamy, (b)Andrew Payti; **130** (tl)Tetra Images/Getty Images, (tr)file photo, (bl)©Ingram Publishing/Alamy, (br)macbrianmun/Getty Images; **133** Ann Summa; **134** Ann Summa; **135** (l)Ann Summa, (r)Ann Summa; **136** Amanita Pictures, (tl)Ann Summa, (c)Amanita Pictures, (c)Matt Meadows, (cr)PhotoDisc, (bcl)Matt Meadows, (br)Matt Meadows; **138** Michelle Chaplow; **140** (l)Aaron Haupt; **141** (l)Luis Delgado, (r)Ann Summa; **142** (l)Laura Sifferlin; **143** (l)Ann Summa, (r)Ann Summa; **146** (t)Andrew Payti, (cw from top)PhotoDisc, (2)PhotoDisc, (3)PhotoDisc, (4)PhotoDisc, (5)PhotoDisc; **147** Andrew Payti; **148** Larry Hamill; **149** (r)Ryan McVay/Getty Images; **150** Larry Hamill, (l)PIXTAL/AGE Fotostock; **152** (t)Ann Summa, (b)Ann Summa; **153** Andrew Payti; **154** Andrew Payti; **155** Aaron Haupt; **156** Andrew Payti; **157** ©JUPITERIMAGES/Creatas/Alamy; **158** (1)Curt Fischer, (2)Curt Fischer, (3)Curt Fischer, (4)Amanita Pictures, (5)Curt Fischer, (6)©Ingram Publishing/Fotosearch, (7)Curt Fischer, (8)Luis Delgado; **159** Larry Hamill; **160** Courtesy Justo Lamas; **162** (l)Pace Gregory/Corbis Sygma, (r)Courtesy Oscar de la renta; **164** (t)Holly Wilmeth/Getty Images, (cl)Oliver Benn/Stone, (b)Bartosz Hadyniak/Getty Images; **165** (tl)Andrew Payti 2004 All Rights Reserved, (bl)Curt Fischer, (bc)Curt Fischer, (br)Curt Fischer; **167** Nancy Louie/Getty Images; **169** (l)Curt Fischer, (c)Curt Fischer, (r)Curt Fischer; **170** (b)Larry Hamill; **171** (l)Larry Hamill, (r)Andrew Payti; **172** Andrew Payti; **173** Andrew Payti; **174** (t)Andrew Payti, (b)Andrew Payti; **175** (t)Keith Dannemiller/CORBIS, (b)Andrew Payti; **176** (l)Andrew Payti, (r)Andrew Payti; **178** (l)Aaron Haupt, (r)Pablo Corral Vega/CORBIS, (1)John Evans, (2)John Evans, (3)PhotoDisc, (4)John Evans, (5)John Evans; **179** Andrew Payti; **180** (t)Ann Summa, (tr)Ann Summa; **181** (1,2,3,4,5)PhotoDisc, (6,7,10,11,12)Andrew Payti, (8)Aaron Haupt, (9)Doug Bryant/DDB Stock Photo; **182** (r)Andrew Payti; **183** (b)Andrew Payti; **185** (t)Pixtal/AGE Fotostock; **186** (r)Andrew Payti, (b)Michelle Chaplow; **187** Owen Franken/CORBIS; **188** Michelle Chaplow; **190** (t)The McGraw-Hill Companies, Inc./John Flournoy, photographer, (b)Danny Lehman/CORBIS; **191** (t)Royalty-Free/CORBIS, (c)Charles Michael Murray/CORBIS, (b)Larry Hamill; **192** Bob Krist/CORBIS; **193** (l)Andrew Payti, (r)Andrew Payti; **194** (l)PictureNet/CORBIS, (r)Andrew Payti; **195** Andrew Payti; **196** (t)Andrew Payti, (7)Realia, (8)Realia; **197** Arvind Garg/CORBIS; **198** Courtesy Justo Lamas; **202** (t)Nik Wheeler/CORBIS, (c)Andrew Payti, (b)Andrew Payti; **203** (l)Larry Hamill, (r)Andrew Payti; **205** ©Iconotec/Alamy; **208** Larry Hamill; **209** ©David R. Frazier Photolibrary, Inc./Alamy, (r)Ann Summa; **210** Danny Lehman/CORBIS; **213** Tim De Waele/Corbis TempSport; **214** Martin Rogers/CORBIS; **215** (l)Andrew Payti, (r)©David R. Frazier Photolibrary, Inc./Alamy; **218** Andrew Payti; **219** Enrico Calderoni/Aflo/Getty Images; **220** (l)U.S. Air Force photo by Staff Sgt Alan Garrison; **221** (t)Aaron Haupt, (c)Aaron Haupt, (b)Curt Fischer; **222** Andrew Payti; **223** Media Minds/Alamy; **224** Michelle Chaplow; **225** Reuters NewMedia Inc./CORBIS; **226** Andrew Payti; **227** Robert van der Hilst/CORBIS; **230** Ingram Publishing, (t)Ross Kinnaird/Getty Images, (b)Vincent MacNamara/Alamy; **231** (tl)©ZUMA Press, Inc/Alamy, (tr)John A. Angelillo/Corbis; **234** (t)Andrew Payti, (b)Kirk Strickland/Getty Images; **235** (t)Andrew Payti, (b)Simon Bruty/Getty Images; **237** Andrew Payti; **238** Courtesy Justo Lamas; **240** (t)Bettmann/CORBIS, (b)Design Pics/Don Hammond; **242** Corbis/age fotostock, (b)Reuters NewMedia Inc./CORBIS, (b)Simon Bruty/Getty Images; **243** (t)Ron J. Berard/Duomo/CORBIS, (b)Chris Trotman/Dumom/CORBIS; **244** Luis Delgado; **248–249** Digital Stock/CORBIS; **252** (r)McGraw-Hill Education; **253** Eric R. Hinson; **255** (t)James Gritz, (b)©Dynamic Graphics Group/Creatas/Alamy; **256** (inset)Cheryl Fenton; **256–H1** Ann Summa; **H7** (t)Ann Summa, (b)Larry Hamill; **H8** (tl)Amanita Pictures, (tl)Matt Meadows, (tl)Matt Meadows, (bc)PhotoDisc, (bcr)Matt Meadows **H10** (t)Andrew Payti; **H11** (tl)PhotoDisc, (tr)PhotoDisc, (bl)Ann Summa, (bcl)PhotoDisc, (bc)PhotoDisc, (bcr)PhotoDisc, (br)Ann Summa; **H15** (b)Realia;.